IMAGES
of America

DERRY

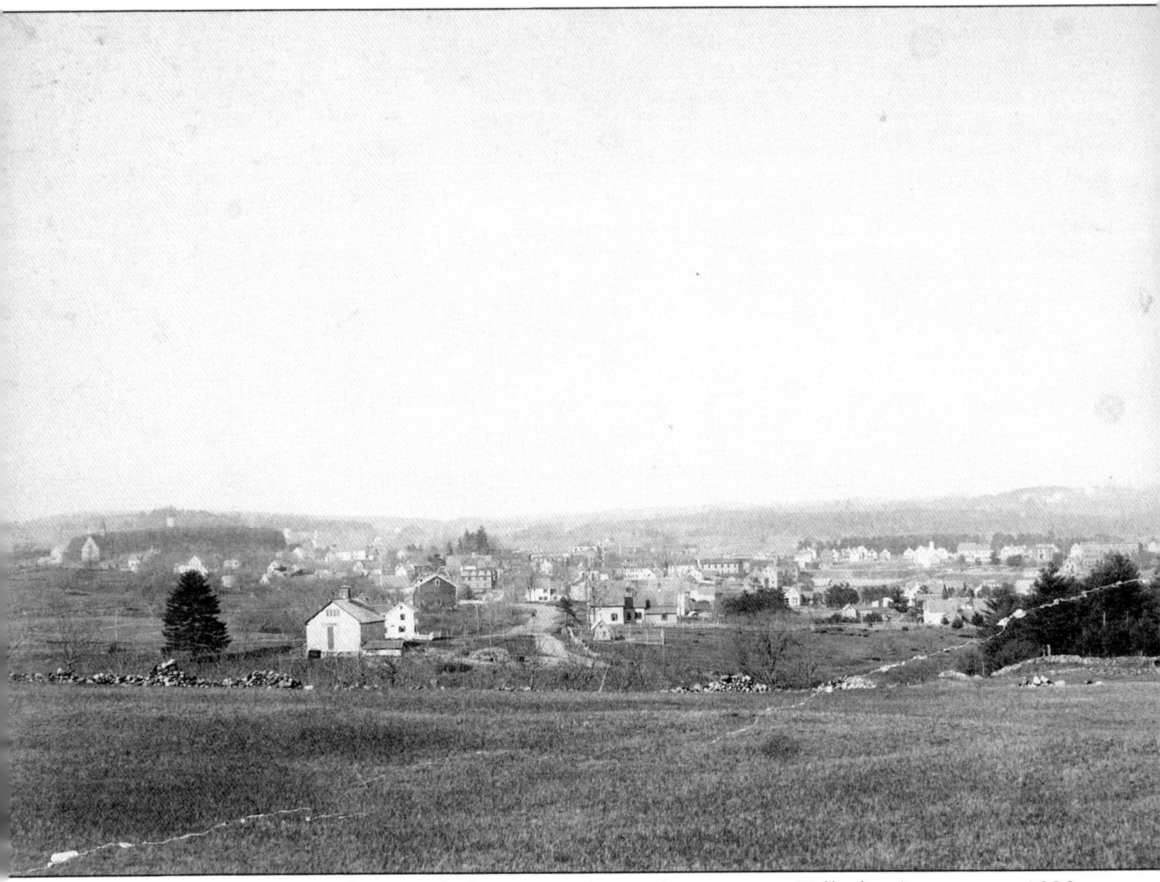

A panoramic view of Derry looking east from the present Hillside Avenue c. 1890. (Library collection)

IMAGES
of America

DERRY

Compiled by

William F. Dugan and Richard Holmes
with the cooperation of the Derry Historical Society

ARCADIA
PUBLISHING

ISBN 978-0-7385-8836-9

Published by Arcadia Publishing
Charleston, South Carolina

Printed in the United States of America

Library of Congress Catalog Card Number: Applied for

For all general information contact Arcadia Publishing at:
Telephone 843-853-2070
Fax 843-853-0044
E-mail sales@arcadiapublishing.com
For customer service and orders:
Toll-Free 1-888-313-2665

Visit us on the Internet at www.arcadiapublishing.com

Contents

Introduction 7

Acknowledgments 8

1. East Derry 9

2. Derry Village 17

3. Beaver Lake 29

4. West Derry
   - Residential 35
   - Mills 45
   - Commercial 59

5. Institutions 81

6. Social 107

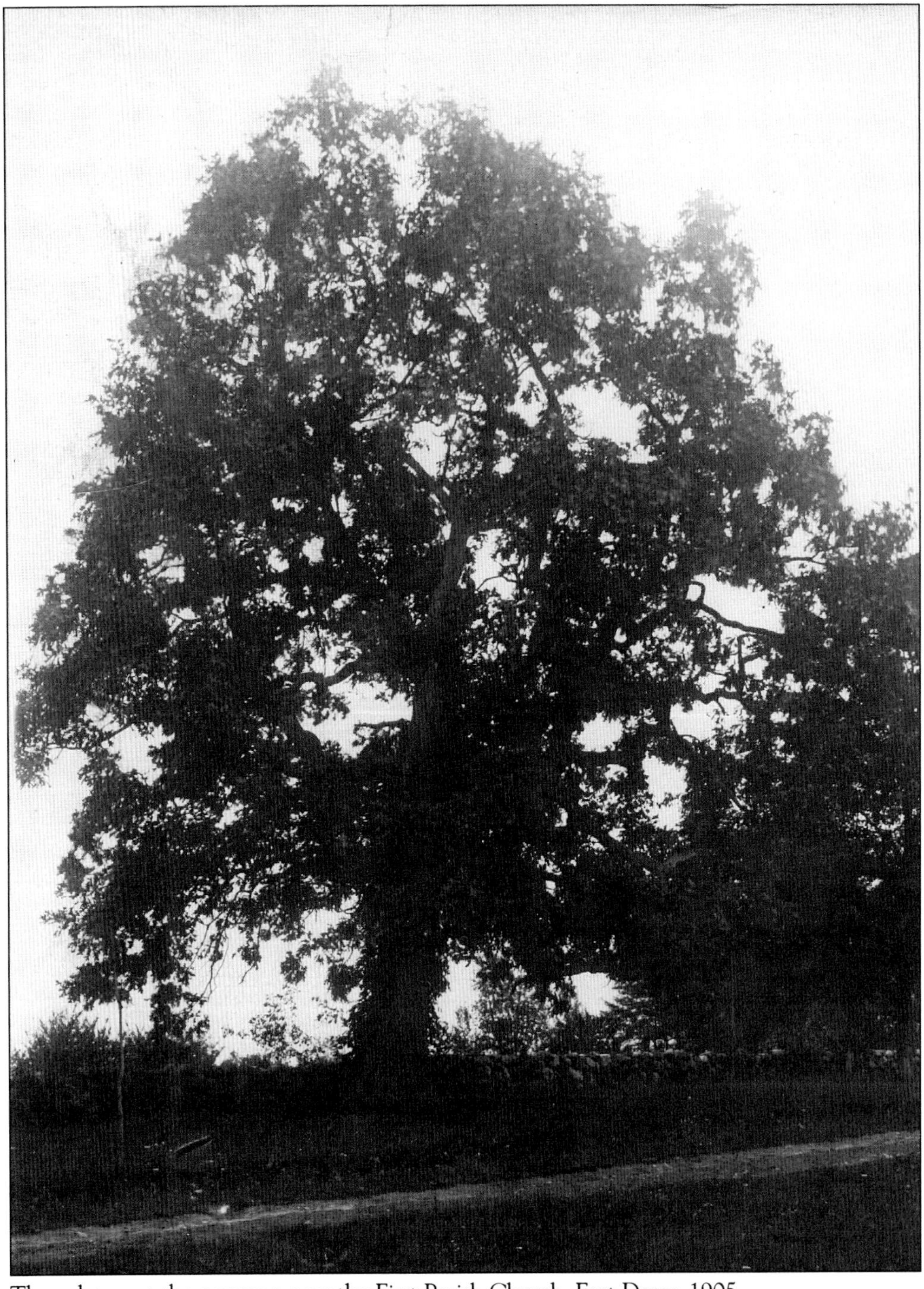

The oak tree at the common near the First Parish Church, East Derry, 1905.

Introduction

In 1719 a small group of Scottish pioneers laid claim to a wilderness that would in time become Derry. On a high hill close to a young oak tree they built their meetinghouse, and between the morning and afternoon services the worshippers would rest and lunch beneath its branches. Once a week a post rider carried to the town a single newspaper. A strong-voiced deacon would stand under the tree and read to the information-starved citizens the news of a greater world.

For nearly ten generations the oak stood on the hill as a respected presence within the community. The gray-haired rememberers taught their children the history that the tree had witnessed. Their word-pictures invoked images of the funeral processions of Derry's great men as they paused by the oak before resuming the final slow march to the grave; of stirring times and long ranks of soldiers in formation proudly squared off with the old tree; of listening to long orations; of children's games and lover's pledges, all witnessed by this ancient sentry oak.

Gypsy moths attacked the East Derry oak in 1906, but somehow it lived and in time recovered. Twenty years later a workman walked past the tree—he saw it only as an old oak—and when no one was around he cut it down and took the wood home to burn in his fireplace. There was a lot of handwringing and tears after the tree's fate became known, but nothing could be done. It was gone forever.

This book is intended to give to the modern resident a photographic record of a Derry that used to be. Just like that old oak tree in East Derry, many of Derry's ancient landmarks are now no longer with us. Some were lost to the ravishes of fire or decay; most, however, were taken from us by the bulldozers of progress. Every year less and less of our past remains standing. Our link with our past is fast disappearing.

The hills where a thousand cows once grazed have now been covered with apartment complexes and housing developments. Some former residential neighborhoods are now home only to strip malls and car lots. Each year an ever increasing number of intersections are taken over by new pizza parlors and gas stations. Roads designed for horses and wagons are now clogged with automobiles. Taxes are up and services are down.

Within these pages are views of a quieter Derry frozen in time by photographs. This book will hopefully bring back many happy memories to long-time residents. We further hope that all readers will recognize the need to preserve what still survives of old Derry. Our legacy to the future is not just what we build today but also what we preserve from yesterday. We cannot and should not stop all progress; but growth should be structured so that the character and history of Derry can be maintained for our children and for generations to come.

Acknowledgments

We wish to thank the Derry Historical Society for the use of the photographs in their collection. The hours of their well-structured museum can be found by calling the Derry Town Hall. The authors are also grateful for the assistance of the following: Edward Newell; George Grinnell; Anthony Galluzzo; Ralph Bonner; Perfecta Camera; Donald Houston; Carol Holmes; Lois Dugan; Bertha MacDougall; the staff of the Derry Public Library; the men and women of the West Derry fire station; Marilyn Hamm; the Derry Historical Commission; the Londonderry Historical Society for their gift of the Arthur Lear collection of photographs; Louise Audette; Broadway Books; the Chester Historical Society; Dennis Goyette; the young men and women of the Pelham Memorial School; Julian Hayes; Elsie and Marion Richardson; John and Marjorie Holmes; Mr. and Mrs. Francis J. Sullivan; and the late beloved Harriett Newell, whose books on Derry have been our guide in this project.

One

East Derry

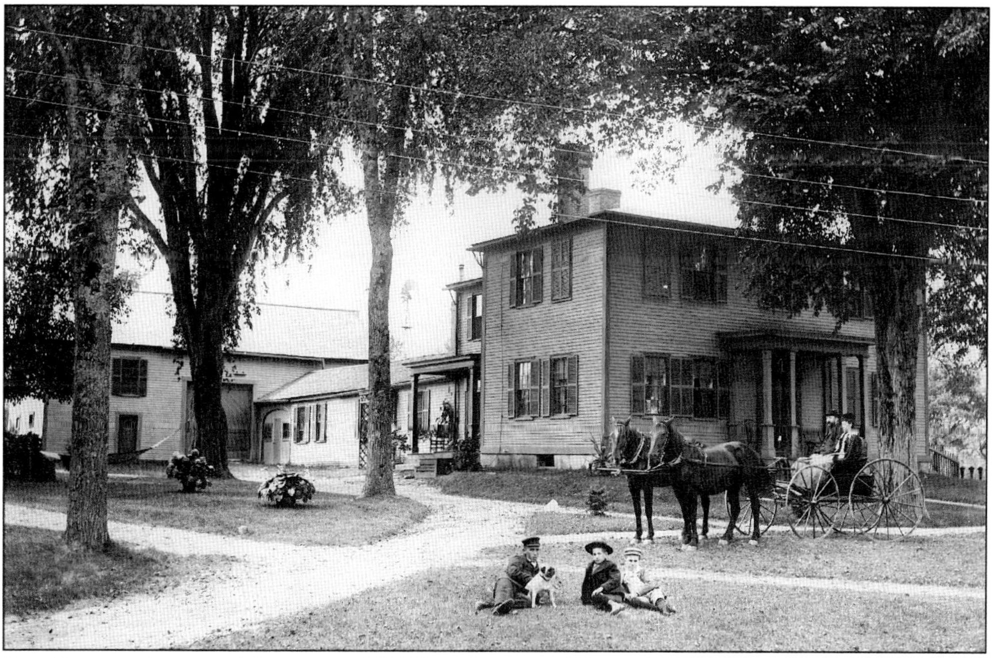

East Derry is the site of the original 1719 settlement of Derry. With its own library, fire station, store, old town hall, and church, it is in some ways a separate self-sufficient community within greater Derry. East Derry's most distinguished area is Hampstead Road, with its long row of well-kept nineteenth-century houses. The Reverend Edward L. Parker built this house on Hampstead Road in 1810 and lived there until his death in 1850. While pastor of the First Parish Church he wrote the first history of Derry, which was published posthumously in 1851. The man in the carriage in this c. 1895 photograph is likely his son, Edward T. Parker. Notice the windmill in the background; it was used to draw fresh water for the house and horse barn.

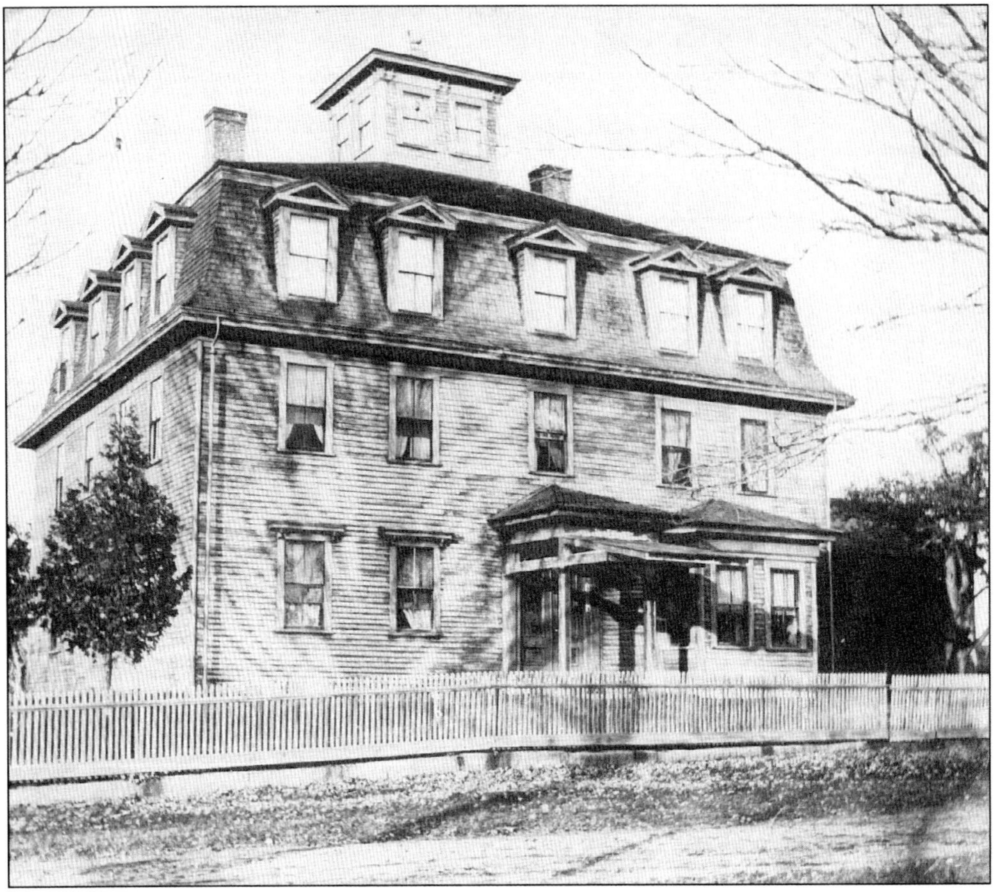

The Lane farmhouse was one of the grandest manor houses in New Hampshire. In 1825 Lafayette stopped here to visit his old comrade, General Derby. The 3-story, 50-by-45-foot building was crowned by a massive cupola. A 2-story, 22-by-84-foot ell extended down Lane Road. The home burned in 1926.

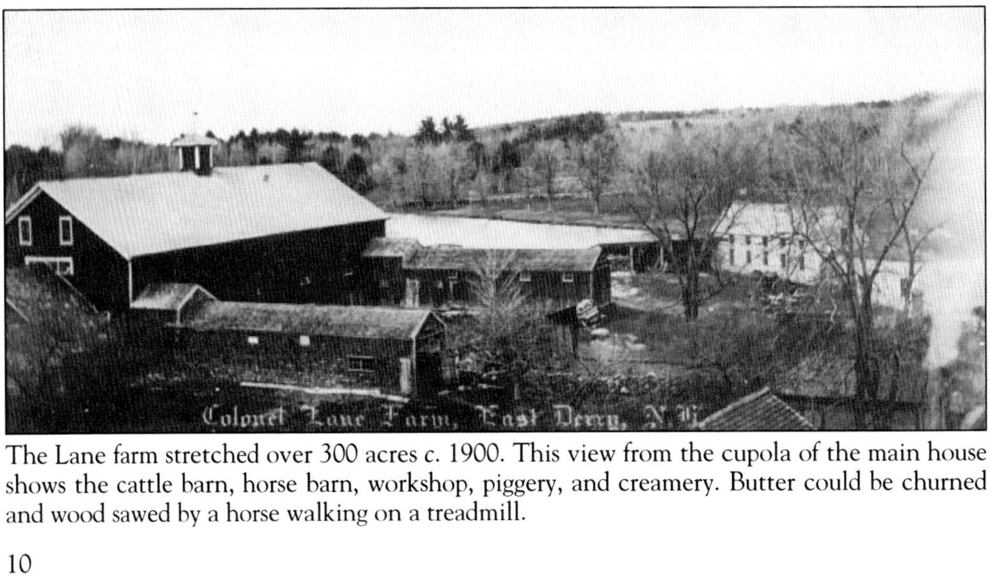

The Lane farm stretched over 300 acres c. 1900. This view from the cupola of the main house shows the cattle barn, horse barn, workshop, piggery, and creamery. Butter could be churned and wood sawed by a horse walking on a treadmill.

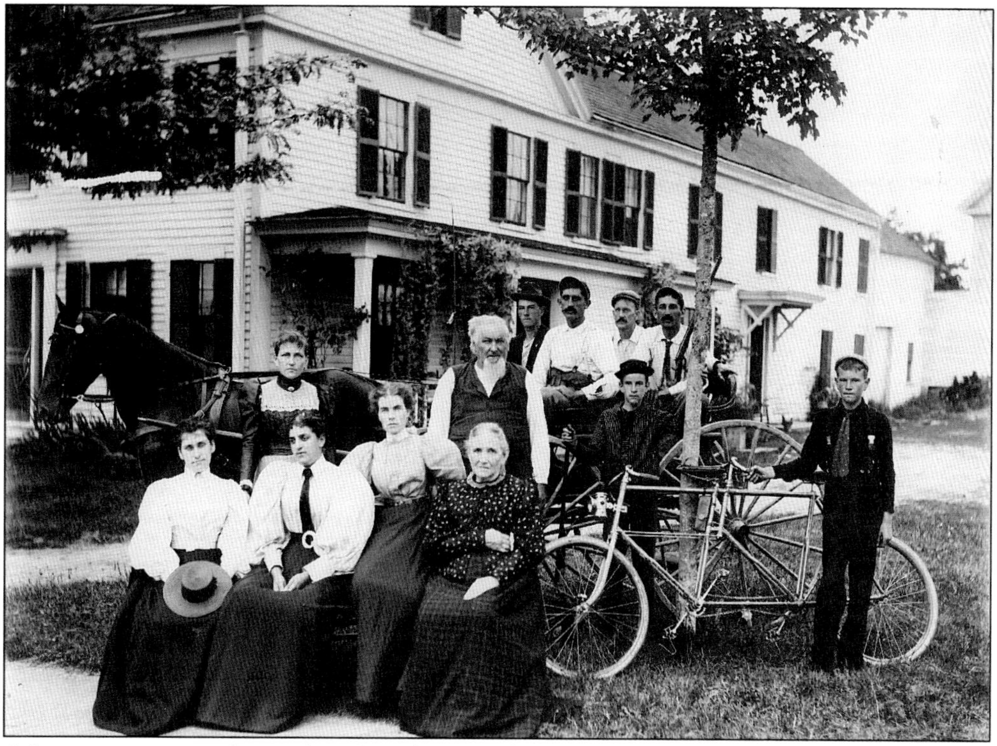

A hunting excursion leaves from Jonathan Sanders' home on East Derry Road *c.* 1895. These boys are proudly showing off their rather oddly-built tandem bicycle. The house on Horse Hill burned before World War I and was replaced by a bungalow-style building.

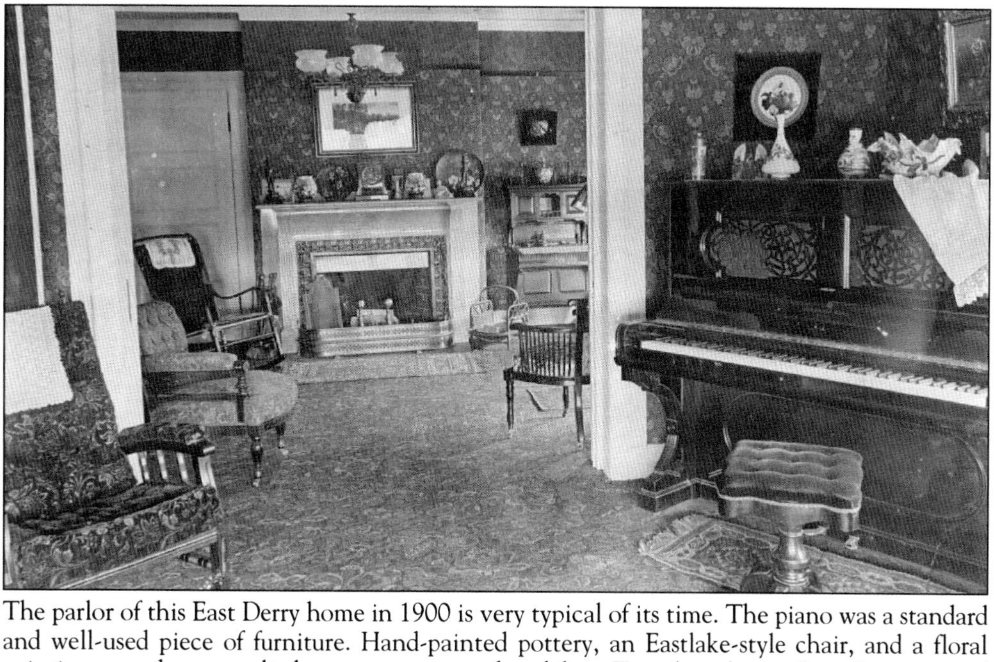

The parlor of this East Derry home in 1900 is very typical of its time. The piano was a standard and well-used piece of furniture. Hand-painted pottery, an Eastlake-style chair, and a floral painting crowd a room lit by an ornate gas chandelier. Together they reflect their owners' acceptance of the prevailing Victorian taste.

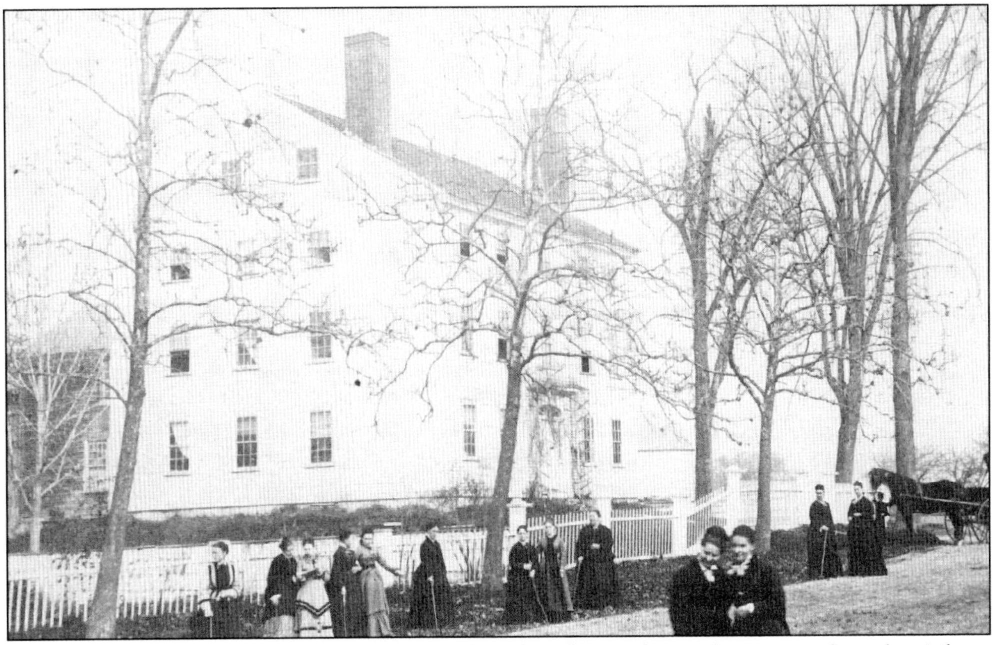

The Elms was built in 1824 and served as a boarding house for students attending the Adams Female Academy. Students of the school are shown out for a stroll in this c. 1870 photograph. The Elms would later become a summer hotel. It was destroyed in a fire in 1907.

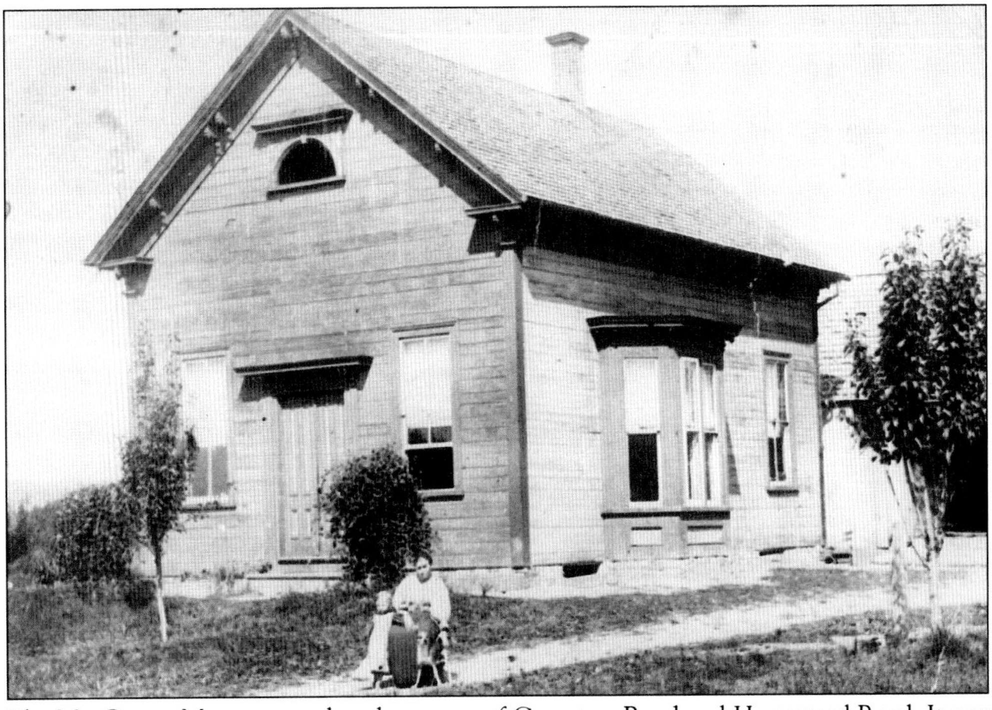

The MacGregor Museum stood at the corner of Cemetery Road and Hampstead Road. It was built privately in 1877 to display curiosities and items of local interest—admission was only 25¢. After a few years it was sold and moved further down the road where it was soon destroyed in a fire.

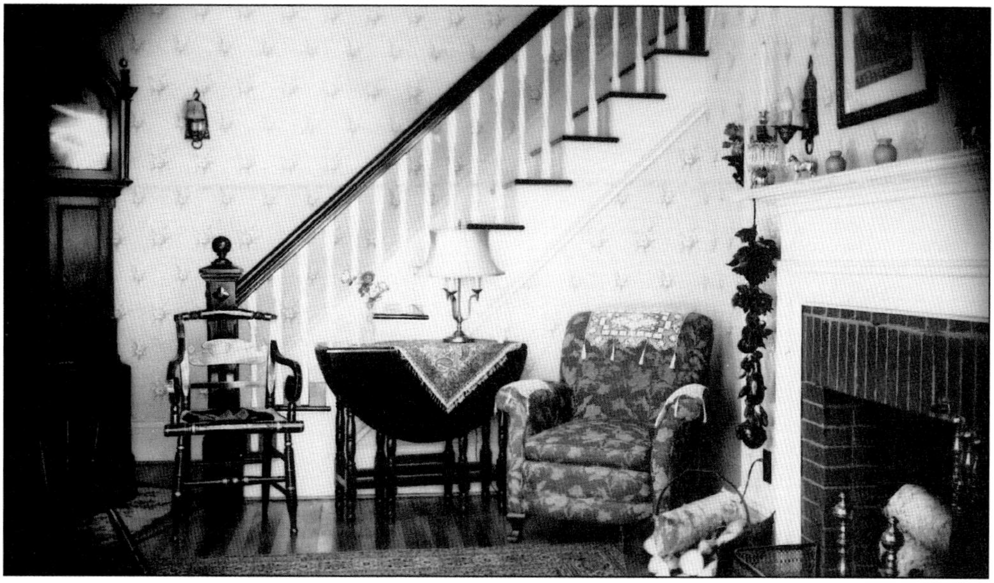

The residence of Mr. and Mrs. Paul Brickett of East Derry was typical of the homes belonging to the area's upper middle class in 1939. Old-fashioned elegance is combined with modern appliances, as evidenced by the electric lights hidden within the candle sconces. (Lear photograph)

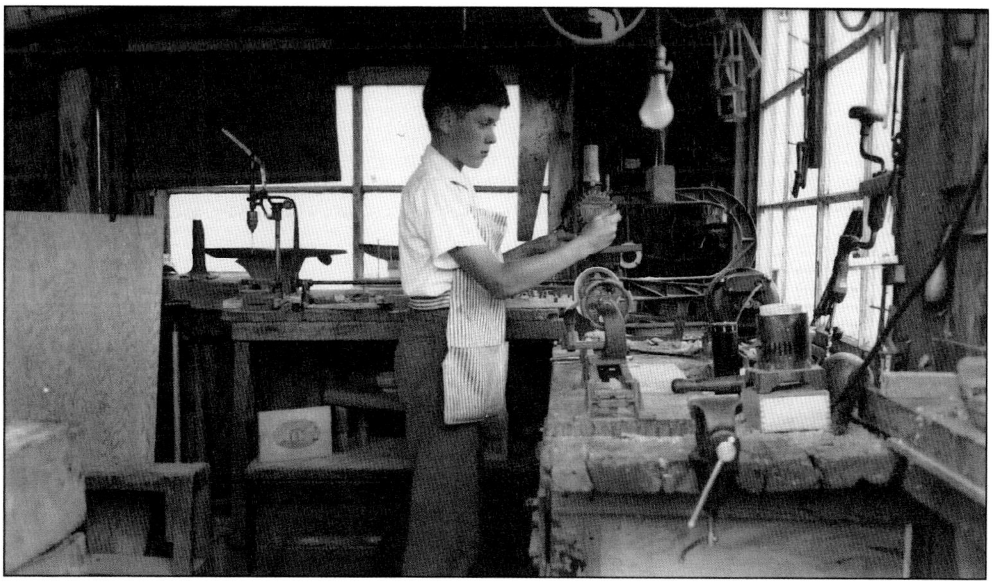

This well-equipped workshop would have been the answer to the dreams of many a teenage boy during the Depression. Young Sherm Brickett is shown working intently on a wooden gear at his East Derry home in June 1939. (Lear photograph)

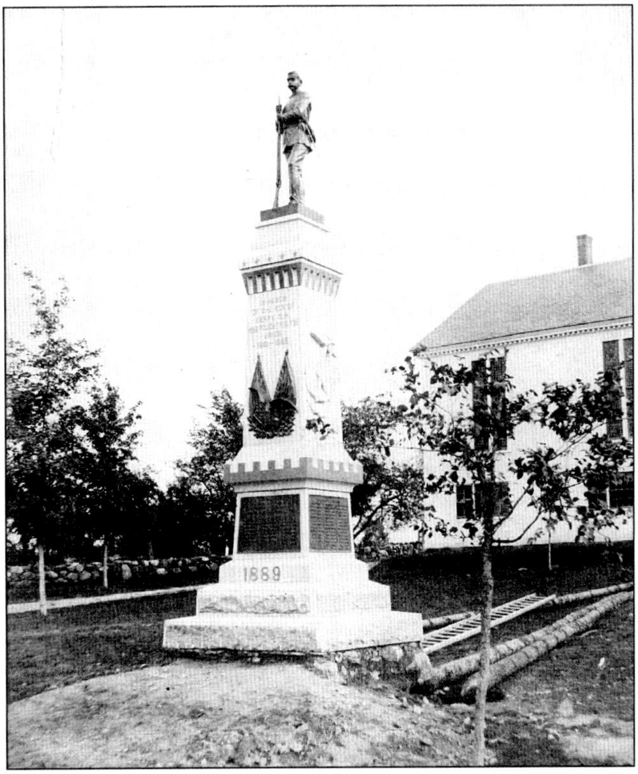

The Soldiers Monument on the day of its erection in 1889. Designed to honor the men of Derry who fought in the Civil War, it stands 27 feet tall, and on its base are inscribed the names of all of the local veterans of the war. Much of its $3,000 cost was borne by Miss Emma Taylor.

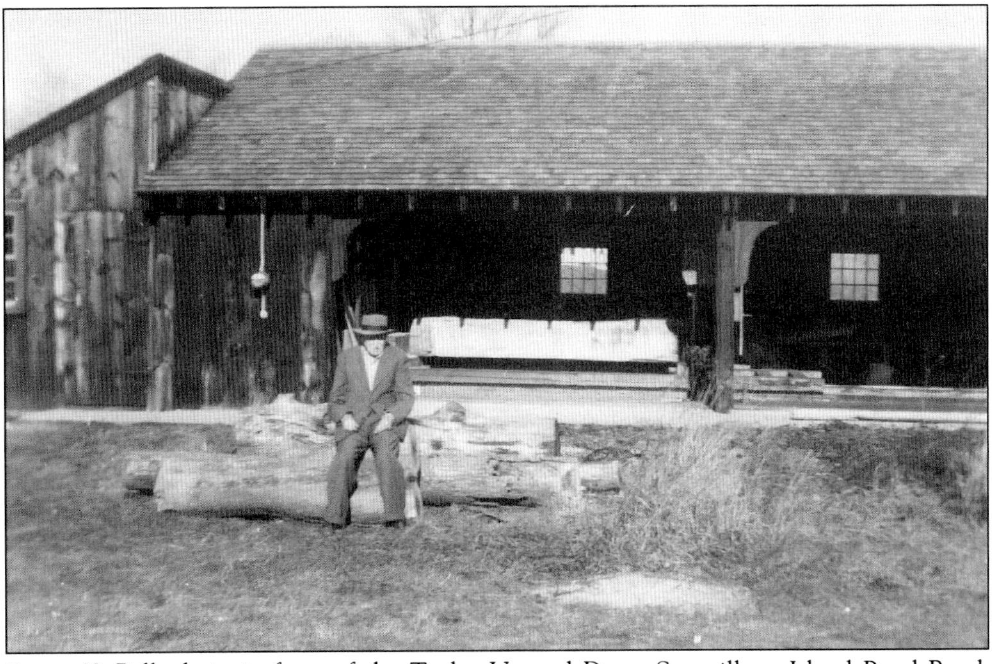

Ernest K. Ballard sits in front of the Taylor Up and Down Sawmill on Island Pond Road. He constructed the water-powered mill with a combination of new material and pieces from abandoned area mills. Upon his death in 1953 Mr. Ballard left the mill to the state to be used as a working museum.

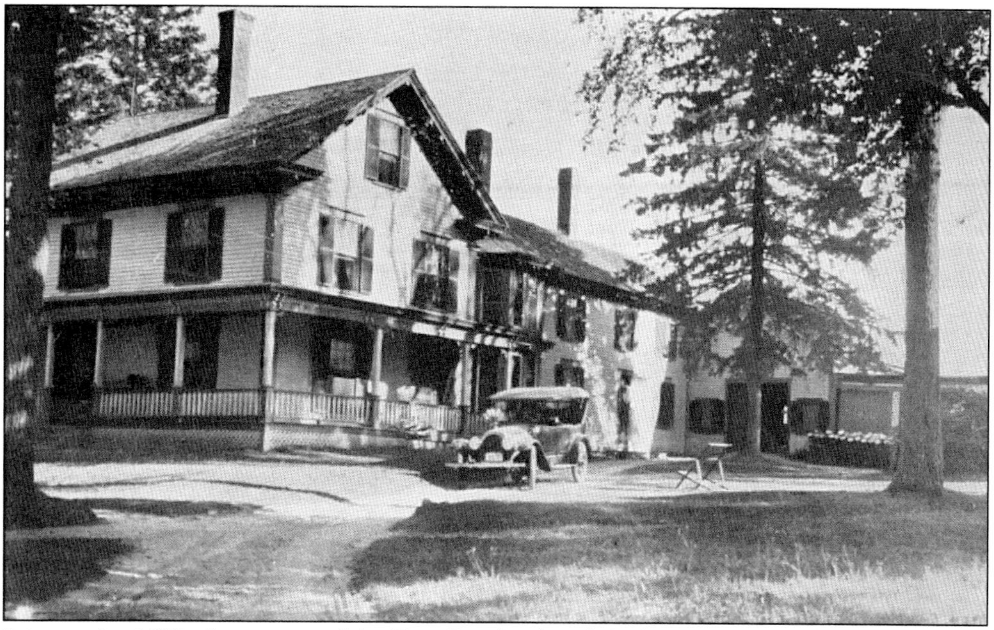

Prior to the 1850s the pastors of the First Parish Church had to provide their own parsonage. This changed during the ministering of Reverend James Wellman (1851–1857) who was provided with this residence on Hampstead Road. It was sold by the church in 1863 after a larger parsonage was purchased.

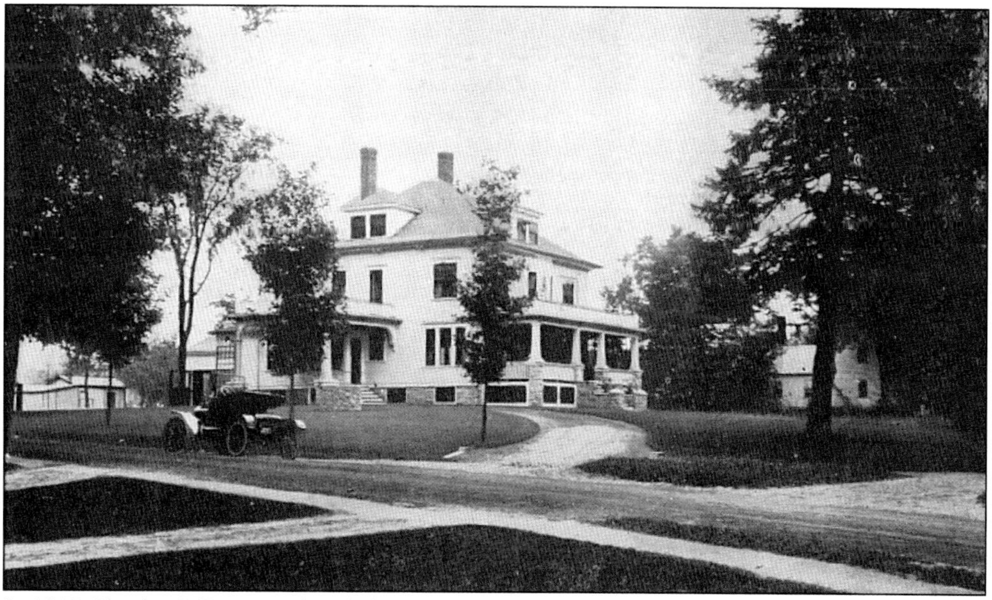

In 1913 Charles S. Emerson decided to erect an imposing residence, appropriate for a man of his means and status within the community. He was the owner of several shoe factories, stores, and apartment buildings in West Derry but he chose to live in East Derry.

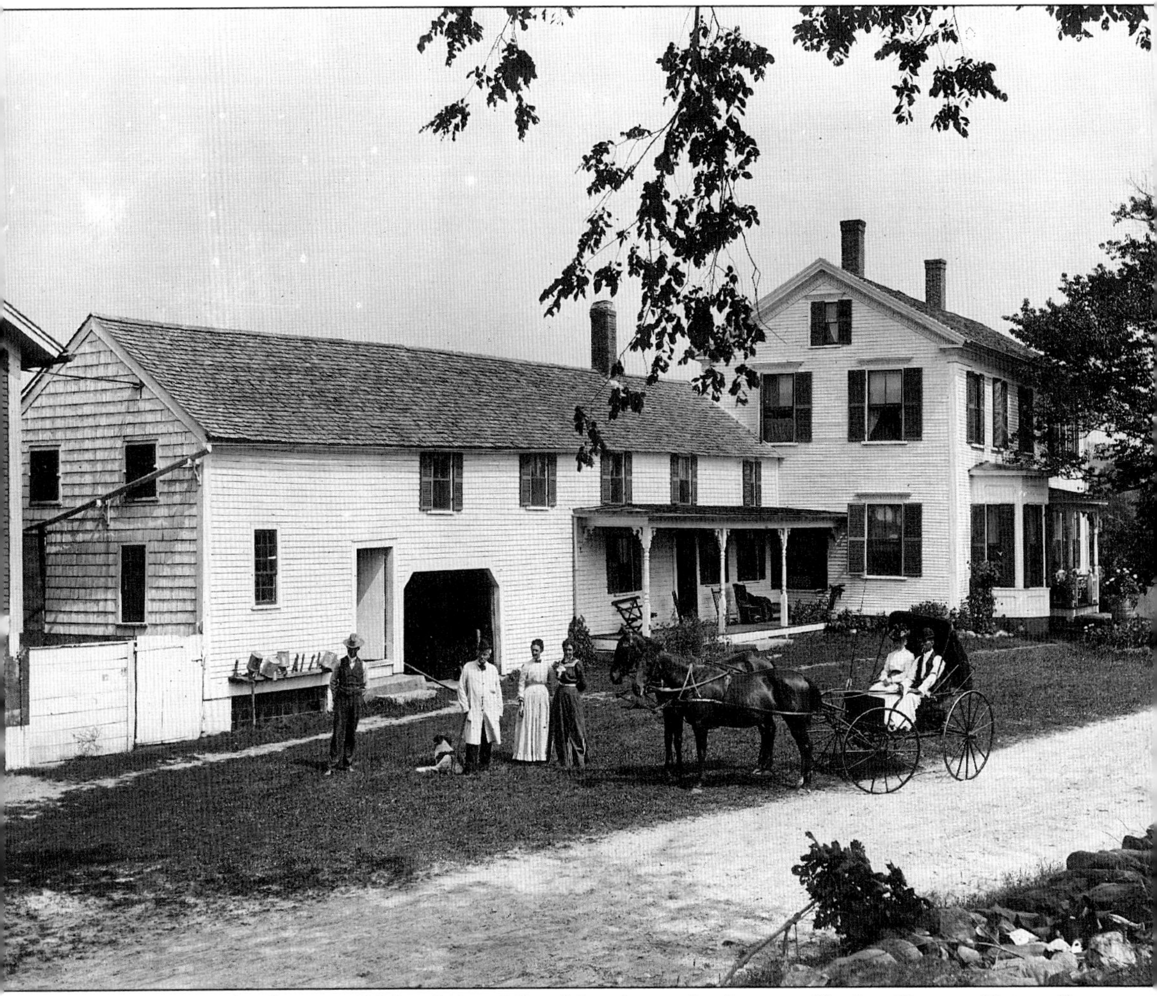

Since 1947 this house off Island Pond Road has been the home of Judge George Grinnell. This 1895 picture shows the Noyes family and their hired hand. The barn, sheds, and house are connected to make travel between them easier during the snowbound winters. (Grinnell collection)

Two

Derry Village

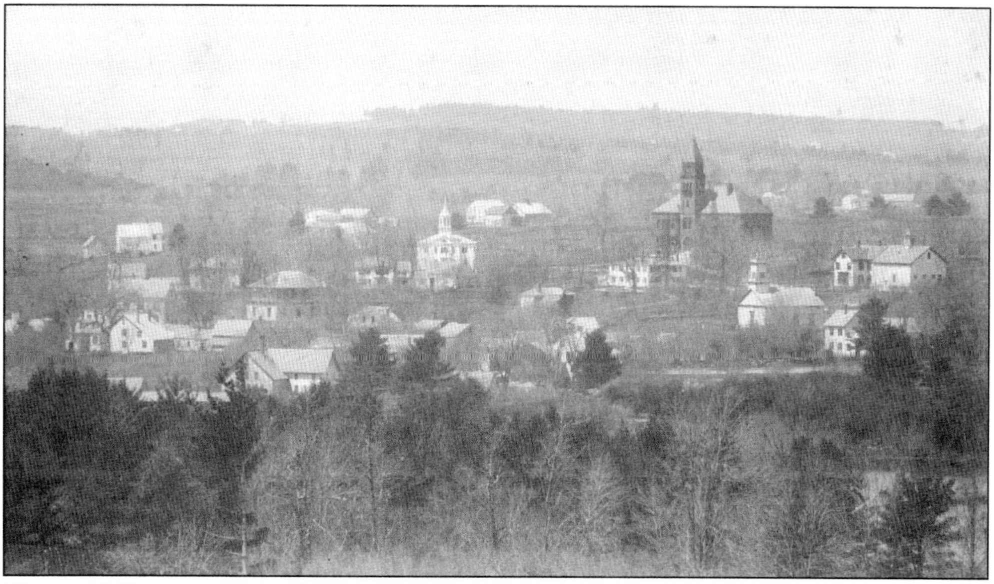

This *c.* 1900 view of Derry Village from East Derry Hill reveals a few recognizable buildings. Dominating the whole area is the brick tower of the Pinkerton Academy building. The old academy building is off to its left. In the center right is the First Methodist Church.

In 1806 a turnpike was built through the center of what would eventually become Derry Village. This new road from Massachusetts to Concord, NH, was soon clogged with freight wagons and coaches, and stores, inns, and mills quickly sprang up in the so-called "Lower Village." The area remained the commercial center of the town until the railroad laid tracks through West Derry.

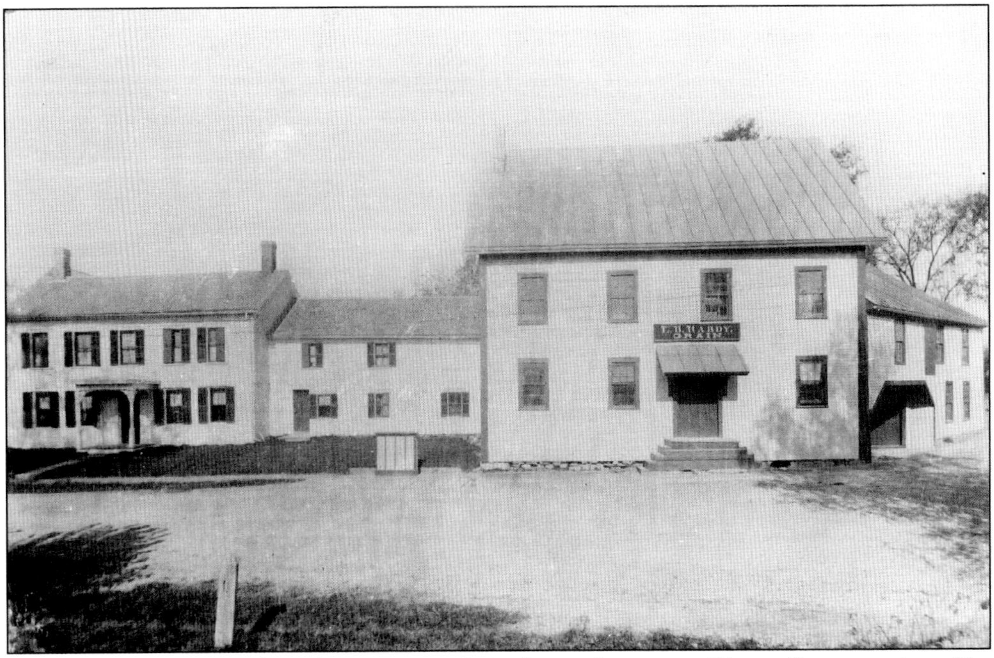

Grist mills have operated on this site since the eighteenth century. This mill was purchased by Lando B. Hardy in 1889 and after his death was operated by the Rockingham County Farmers Association. It was sold to the Chase Mill during the Depression and then demolished.

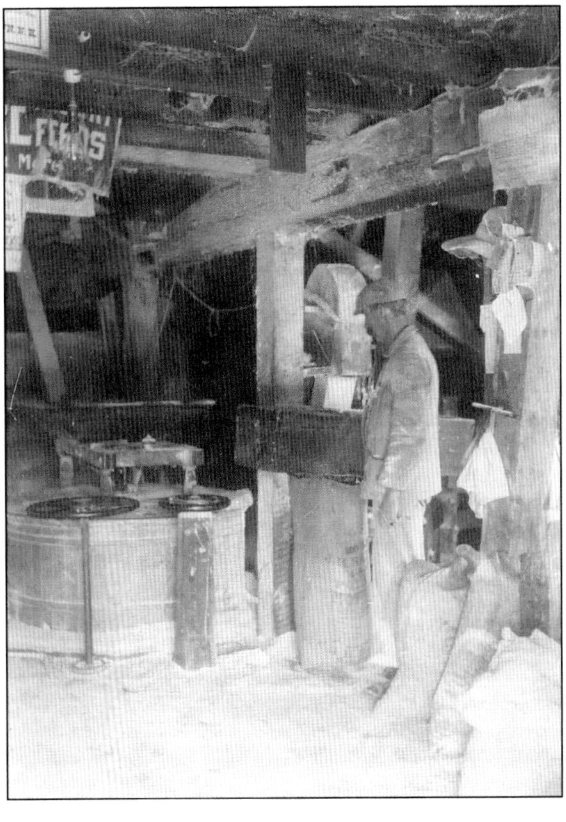

Lando B. Hardy is shown in his grist mill carefully watching flour being ground. He owned the Thornton Street business from 1889 until his death in 1921. Local farmers could bring their corn, wheat, and other grains to be ground at the mill.

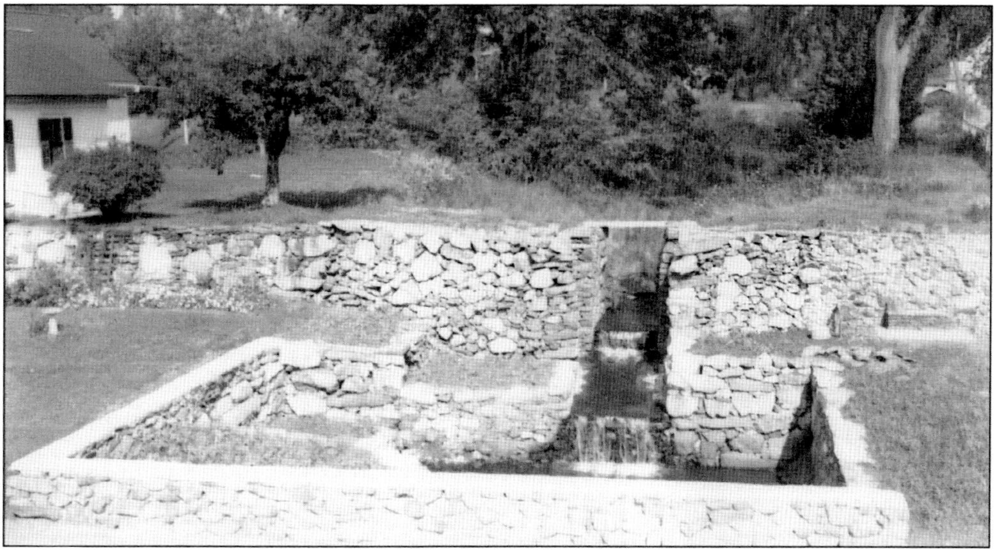

Hardy's Grist Mill was razed during the Depression. In 1939 Harry A. Gregg of Nashua, a wealthy banker, repaired the foundation and established a minipark in honor of one of his ancestors, who had built the original mill in 1719.

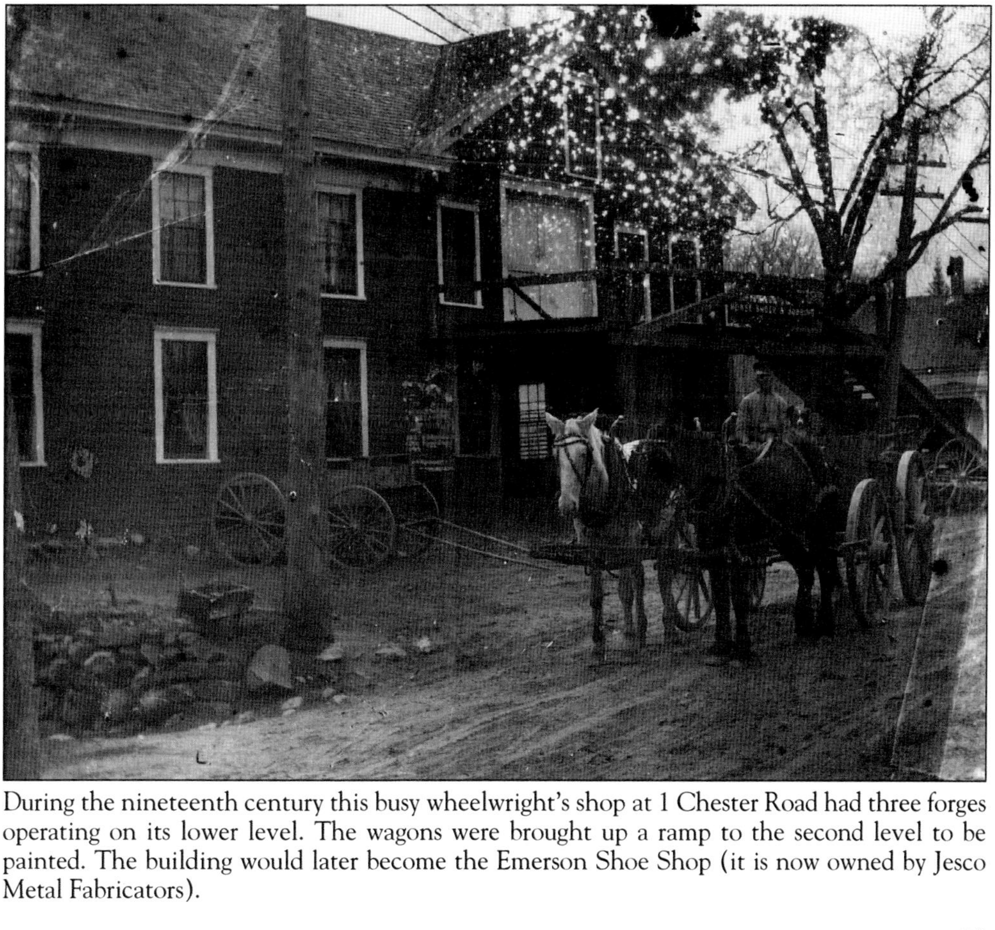

During the nineteenth century this busy wheelwright's shop at 1 Chester Road had three forges operating on its lower level. The wagons were brought up a ramp to the second level to be painted. The building would later become the Emerson Shoe Shop (it is now owned by Jesco Metal Fabricators).

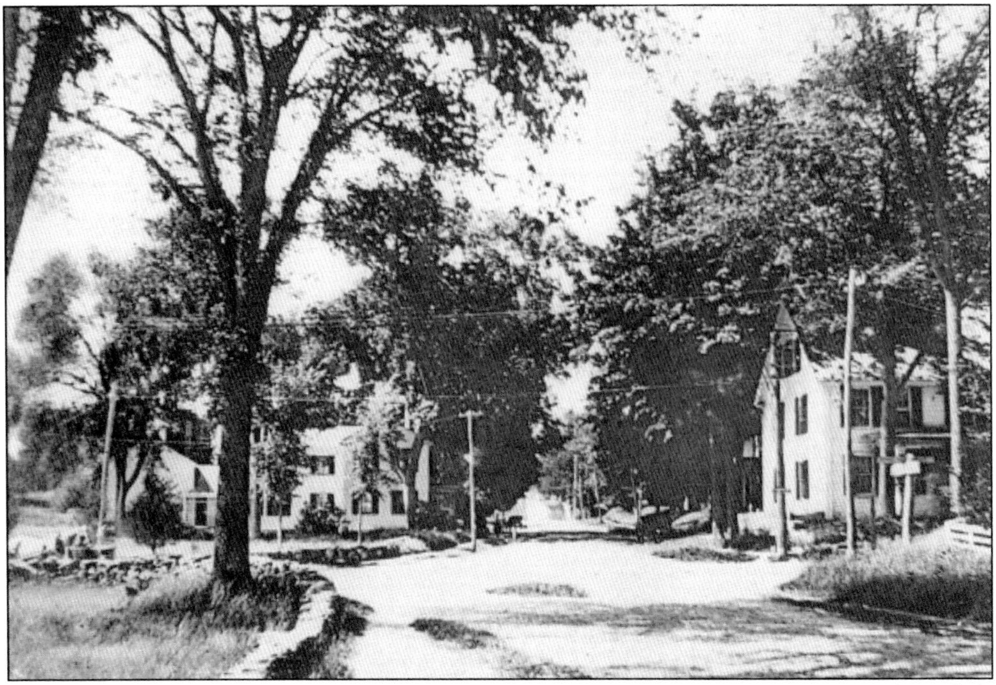

This 1905 photograph shows the former boarding house for the H.P. Hood Farm (on the right). The house on the left was moved in 1926 by Everett R. Rutter to Lane Road in East Derry. The Danforth traffic circle was built at this intersection in 1937.

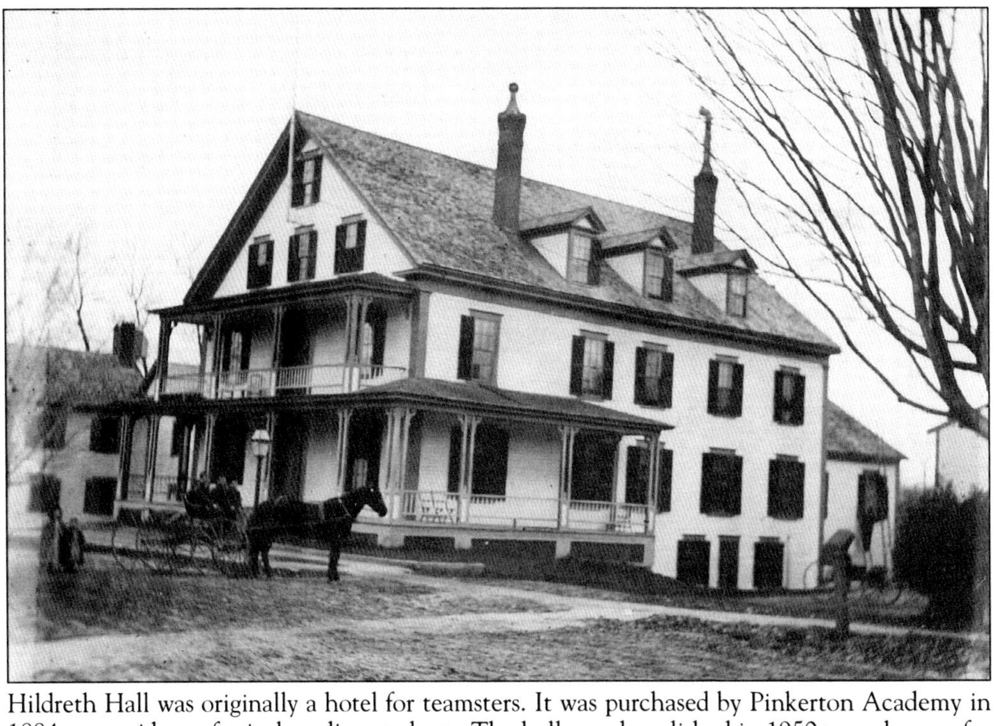

Hildreth Hall was originally a hotel for teamsters. It was purchased by Pinkerton Academy in 1884 as a residence for its boarding students. The hall was demolished in 1950 to make way for the new Shepard Field House.

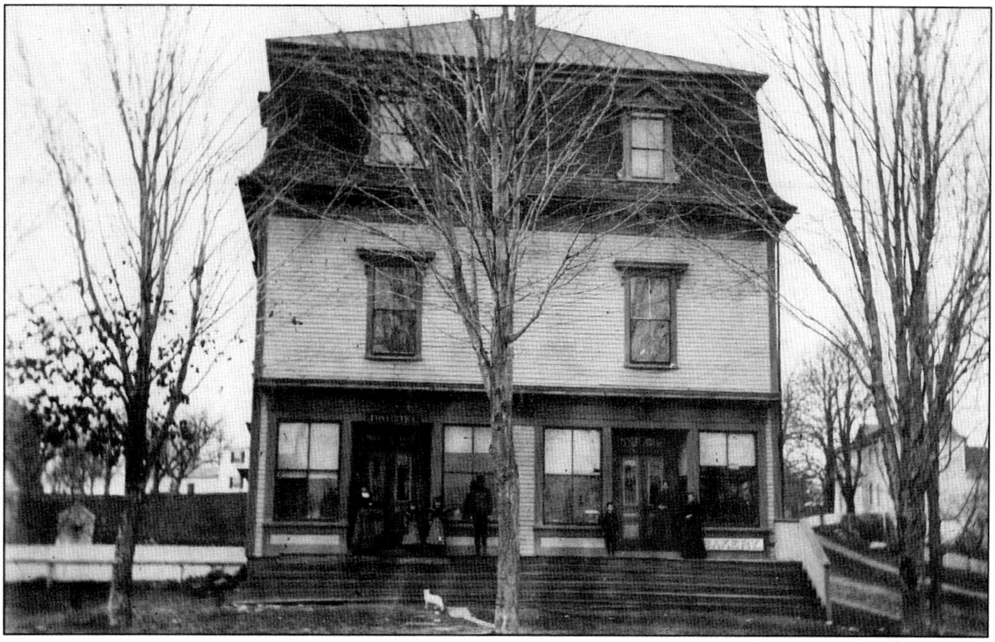

When this photograph was taken in 1895 the Association Hall was the local post office and bakery. For the next half a century it was used by the Central Congregational Church as its fellowship hall. The public hall upstairs has been the site of speeches by Ralph Waldo Emerson, Oliver Wendell Holmes, and Nelson Rockefeller, among many others (it is now an antique shop).

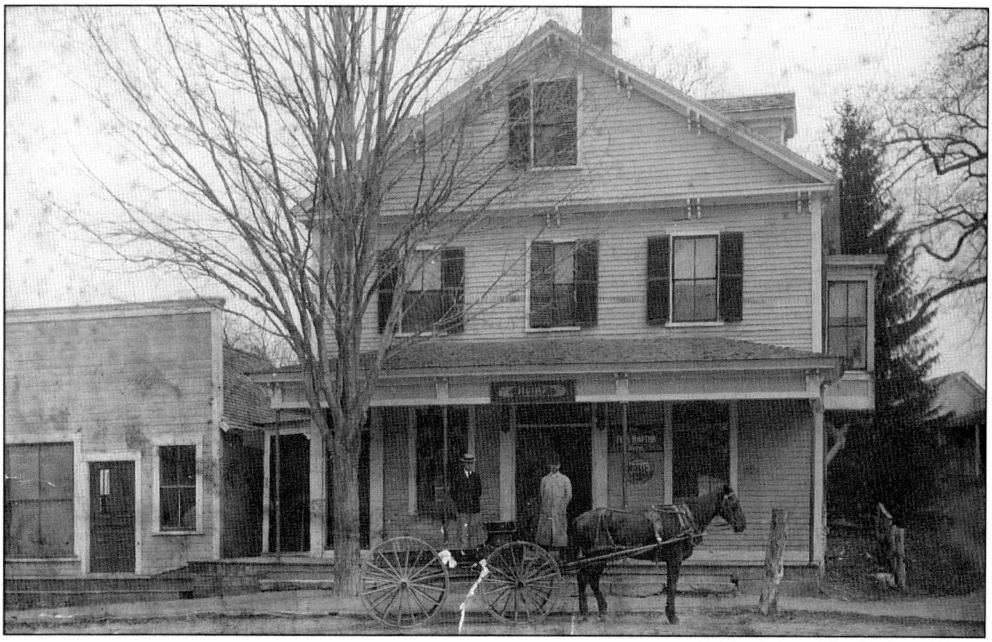

In 1858 this former young ladies' seminary was moved from Crescent Street to become a general store at Thornton Square. One summer day in the 1920s storekeeper Sarah Couch received a shock when Harvey Firestone, Henry Ford, and Thomas A. Edison all came through the door together to buy cigars.

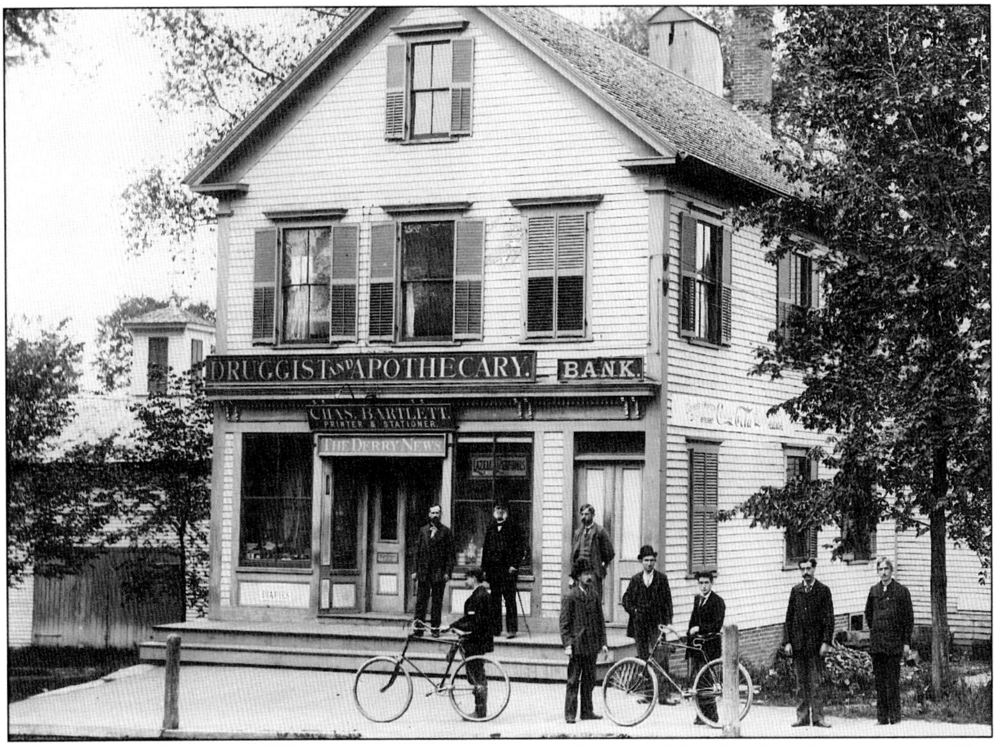

In 1880 the first issue of the *Derry News* was printed in this North Main Street store. The presses were powered by a wire rope and pulley which was strung from the distant Chase Mill. The rope crossed two roads and a field, ending up at the "dog-house" on the roof. The building was also at various times a drugstore, bank, and post office.

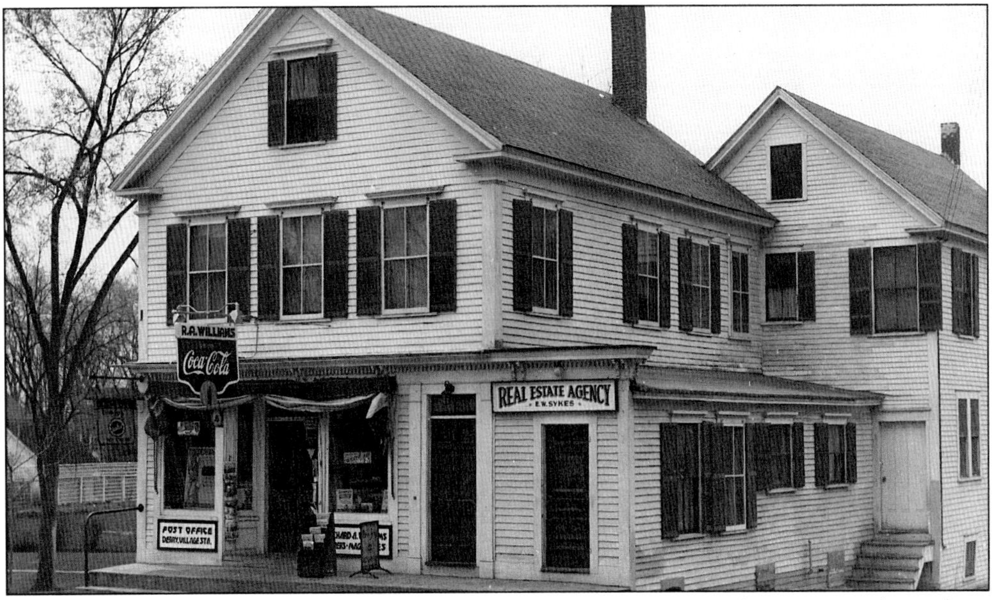

The Bartlett building would be the village post office from 1883 through 1945. It is shown here at the start of World War II operating as a general store, but it would later become a public accountant's office (it is now a private residence).

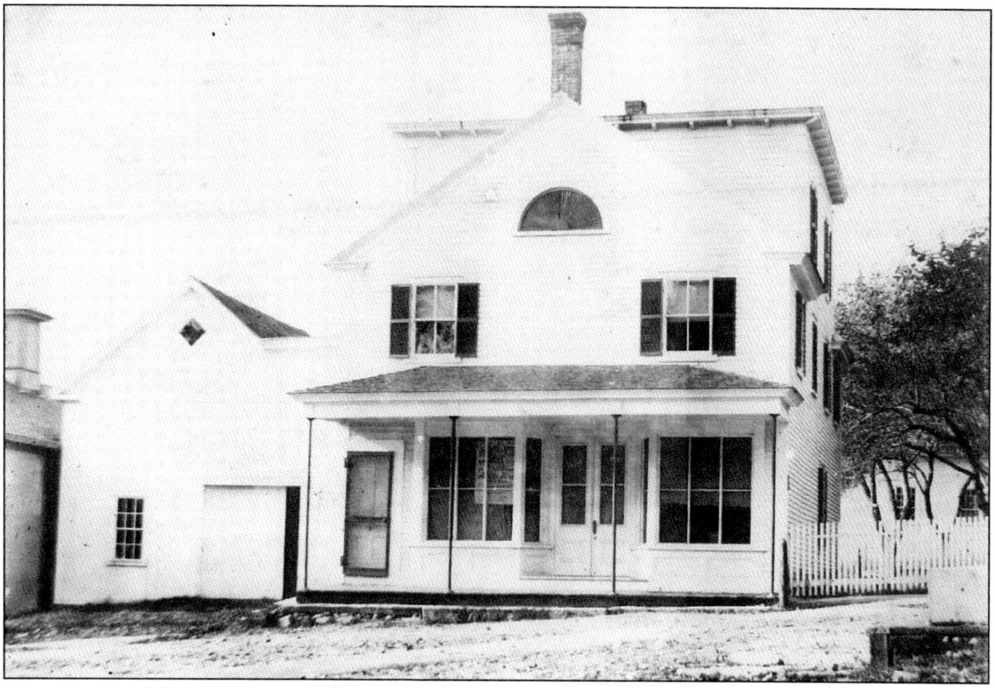

The Charles Adams house on the west side of Thornton Square operated as a general store for nearly a century. It stood to the right of the present Village Store. The building was torn down in 1945 and replaced with a modern house.

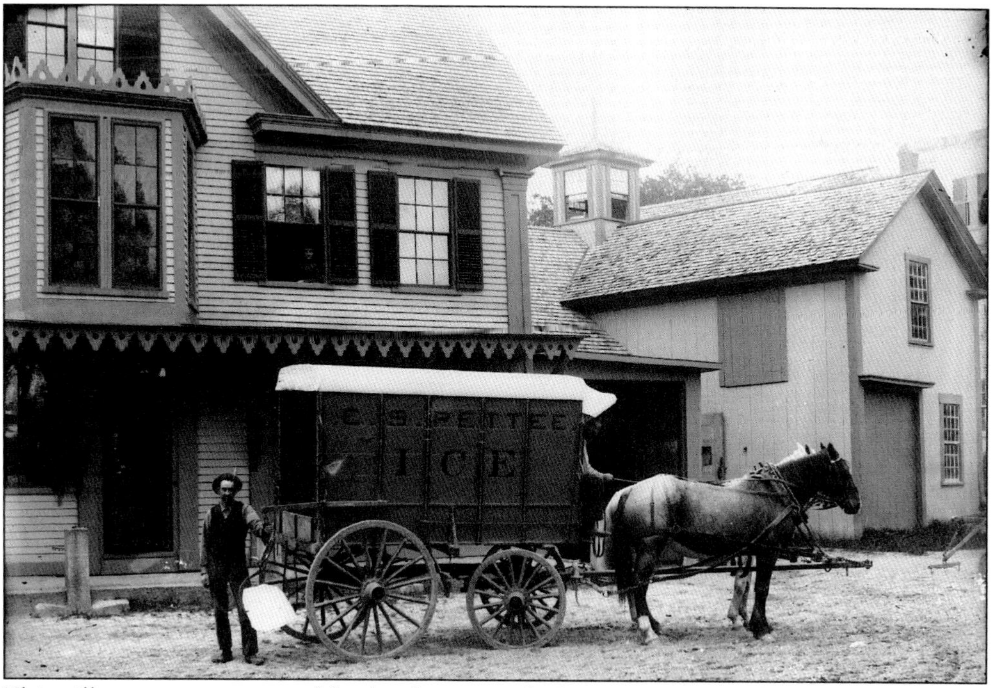

This village store was owned by local iceman C. Seneca Pettee at the time of this 1895 photograph. The eccentric Victorian building was torn down in 1937 to build the present one-story Derry Village Store.

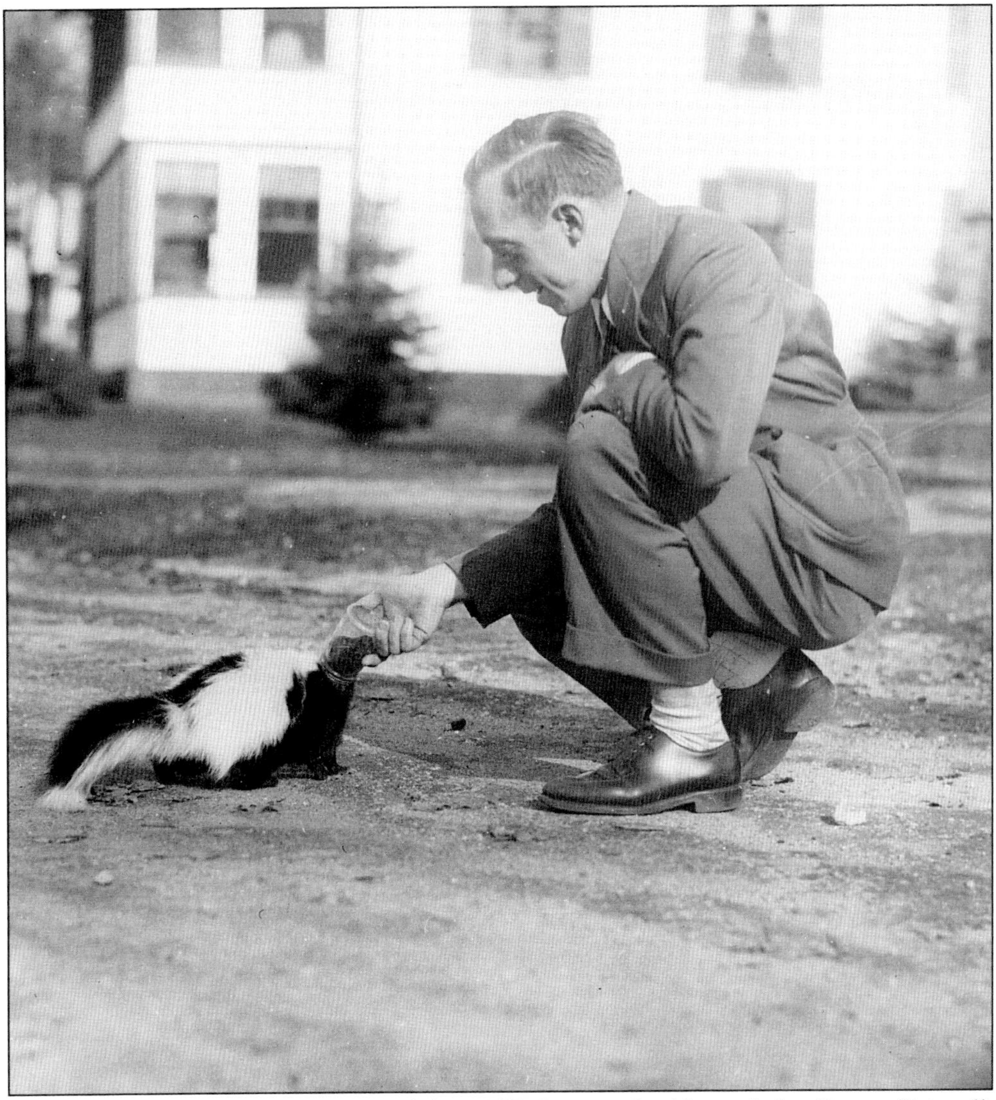

Newspapers all over the country carried this 1937 photograph of future Judge George Grinnell. He is shown at Thornton Square trying to rescue a wild skunk which got its head trapped in a mayonnaise jar. (Grinnell collection)

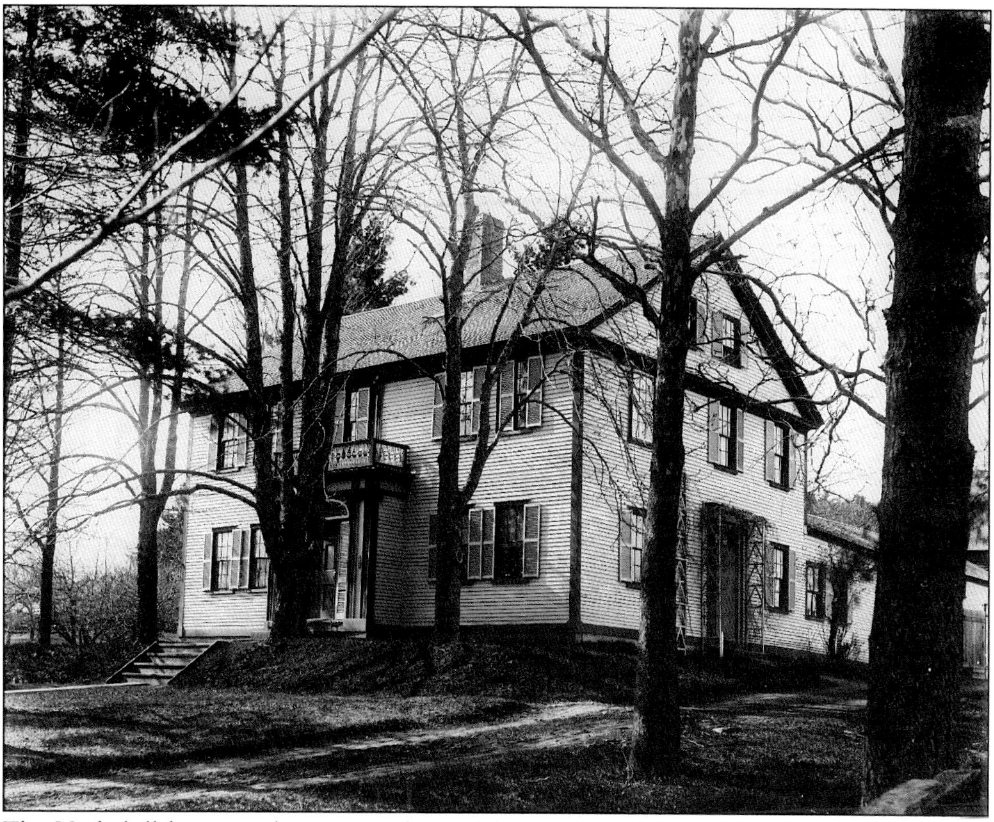

The Underhill home at the corner of Nesmith Street and Chester Road was likely built by James W. Nesmith c. 1835. Soon after the death of Miss Dorothy Underhill it was razed to make way for the Forest Hills Estates.

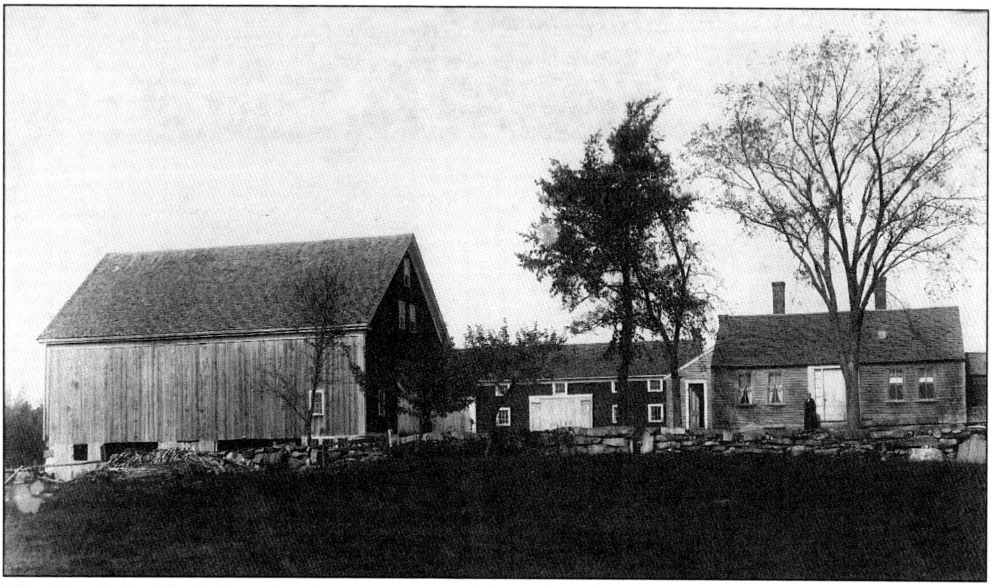

The Frank P. Clark farm (with its connected dairy barn) on English Range Road c. 1895 was typical of outlying farms. It burned in 1950 and a modern house has been erected on the site.

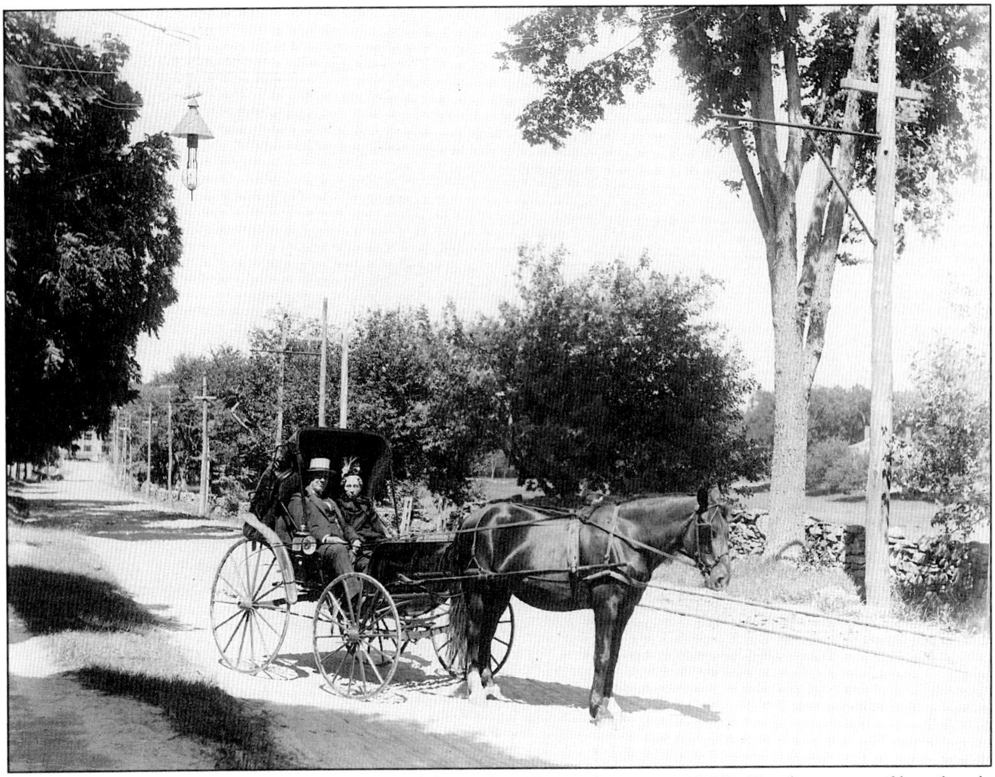

Harvey P. and Caroline Hood in front of their East Derry home *c.* 1895. By the time of his death in 1900 Harvey's dairy company had become the largest in New England. The benefactions of the family to the town have included three public parks, a school, a golf course, and a hospital.

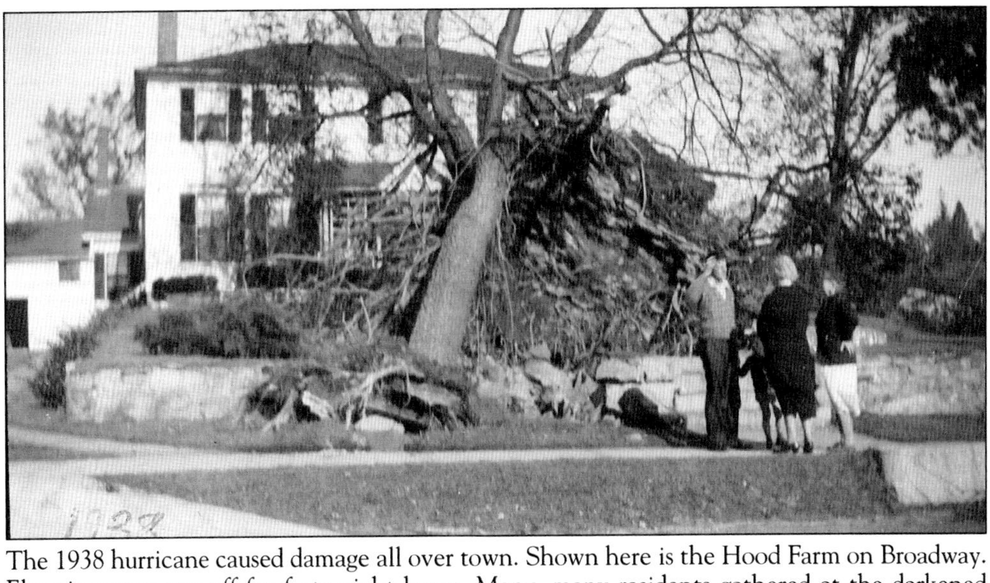

The 1938 hurricane caused damage all over town. Shown here is the Hood Farm on Broadway. Electric power was off for forty-eight hours. Many, many residents gathered at the darkened Plaza Theater to just sit and talk with their friends. Some cottages were blown over at Beaver Lake and 450 fallen trees were counted.

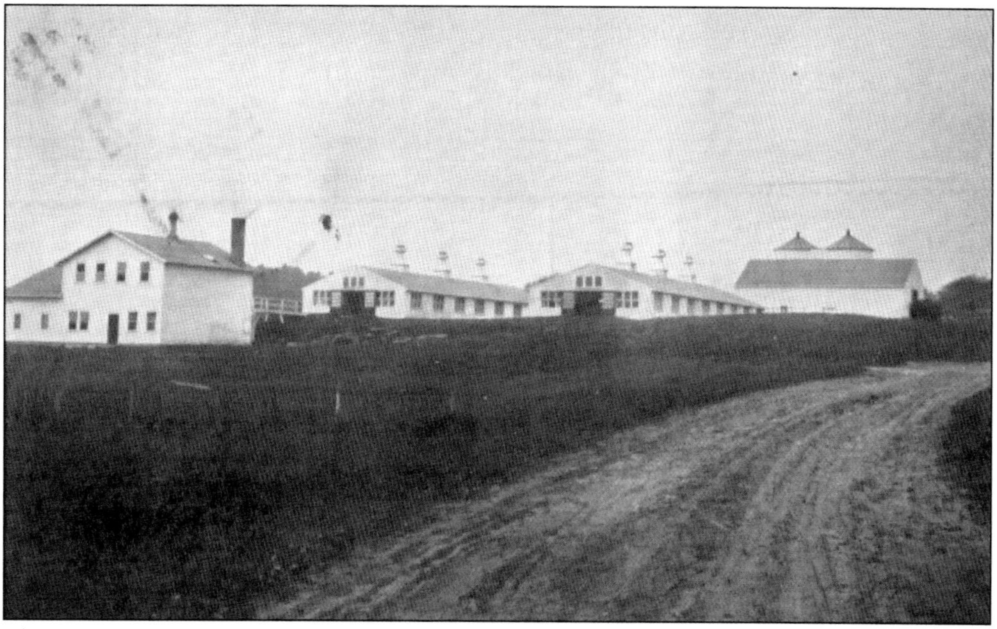

The massive complex of barns at the H.P. Hood Farm as they appeared in the 1920s. The 140-foot-long main barn burned in 1962.

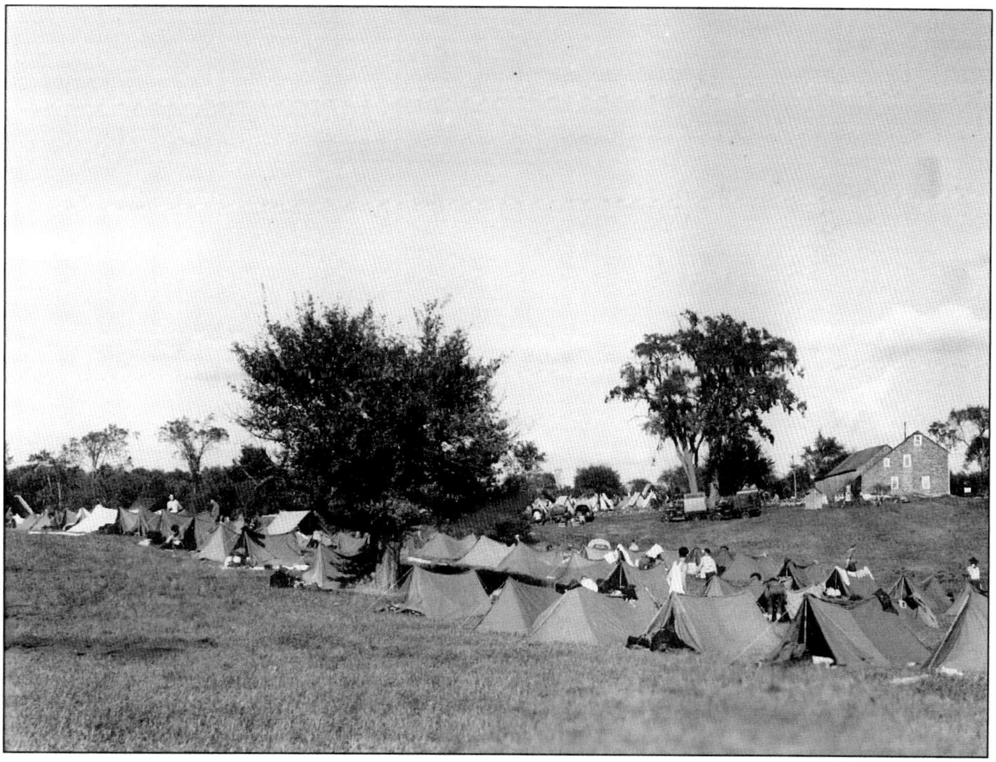

As war clouds gathered over Europe the need for military preparation became more urgent. In the summer of 1938 the 5th Infantry camped on Hood's meadow for field maneuvers.

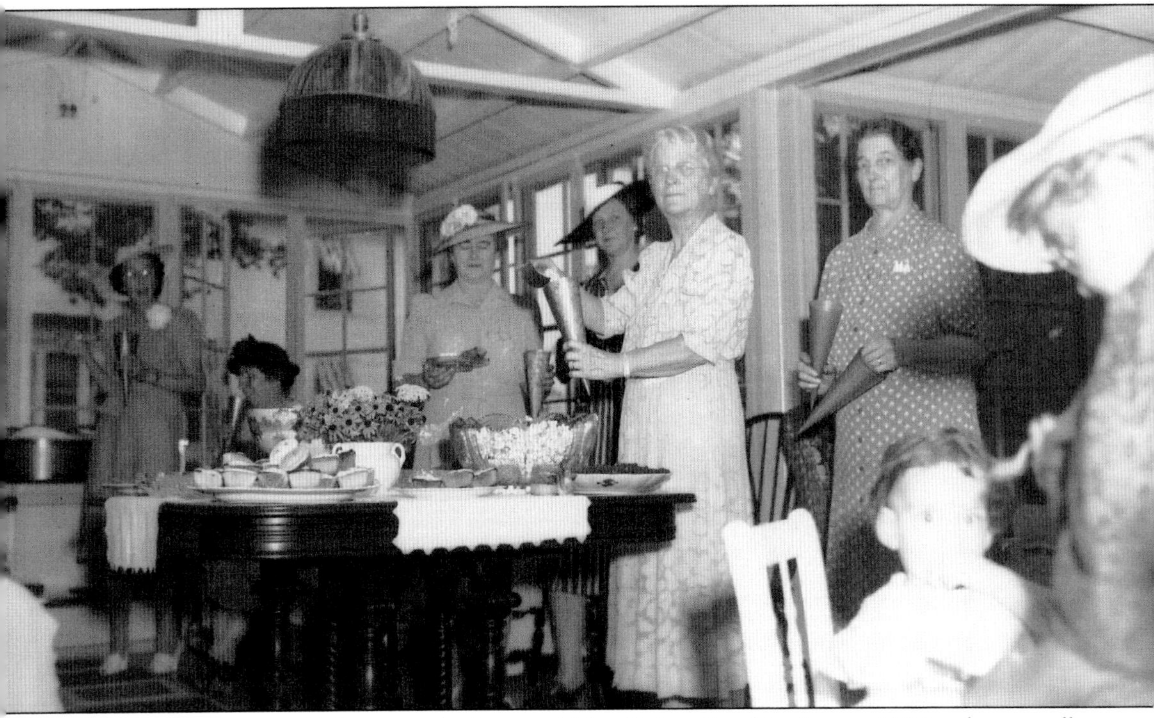

The Derry Garden Club met at the home of Mrs. Helen Hood in August 1939 to hear a talk on trees by a visiting professor. Refreshments included an ice cream cake and cornucopia filled with popcorn. Mrs. Hood is assisted by Mrs. Harriet Low. (Lear photograph)

Three

Beaver Lake

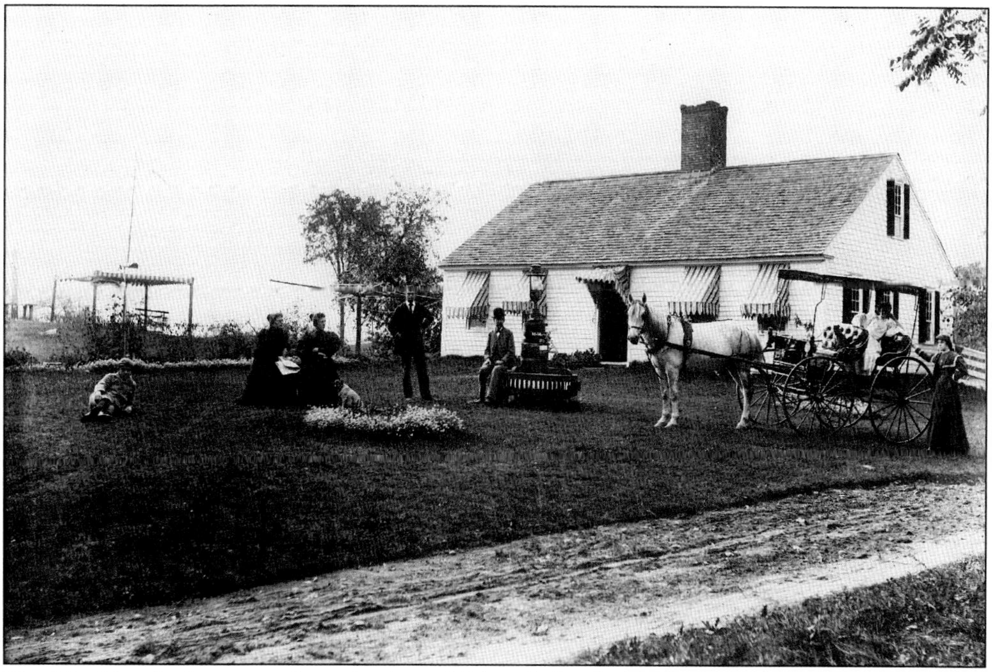

The MacMurphy homestead was built in 1731 on Lake Avenue and is likely one of the oldest houses in the area. It stands close to the site where Reverend James MacGregor preached the first sermon ever heard in Derry on April 13, 1719. The Beaver Lake section would remain primarily agricultural until around the start of the twentieth century, when a trolley line gave the area a direct link to the railroad service of West Derry. This in turn led to the area becoming a summer vacation mecca, centering on a few hotels, public beaches, and a large pavilion. Later, the ease of access provided by the automobile would cause the lake to be encircled by hundreds of small summer cottages.

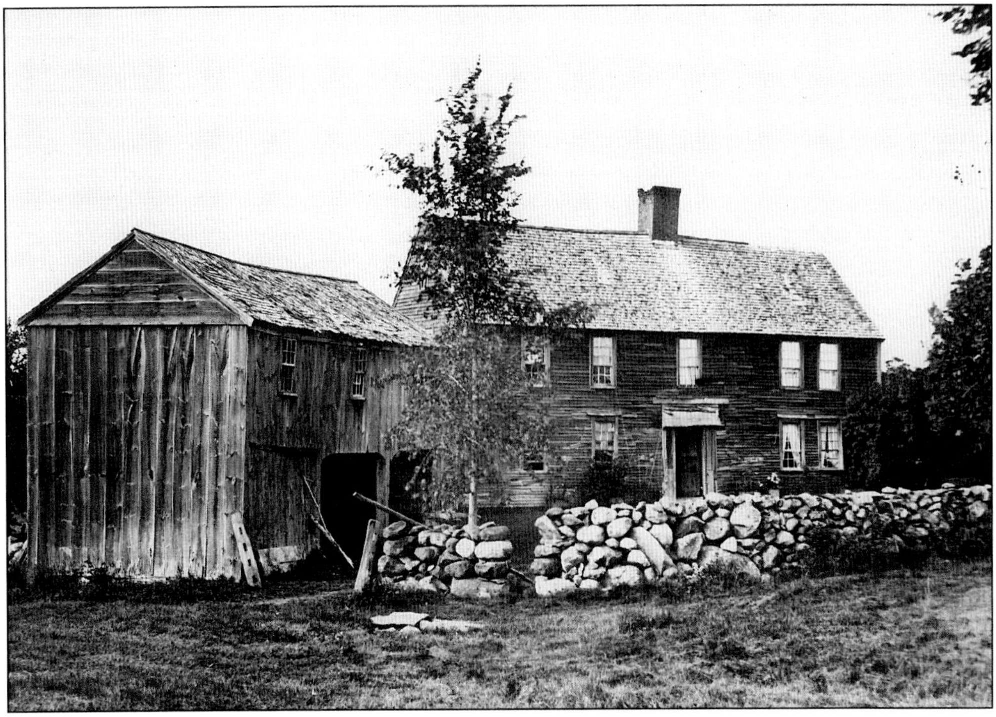

The John MacMurphy homestead was built c. 1730 on Old Chester Road. It was the second framed house to be built in the town and remained in the family for over 150 years. Its dilapidated condition led to its razing shortly after this picture was taken in 1895.

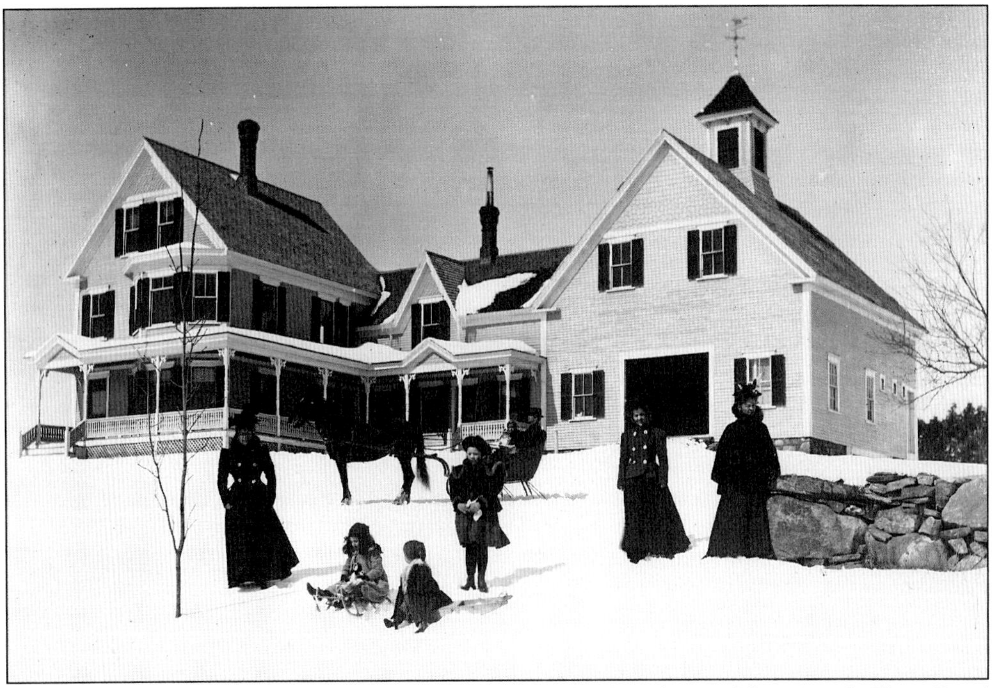

The George W. Benson family playing in the snow on the front lawn of their North Shore Road home c. 1896. The two ladies to the right are likely hired help.

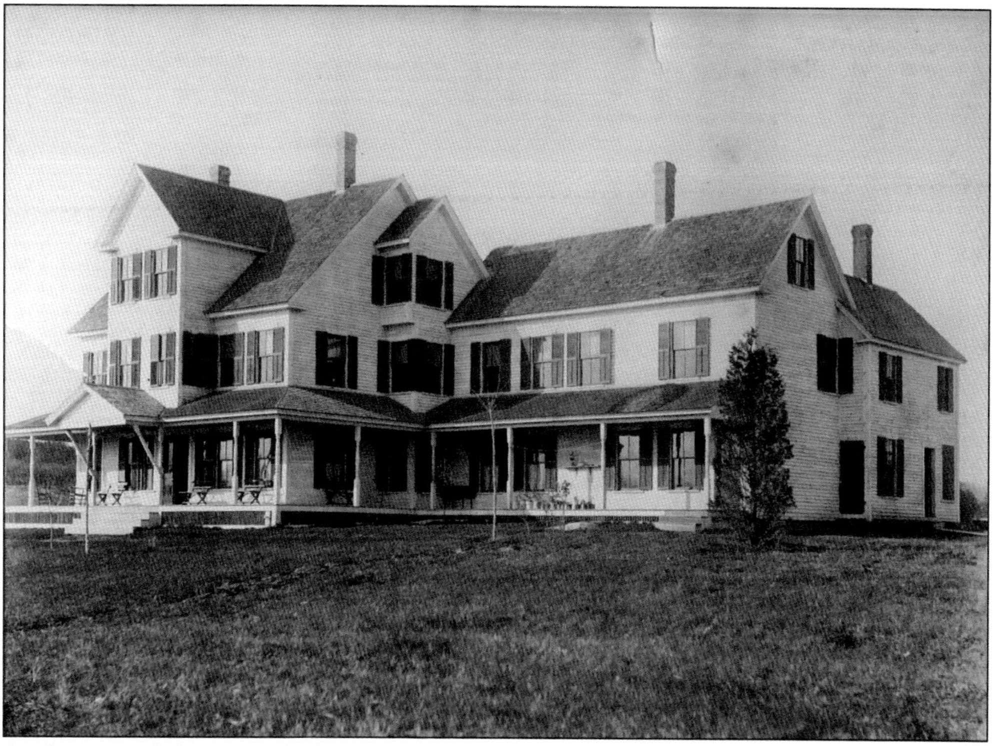

At the time of this *c.* 1895 photograph, the Beaver Lake House was owned by Mr. and Mrs. William H. Bachelder, who ran it as a hotel. Its close proximity to the Chester and Derry trolley helped in its popularity. It is now operated as a Gero Psych community residence.

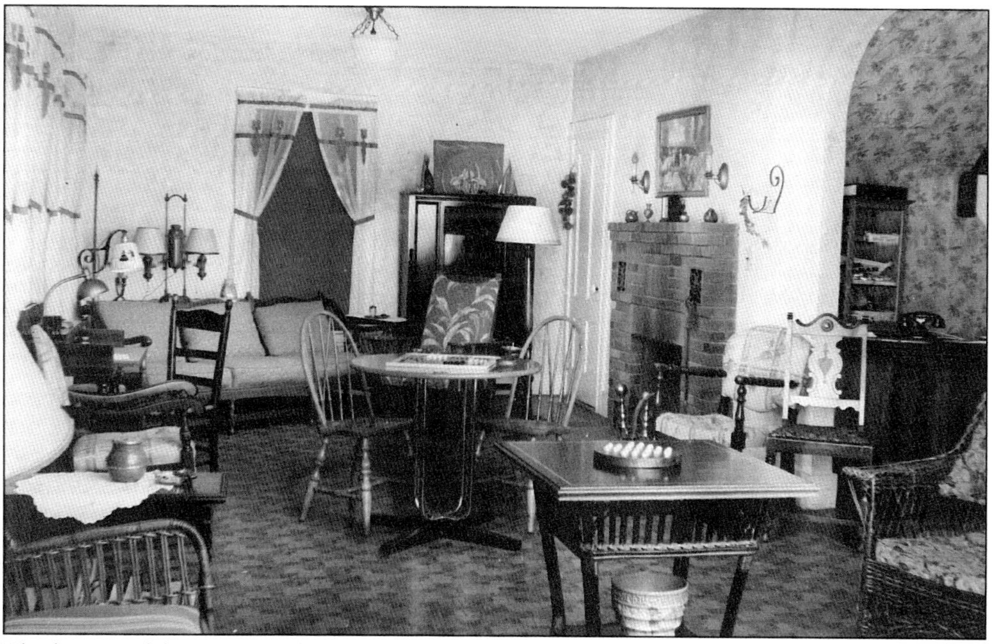

The lounge of the Beaver Lake House *c.* 1940. City folk would come to summer hotels like this to escape the heat and rusticate in the country. (Lear photograph)

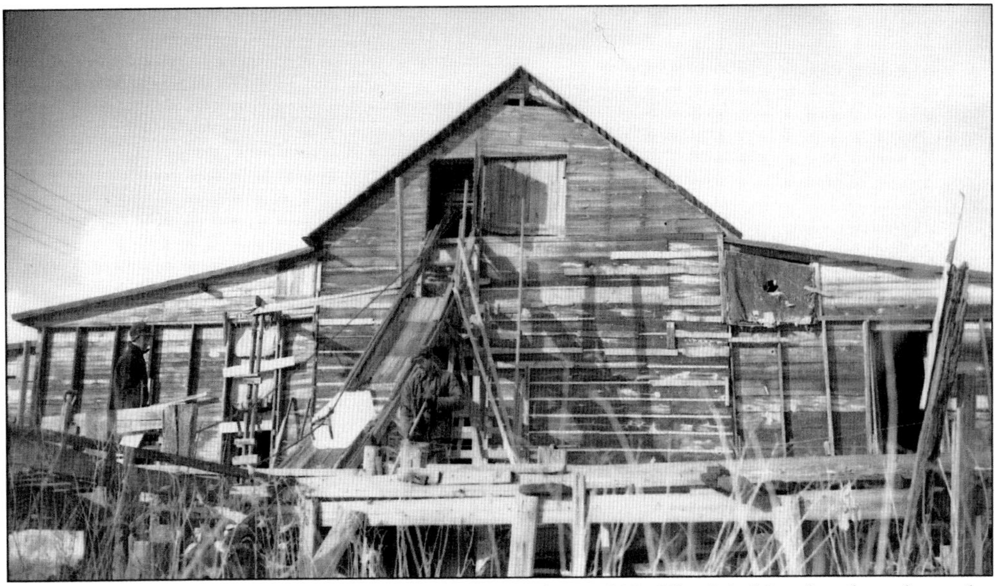

Madden's ice house on Beaver Lake as it appeared in 1940. The Madden brothers kept the business going every winter until 1947. (Lear photograph)

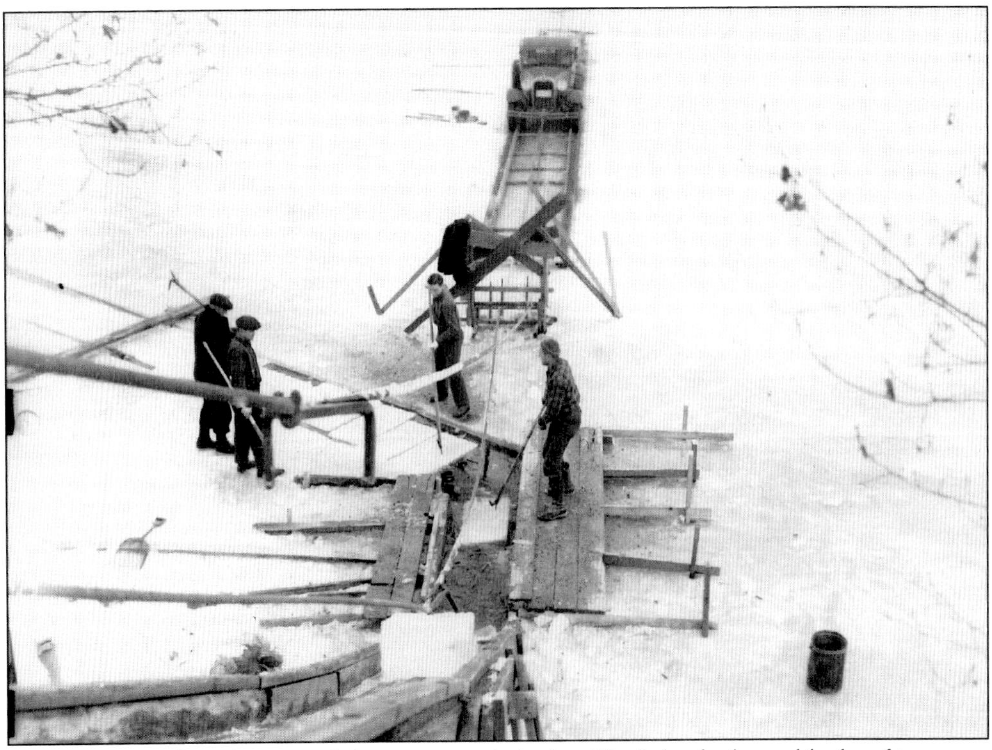

A Model A Ford truck powered the conveyor belt that lifted the fresh cut blocks of ice up to Madden's ice house in 1940. (Lear photograph)

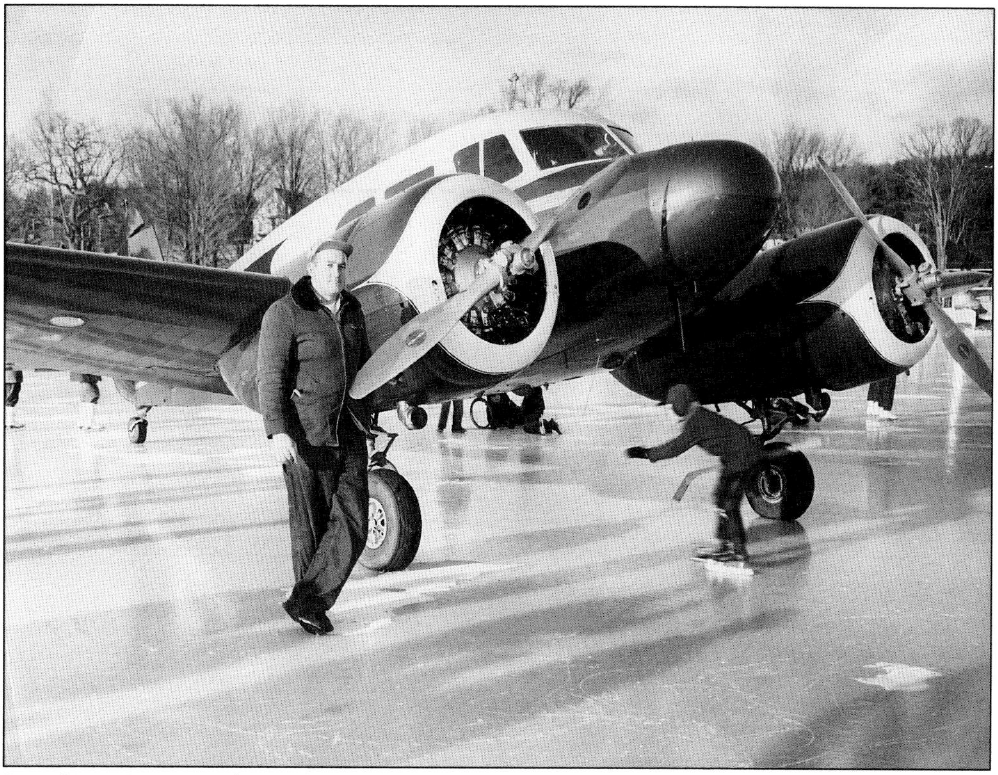

David MacGregor is shown during the 1940s having just landed his airplane on frozen Beaver Lake. The Derry Flying Club started this practice in 1937. During the summer it operated Smith field on the top of Ryan's Hill. (F.J. Sullivan photograph)

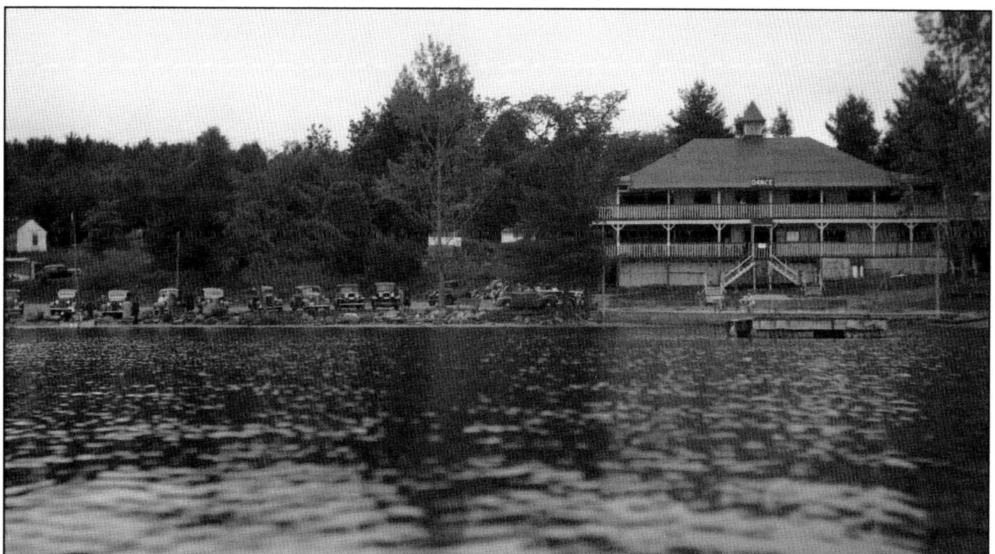

The orange-colored Beaver Lake Pavilion, judging by the number of cars in this 1939 photograph, was a popular summer attraction. It was built by the Chester and Derry Street Railroad in 1896 and rebuilt after a 1915 fire. Besides swimming, it offered bowling, dancing, and slot machines. It burned for a final time in 1960. (Lear photograph)

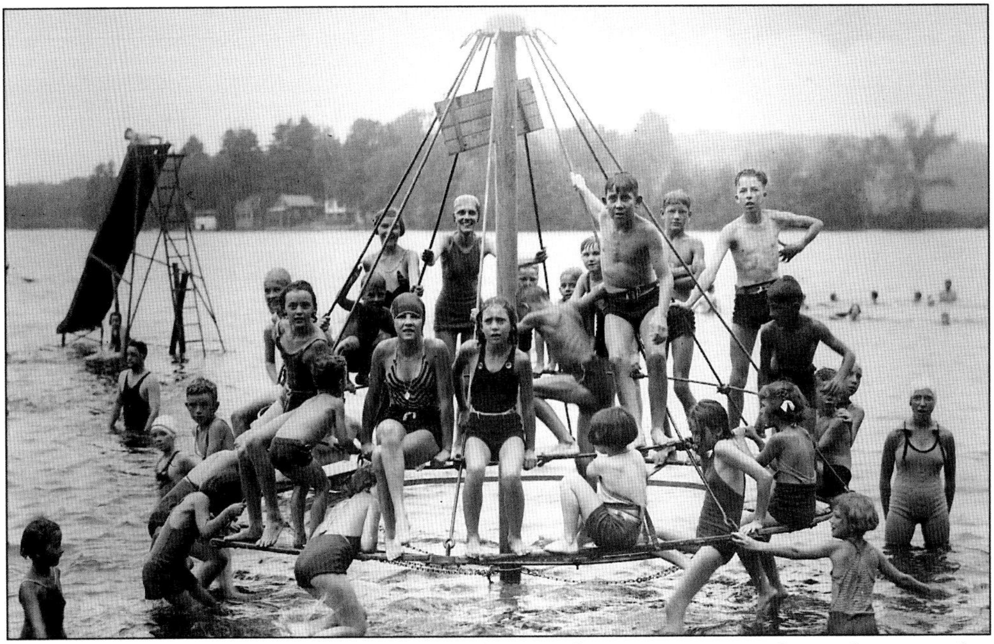

One of the attractions at Comeau's Beach was this water swing shown here in this 1938 photograph.

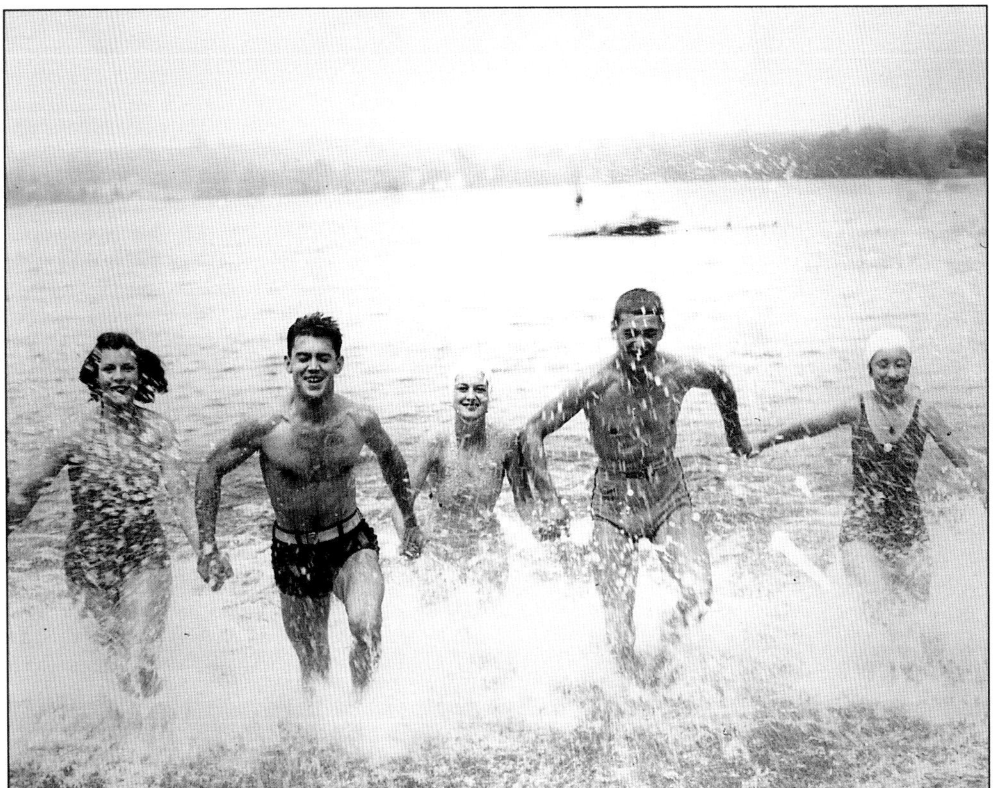

Local teenagers frolicking in 1938 at Comeau's Beach.

Four

West Derry: Residential

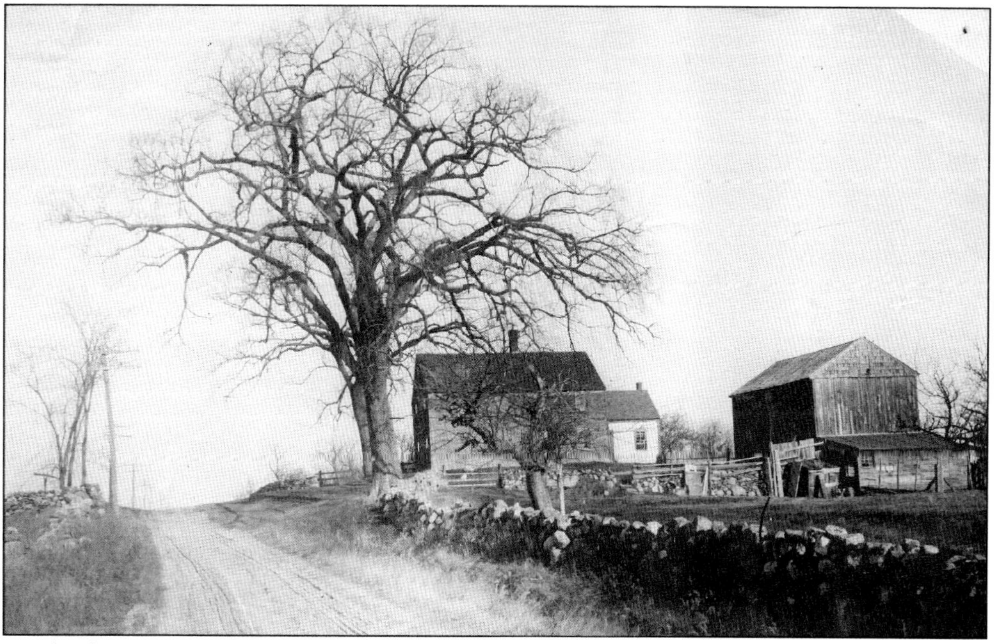

For the first century of Derry's history the western end of the town was decidedly rural. By the time of the Revolutionary War most of the original forests had been cut down to create farms. Stone walls were built to clear the fields and divide the pastures, and large barns and good solid farmhouses were erected on the nearly treeless landscape. George W. McKenney's farm (pictured here) was typical of the time. Located on Fordway, it burned some time before World War I (part of its original pasture is now a trailer park).

The pastoral isolation of West Derry ended with the coming of the railroad. In a few years shoe factories began to be built and the population mushroomed to the point where West Derry became the most densely populated part of the town.

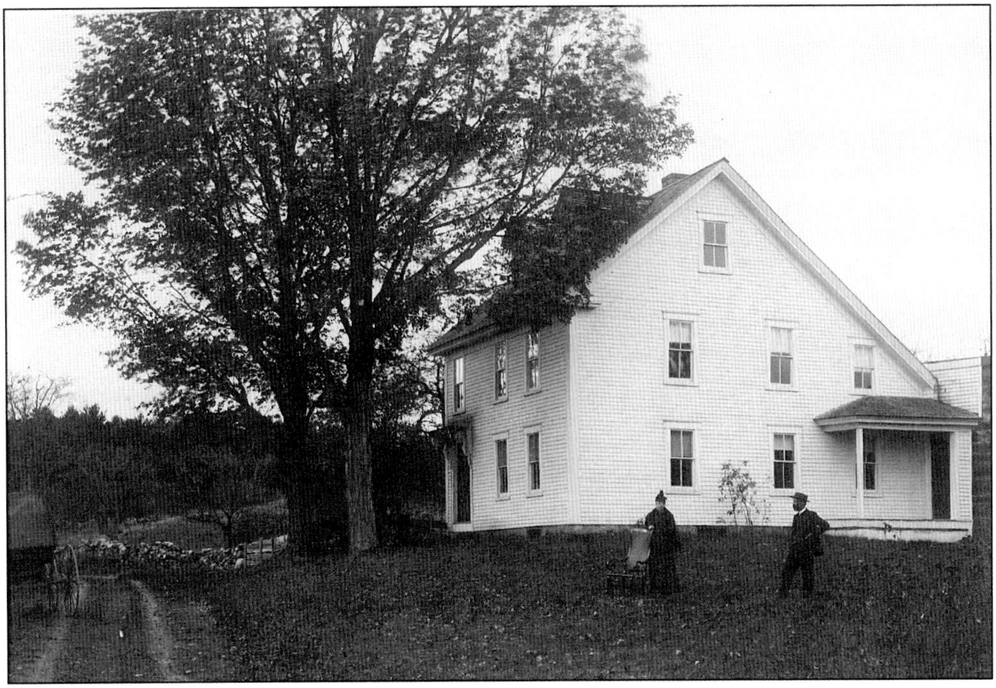

The James and Sarah MacMurphy homestead on the Franklin Street Extension dated back to the 1720s. Sarah Reid MacMurphy achieved local fame for her thrift: she worked two years as a maid for James Pinkerton at a salary of 50¢ a week (with board), and during that time she saved $50.

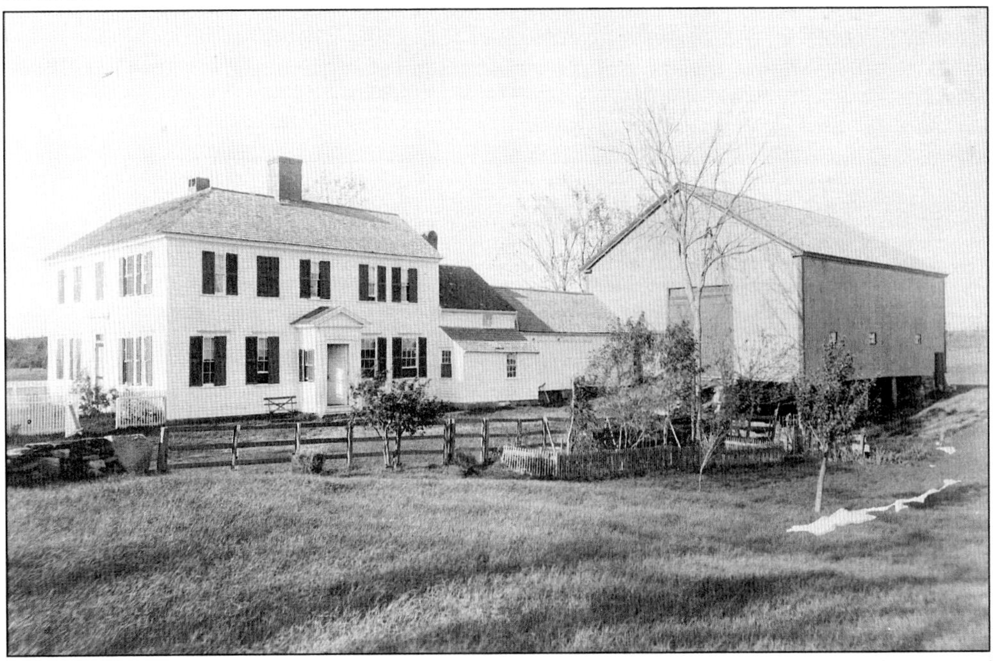

The Alexander MacMurphy homestead on the Franklin Street Extension was the seat of this founding family for two hundred years. It was razed in the 1960s to make way for a brick apartment complex.

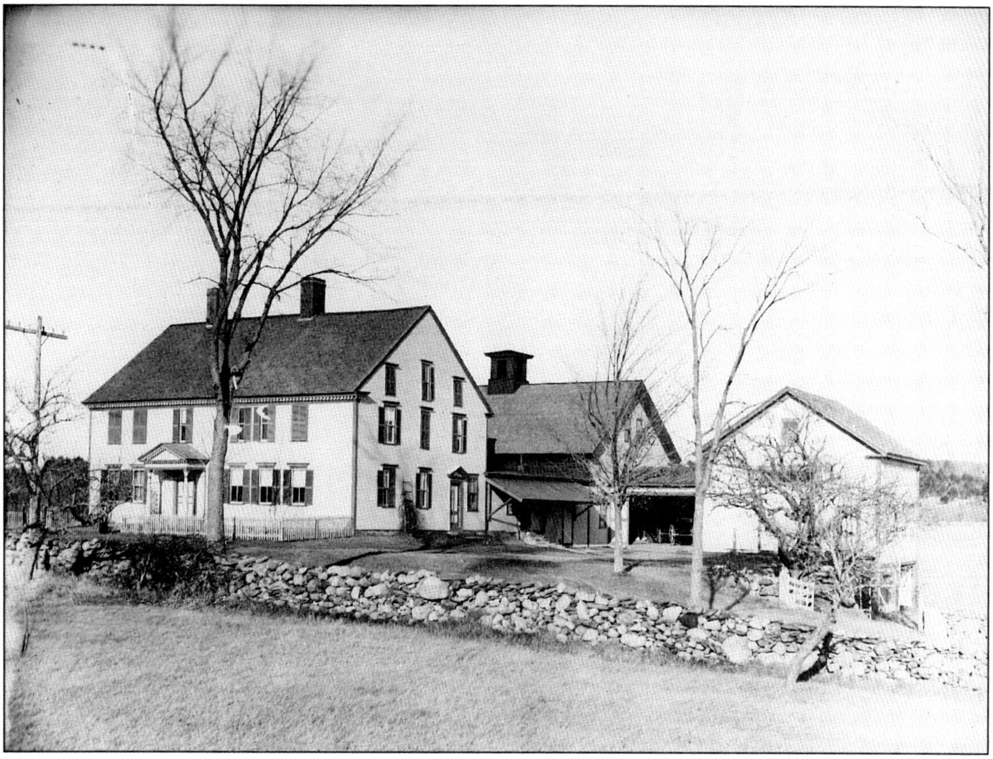

Elder James Pinkerton, co-founder of Pinkerton Academy, operated a store in this eighteenth-century home on Manchester Road. It is now the only house surviving in a neighborhood of factories, car lots, and shopping malls. For many years it was Ralph A. Smith's dairy farm; more recently it was a furniture store.

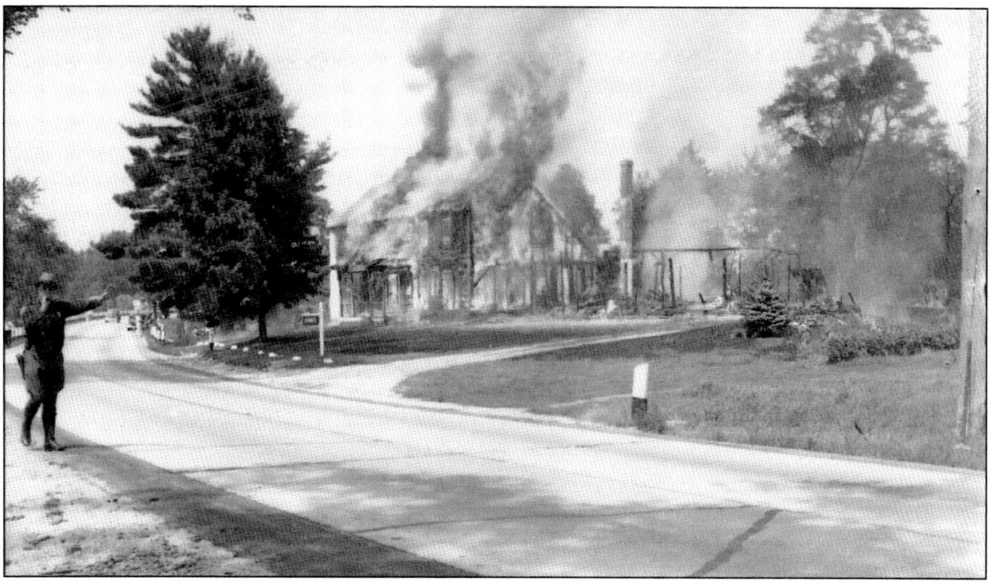

In August 1939 fire destroyed the Vaillancourt residence on Manchester Road. This had been the home and store of Major John Pinkerton, who was a co-founder of the academy which bears his name. State Trooper Gale French is shown here directing traffic. (Lear photograph)

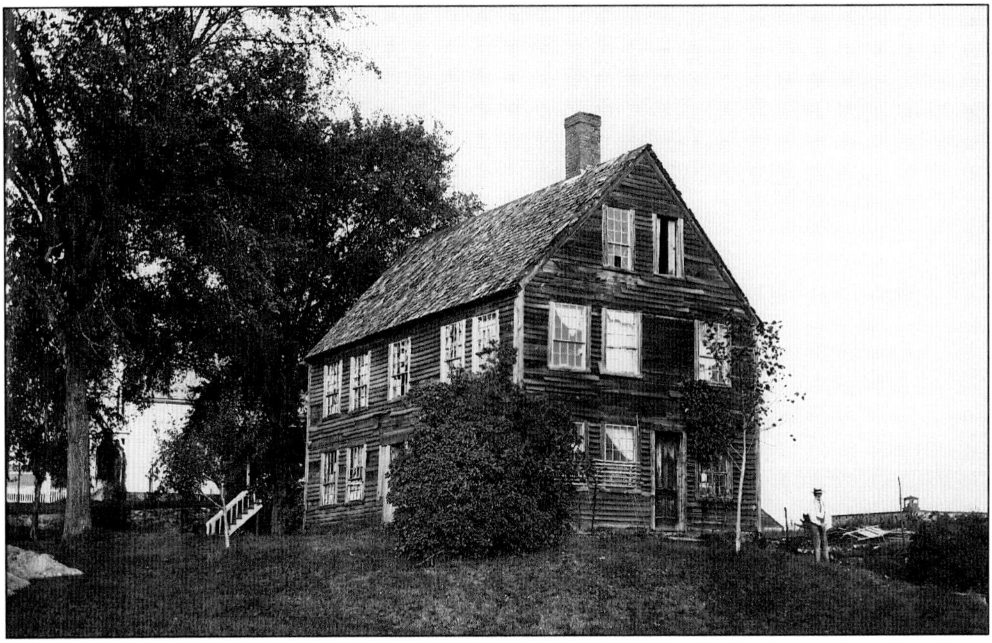

John Holmes is shown in 1895 standing next to his ancestral home, which stood on Broadway across from the present West Side Community Center. Shortly after this picture was taken, the building was torn down to make way for a modern house.

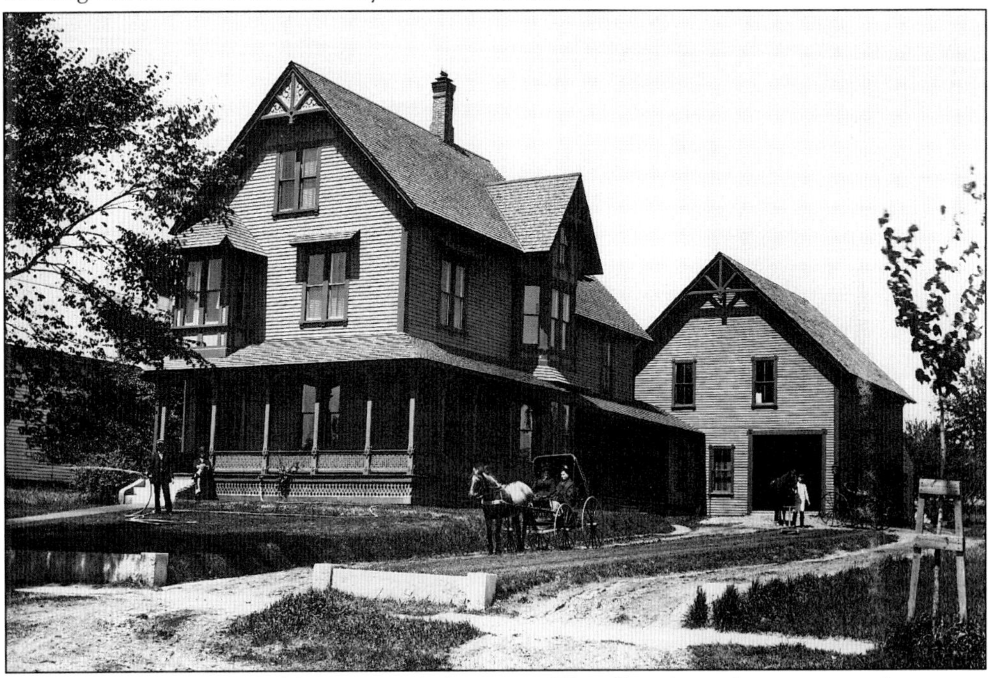

This photograph of the Alden B. Smith home on West Broadway shows a typical scene in the Victorian era. The men have stayed home to do yard work while the ladies go out for a carriage drive. The home was torn down in the 1980s to make room for a proposed addition to the Adams Memorial Building next door, which was never built. The lot remains vacant to this day.

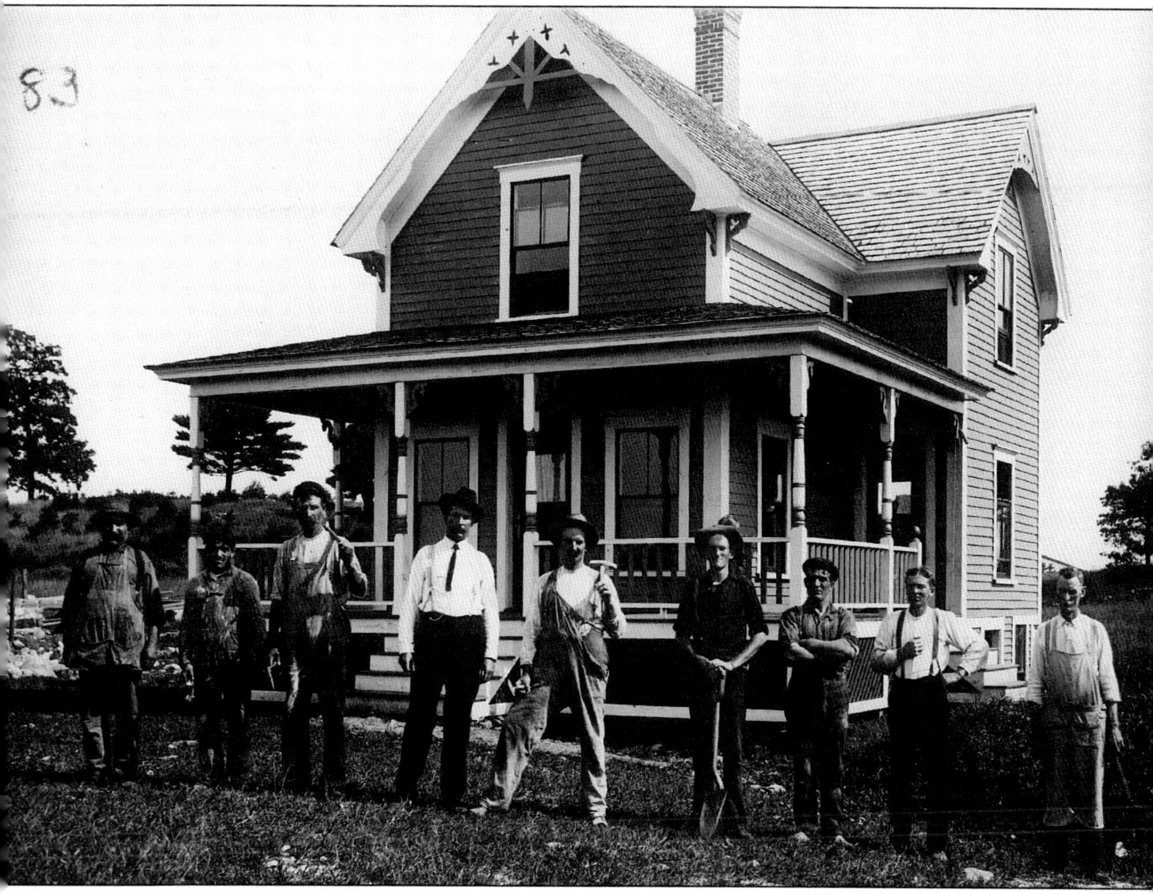

With the expansion of the West Derry shoe factories a constant demand was created for affordable housing. The building crew that built this residence at 21 Wyman Avenue around 1900 seem particularly proud of the results of their labor.

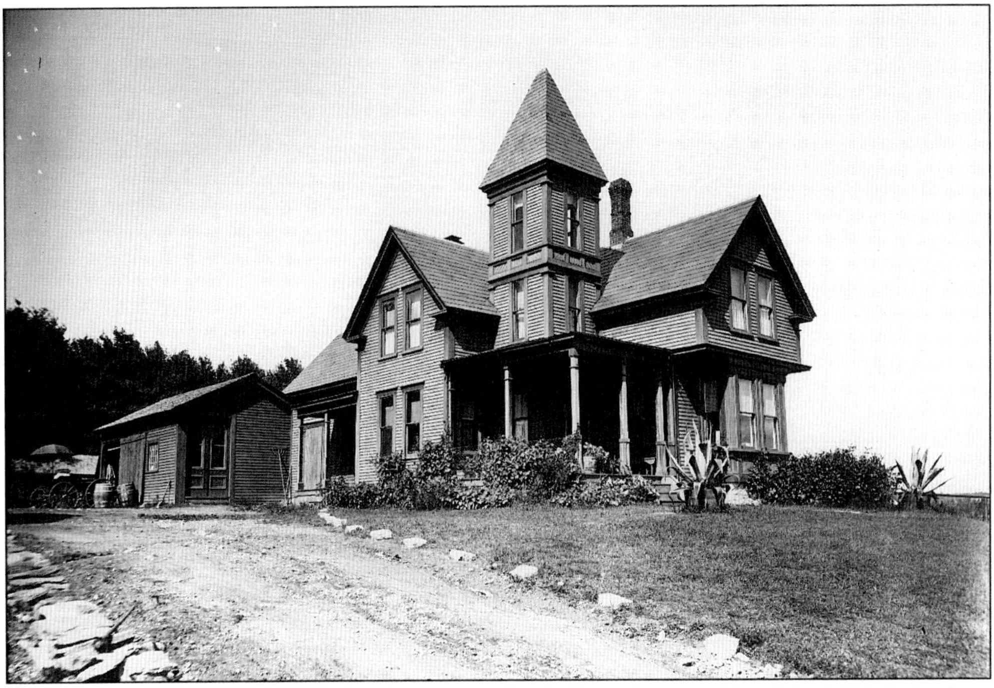

When Ernest L. Abbott built this house on the hill on Lennox Road in 1890 it had an unobstructed view of the whole town. Later the house would remain in the Bachelder family for three generations until the recent passing of longtime school board member Helen Bachelder.

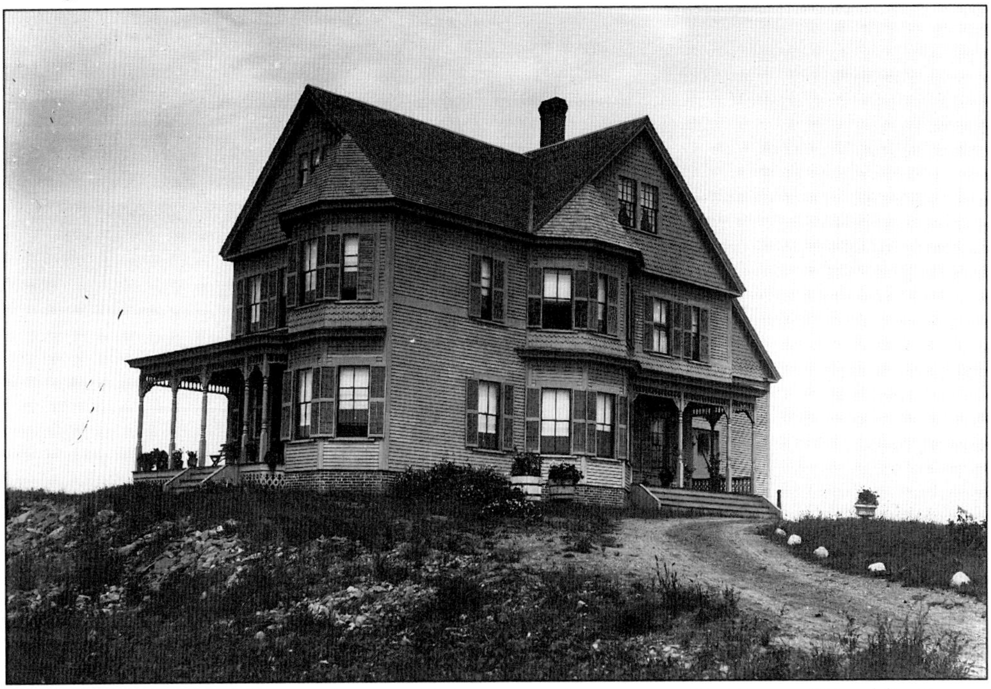

The George and Rosina Rollins house still dominates the corner of Rollins and Franklin Street. It is shown here in 1895 when it was still new and the area was undeveloped. Mr. Rollins was the local freight agent for the American Express Company.

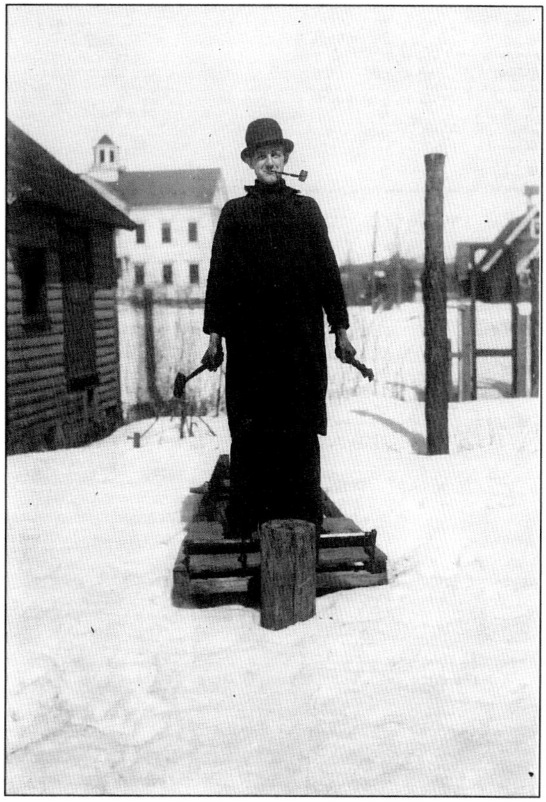

In this c. 1920 photograph Hugh Webb is shown on Birch Street striking a comical pose. In the background is the Oak Street School and the old Episcopal Church.

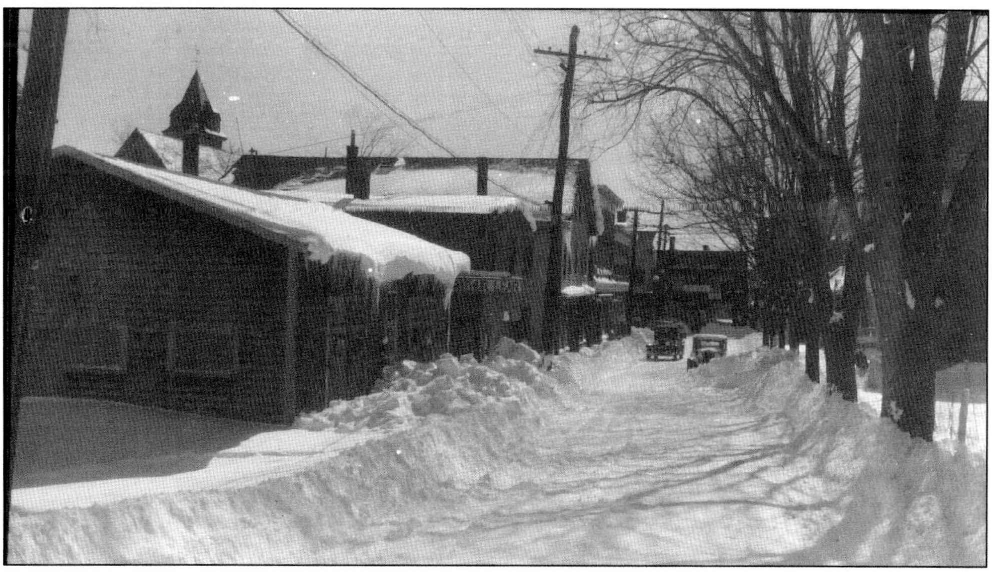

Snow removal during the winter of 1939/40 was hampered by narrow streets hemmed in by trees and buildings. On the left is the Franklin Street office and garage of photographer Arthur Lear. (Lear photograph)

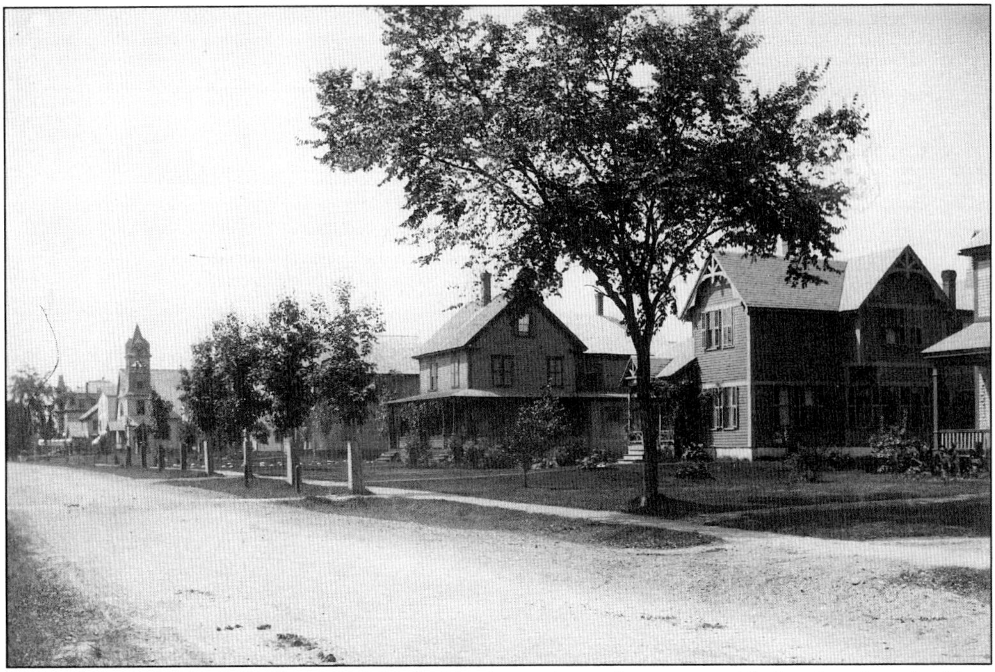

Looking west on Broadway c. 1895. Probably the only easily recognizable landmark is the First Baptist Church on the left. The house with the large tree was recently torn down to build a municipal parking lot. The next house to the left was razed in 1929 to be replaced by the telephone building. (Library collection)

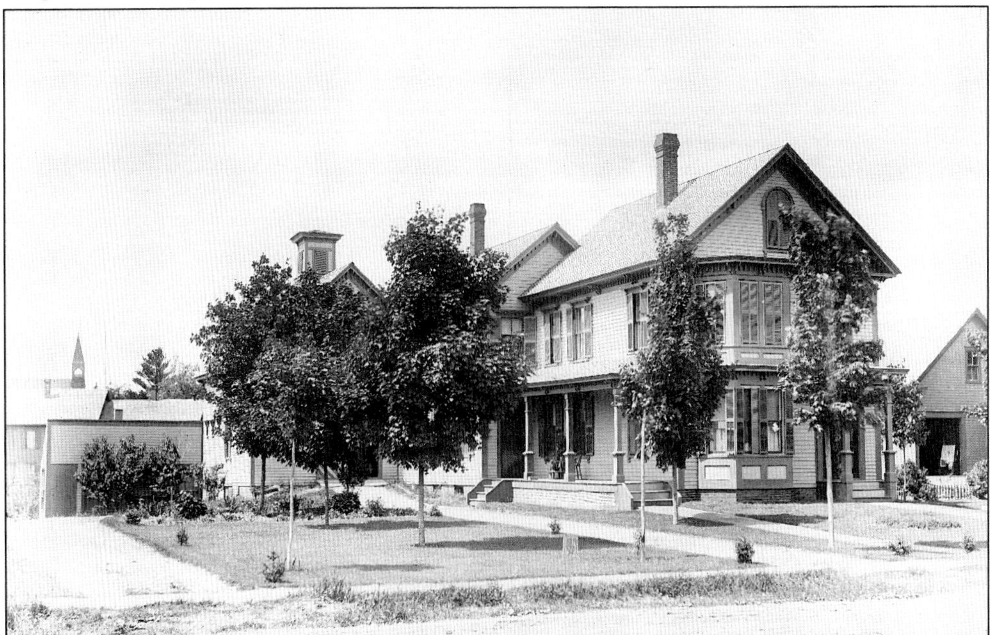

For many years this house to the right of the town hall was the office of Dr. A.D. Teitelbaum. With a new front it is now the Benway-Johnston Insurance Agency. In the back can be seen the steeple of the original St. Thomas Aquinas Church.

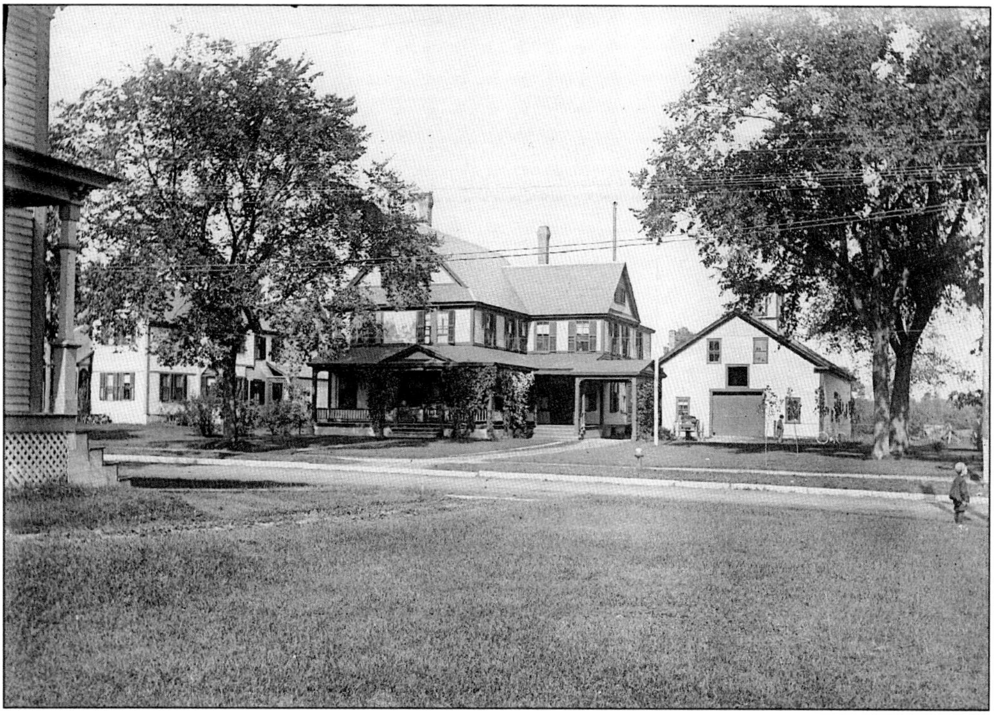

The Broadway residence of Dr. Henry E. Newell *c.* 1895 is scarcely recognizable today. In 1923 it was sold to the local Masonic order and is now fronted with pillars, a porch, and stucco outer walls. Marlboro Road now nearly bisects the site of this barn. (Newell collection)

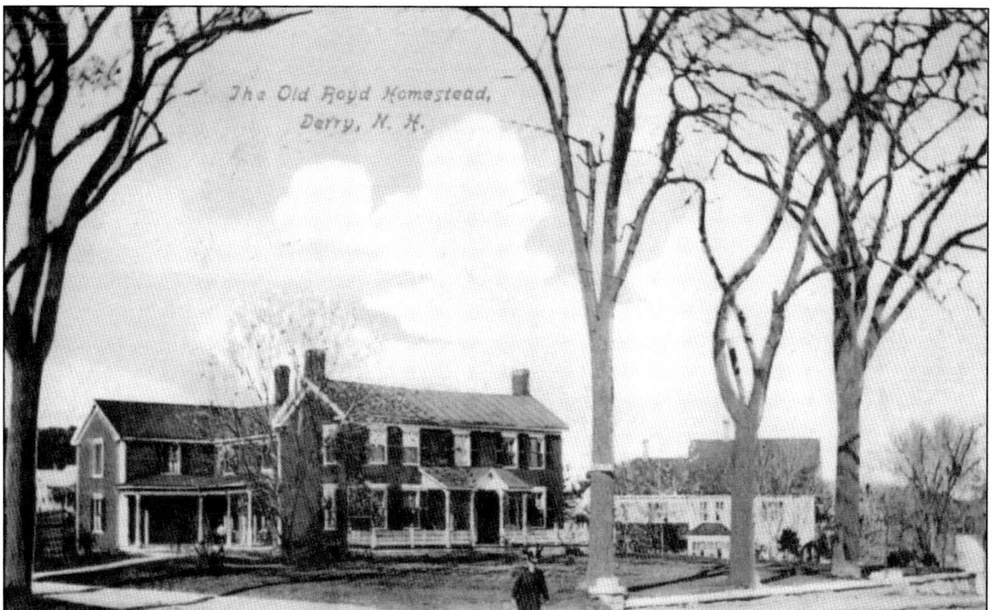

The Boyd homestead was considered one of the finest in West Derry, and it was also likely the only private brick residence in the town. It was razed in 1926 to make room for the MacGregor Library building. The two homes on the right were moved to create the MacGregor Pioneer Park.

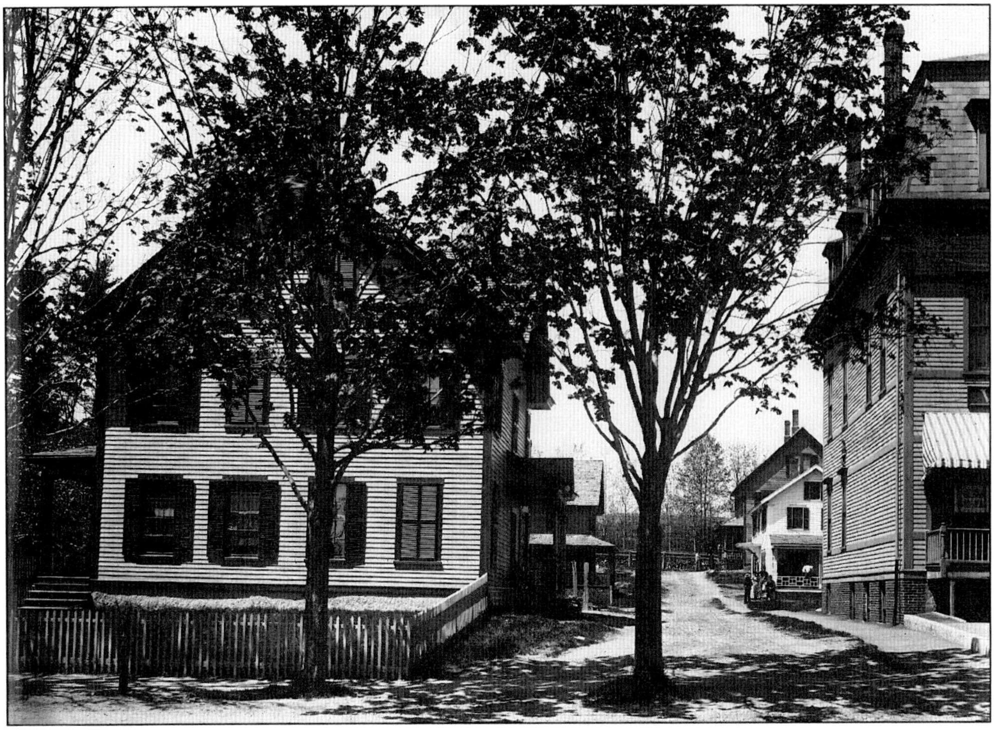

McAllister Court as it appeared *c.* 1895. The house on the left was moved in 1917 to the end of the street to make room for the First National Bank building on Broadway. On the right is the Odd Fellows block, which would be destroyed in a fire in 1897. V.H. Moody's Clothing Store and Derry Shoe occupied the lower floor.

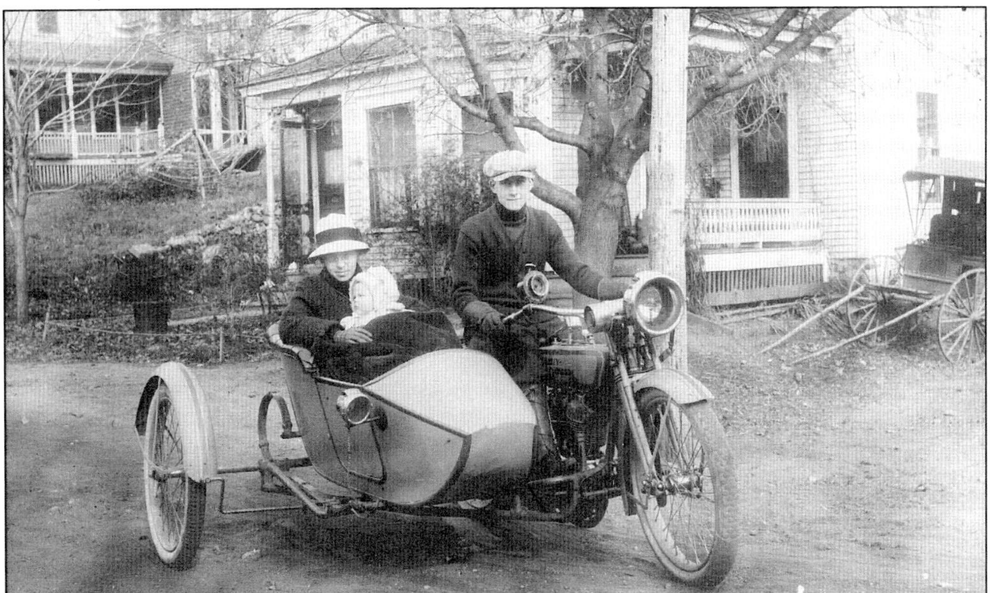

Richard and Bernice Durkee are taking their daughter down Grove Street in 1915. The new Harley Davidson motorcycle with sidecar contrasts sharply with their buggy that sits sadly discarded in the yard.

West Derry: Mills

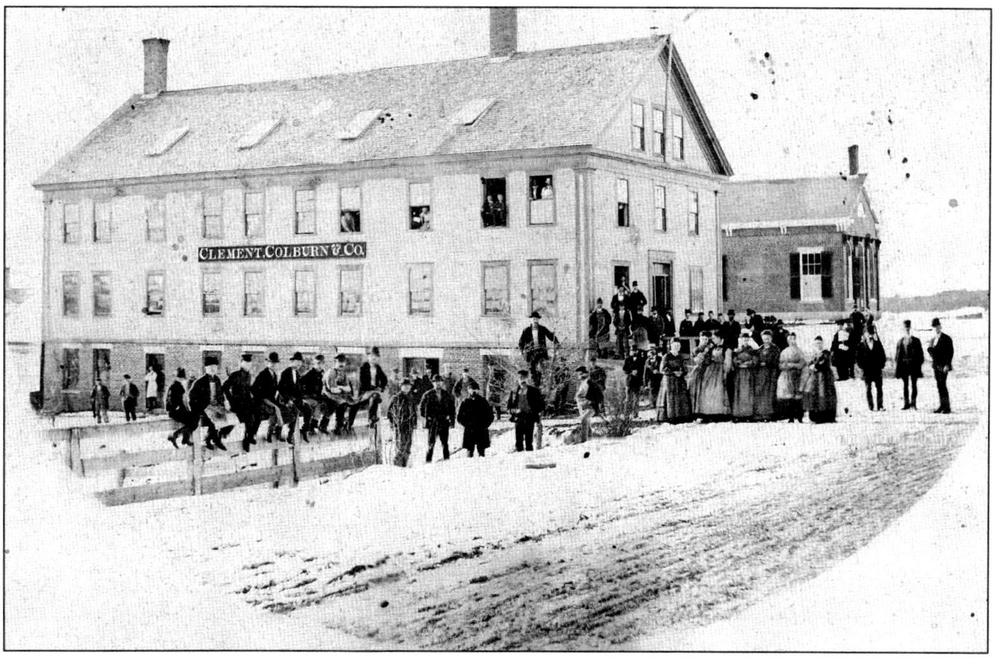

The development of the large mills of West Derry began soon after the Manchester and Lawrence Railroad built its line through the area. In 1855 Currier and Boyd built this shoe shop close to the depot. The enterprise did not prove very successful and was closed in 1868, but it was purchased by Colonel William S. Pillsbury in 1870. He immediately began to buy other buildings in the area and soon entered into a partnership with Clement, Colburn, and Company. They rented his buildings, put up the operating capital, and marketed the shoes, while Pillsbury bought the leather, hired the help, and managed the production. This successful arrangement continued until Pillsbury's retirement in 1908.

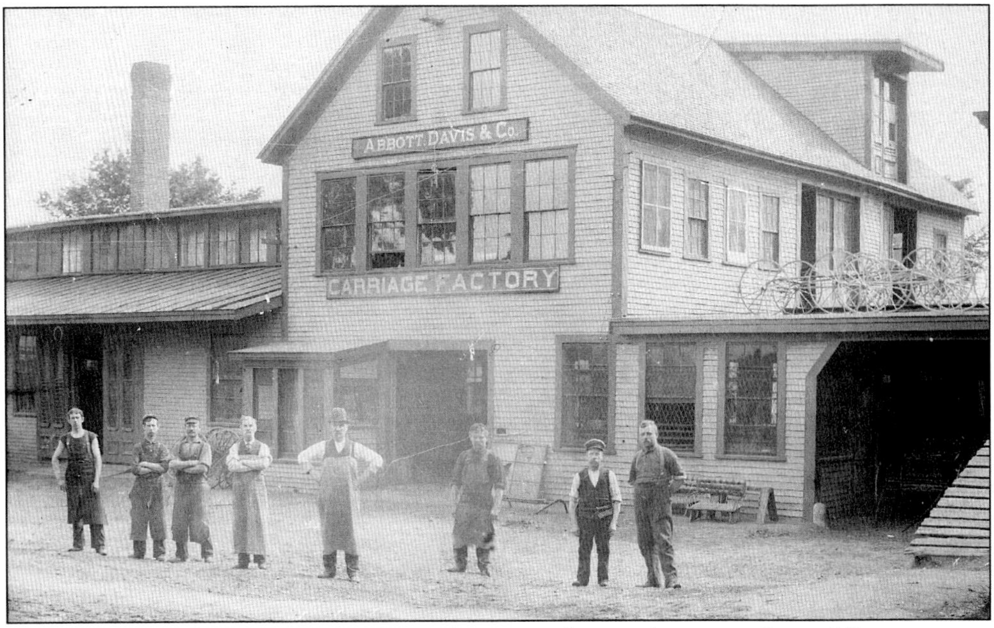

Abbott, Davis, and Company manufactured carriages from its factory on Central Street starting in 1887. The vehicles were painted on the second floor of this 72-by-28-foot building to escape the dust of the unpaved roads outside. The company also owned a 10,000-square-foot warehouse, a blacksmith shop, a wheelwright shop, and a stable.

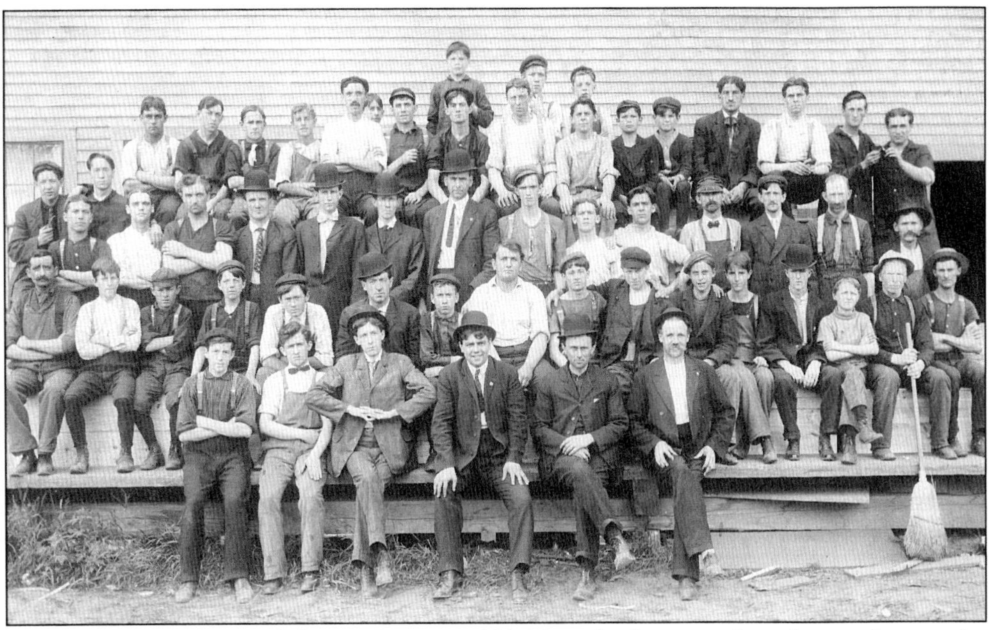

Workers at an unidentified shop in Derry c. 1890. Note the large number of young boys in the group; child labor laws were apparently not yet in effect or were unenforced.

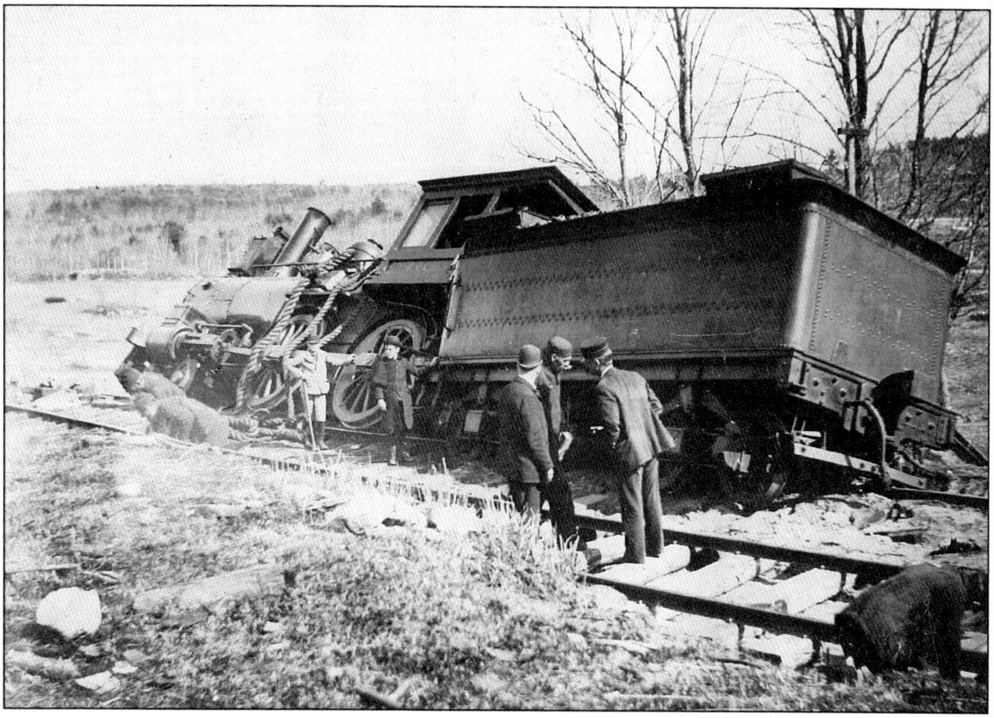

A Boston and Maine passenger train derailed at Hood's Crossing in 1908 when a switch was left open, and it took six hours to get the engine and its tender back onto the track. The first passenger trains passed through West Derry in 1849; the last on July 10, 1953.

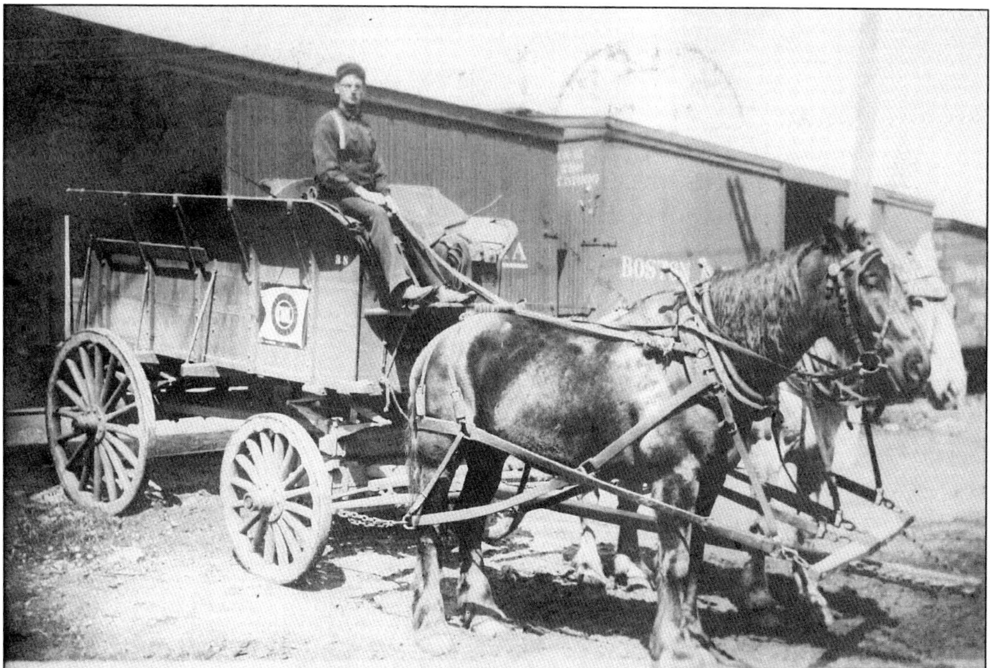

A teamster with a pair of mules picks up freight from a boxcar *c.* 1910. The Boston and Maine Railway was the link between the West Derry shops and the markets of the world.

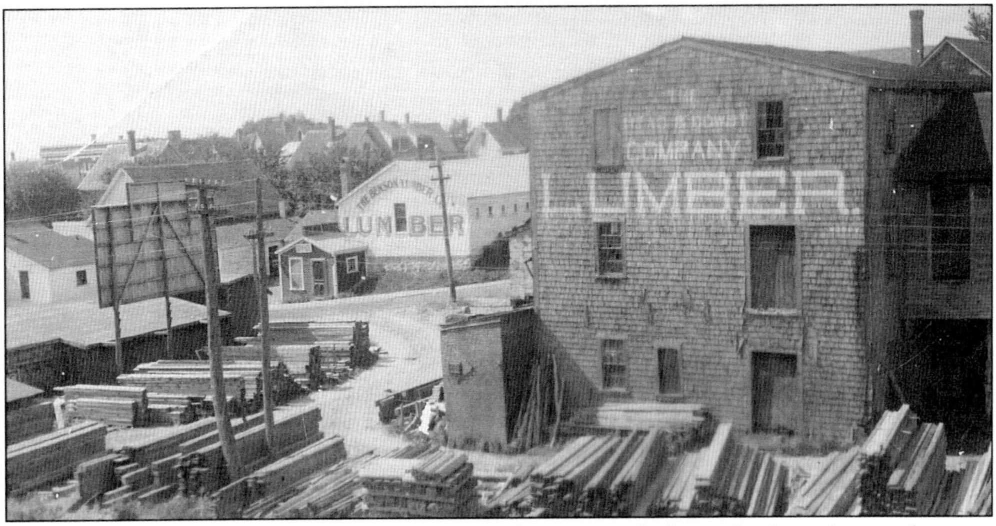

In the beginning of the twentieth century, with more mills being built and more housing necessary for the expanding labor force, lumber mills in the area flourished. Companies such as Benson's, Kimball's, True's, and Head's were selling millions of feet of lumber. Pictured here is Benson's Lumberyard on Martin Street; much of Benson's was destroyed during a Christmas week fire in 1943.

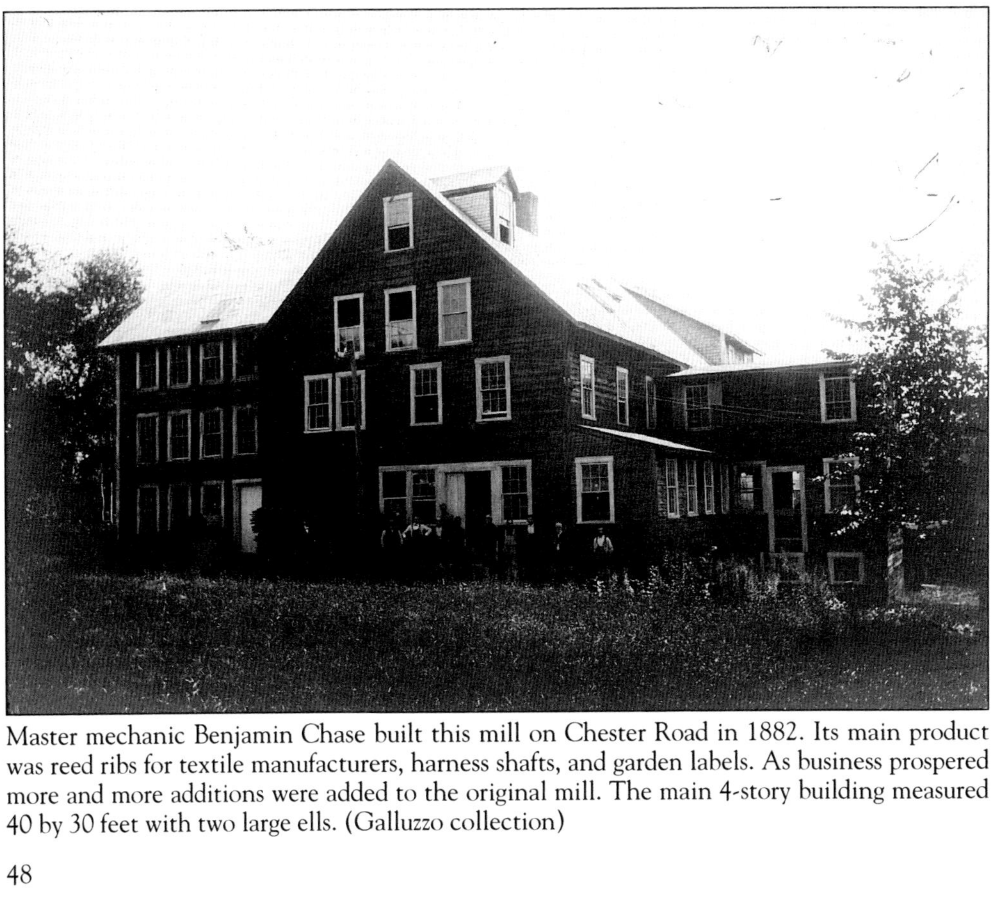

Master mechanic Benjamin Chase built this mill on Chester Road in 1882. Its main product was reed ribs for textile manufacturers, harness shafts, and garden labels. As business prospered more and more additions were added to the original mill. The main 4-story building measured 40 by 30 feet with two large ells. (Galluzzo collection)

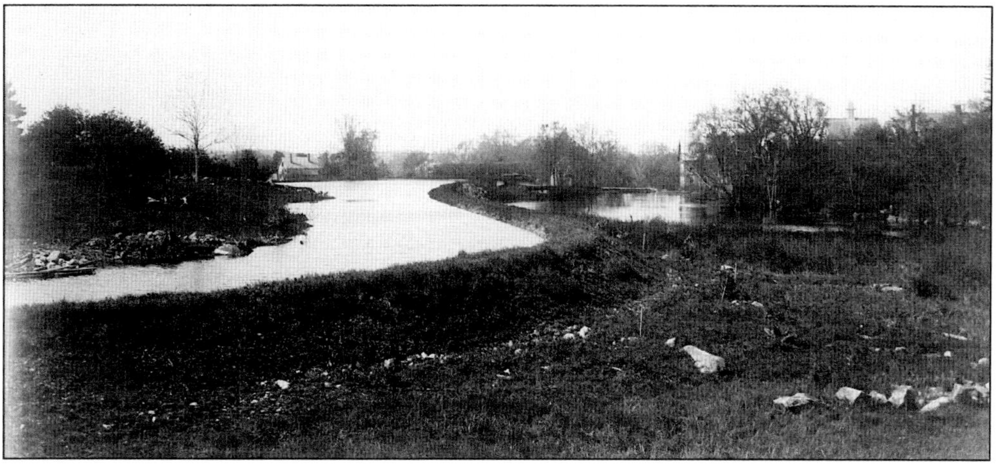

In the summer of 1900 Benjamin Chase brought in a crew of Italian laborers to dig this canal, which went from the Meadow Dam at the west end of Beaver Lake 1,000 feet west to this woodworking mill on Chester Road. It was used to generate the first electric power in the town. (Galluzzo collection)

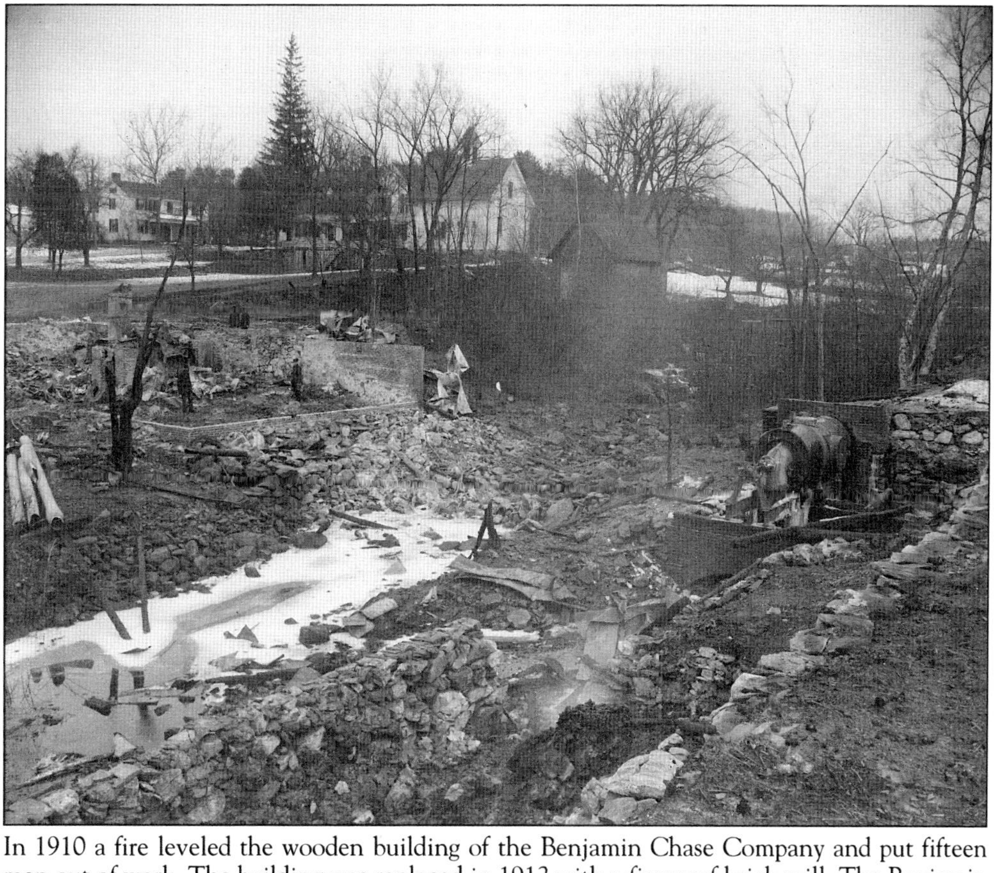

In 1910 a fire leveled the wooden building of the Benjamin Chase Company and put fifteen men out of work. The building was replaced in 1912 with a fireproof brick mill. The Benjamin Chase Company at Chester Road was eventually bought by the Anthony Galluzzo Company, which makes fine commercial furniture and garden labels. (Galluzzo collection)

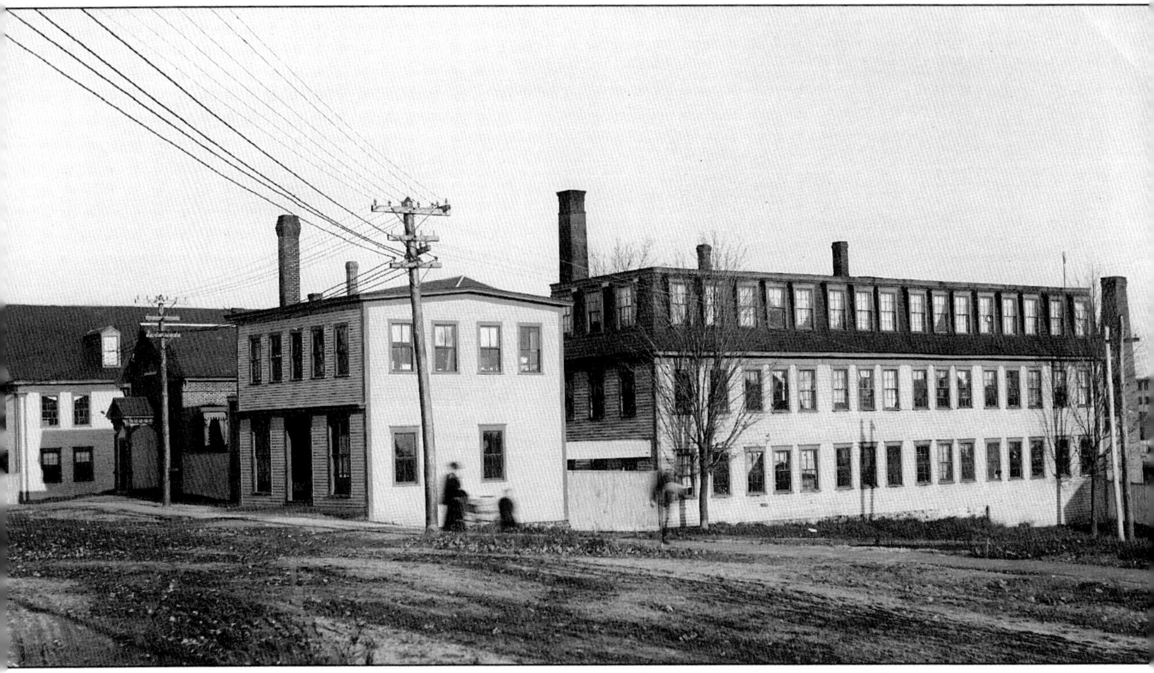

The Pillsbury Shoe Factory complex c. 1900. To the left is the original Benjamin Eastman shop built in 1855. Next in the line is the first school ever built in West Derry; this little brick building was replaced by the West Side School in the 1890s, and it then became the shoe shop's office. The Pillsbury factory extended 220 feet along Broadway and 135 feet down Central Street. In 1915 it was converted into thirty-one kitchenette apartments by Wallace Mack, R.W. Pillsbury, and Charles S. Emerson. Each apartment included a kitchen, pantry, bathroom, living room, and bedroom, and with a gas stove and refrigerator it rented for $5 a month. The front of the shop on Broadway was converted into a number of small shops. Everything in this picture was destroyed in a 1979 fire.

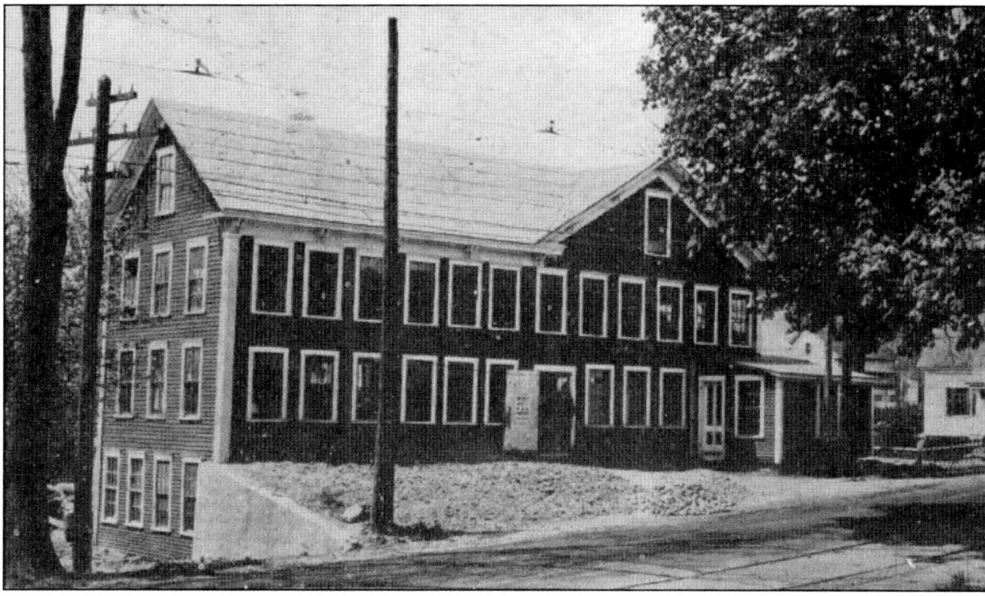

In 1911 brothers Arthur and Myron Emerson remodeled a former wheelwright's shop into a shoe shop at 1 Chester Road. The family also owned a shoe shop on Maple Street and in Hampstead. In 1925 the so-called "Red Shop" became the Essex Casket Company (the building is now owned by Jesco Metal Fabricators).

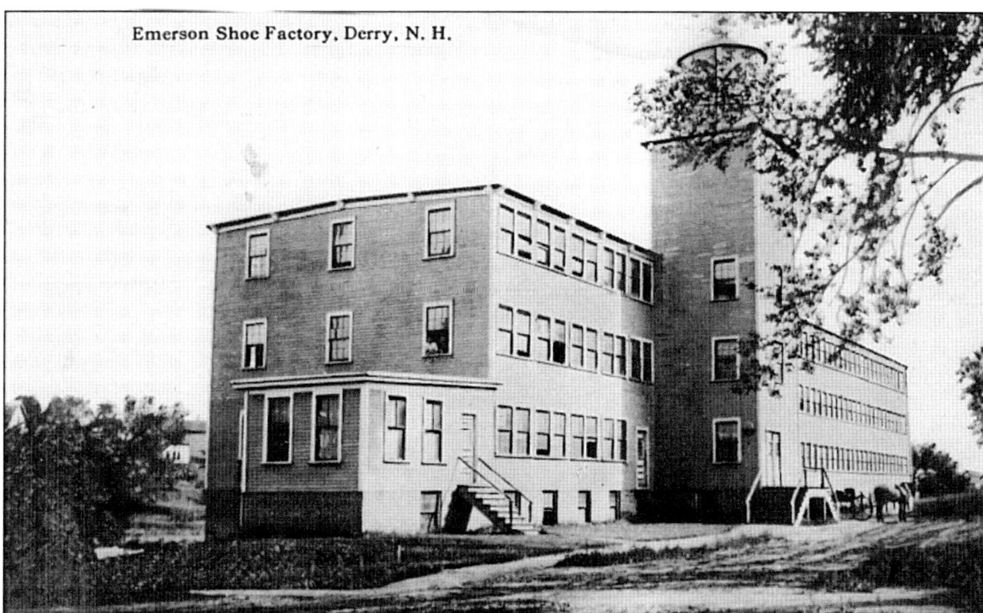

In 1909 Charles S. Emerson rented this newly built 104-foot-long factory on Maple Street from a group of local businessmen. He intended to employ four hundred hands to manufacture shoes for ladies, children, and infants. In 1939 it became the Klev Bro Shoe Factory and later the Jodi Shoe Company (it is now a woodworking shop).

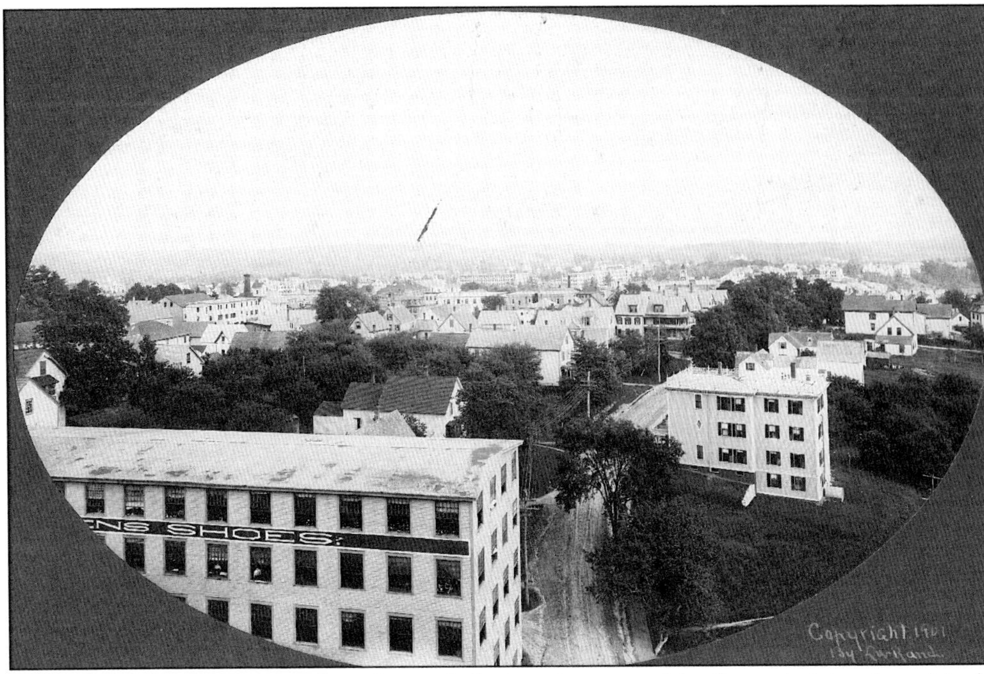

This 1901 photograph is shot from the roof of a shoe factory on Elm Street looking down Maple Street toward Broadway. On the immediate left is the massive Perkins Shoe Shop that would be torn down in 1939 by the Klev Bro Company. (Rand photograph)

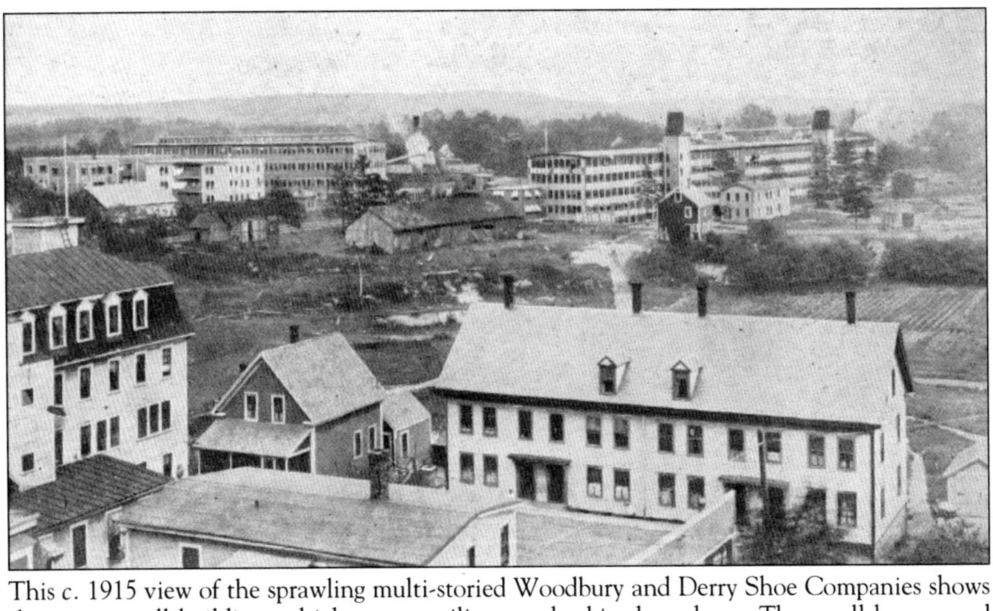

This c. 1915 view of the sprawling multi-storied Woodbury and Derry Shoe Companies shows the many small buildings which were auxiliary to the big shoe shops. The small houses and tenements of the shoe workers can also be seen.

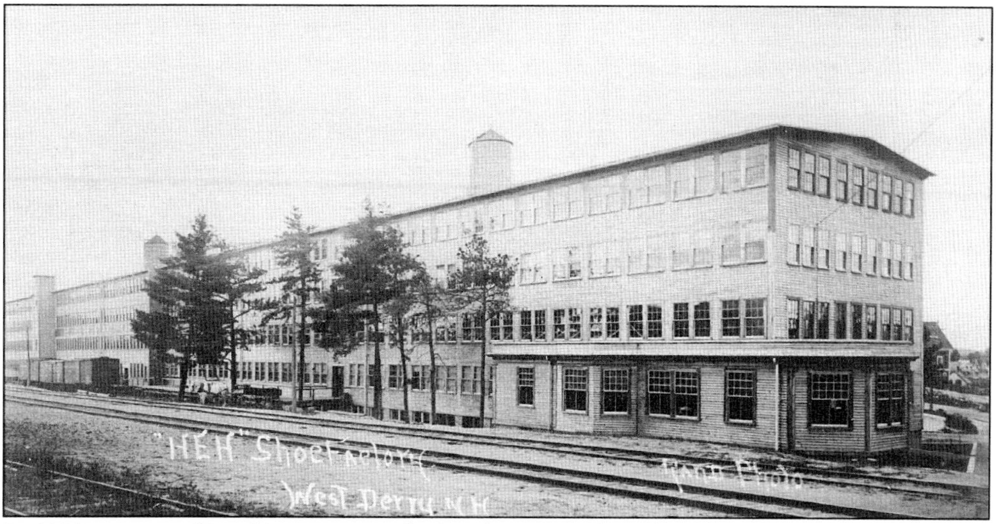

In 1902 a group of local businessmen built a four-story shoe shop on speculation. In time the building was expanded to be 528 feet in length and contain over 3.5 acres of floor space. With a half mile of usable lateral space it was one of the largest wooden factories in the country. After years of disuse "The Big Shop" was torn down in 1939/40.

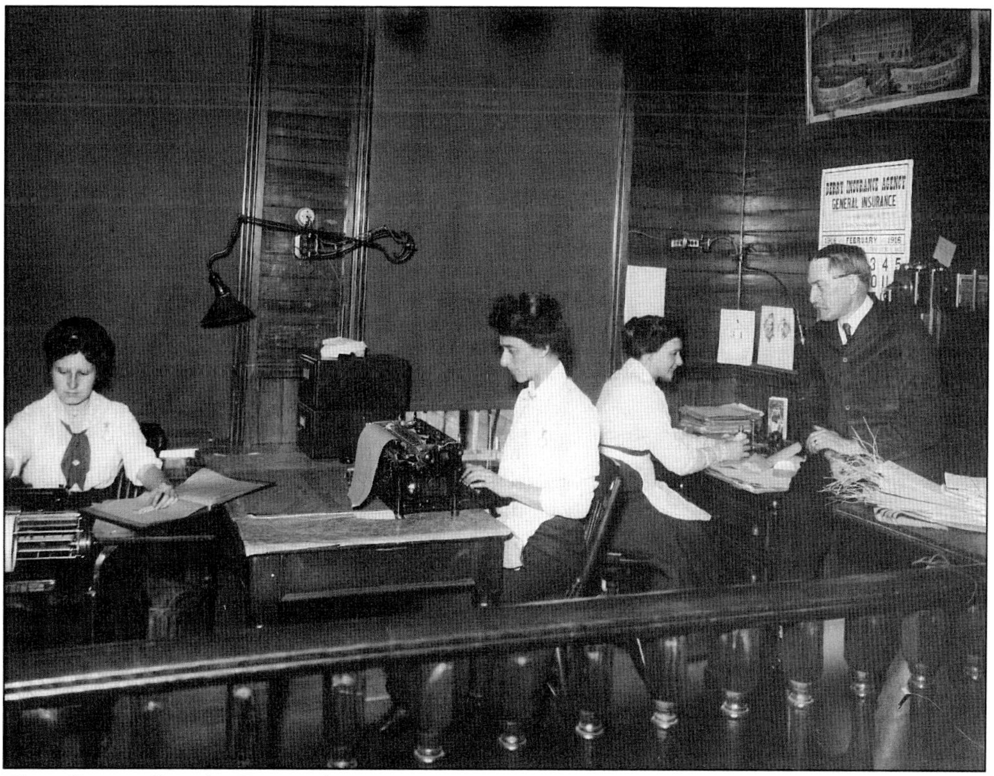

The office staff at the Derry Shoe Factory in 1916. From left to right are Edna Weeks, Anna Moore, Mildred Fitz, and Frederick Wallis.

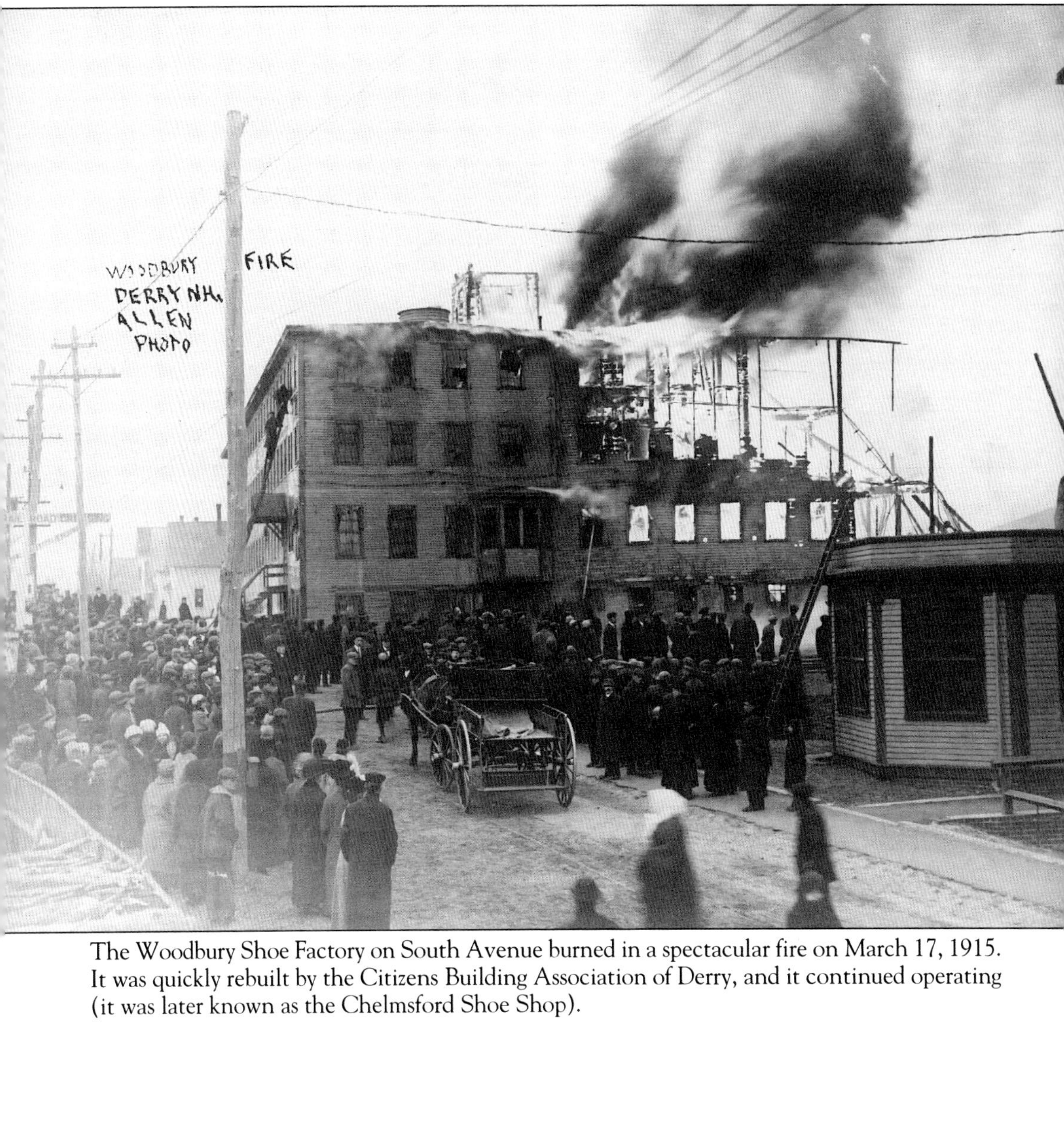

The Woodbury Shoe Factory on South Avenue burned in a spectacular fire on March 17, 1915. It was quickly rebuilt by the Citizens Building Association of Derry, and it continued operating (it was later known as the Chelmsford Shoe Shop).

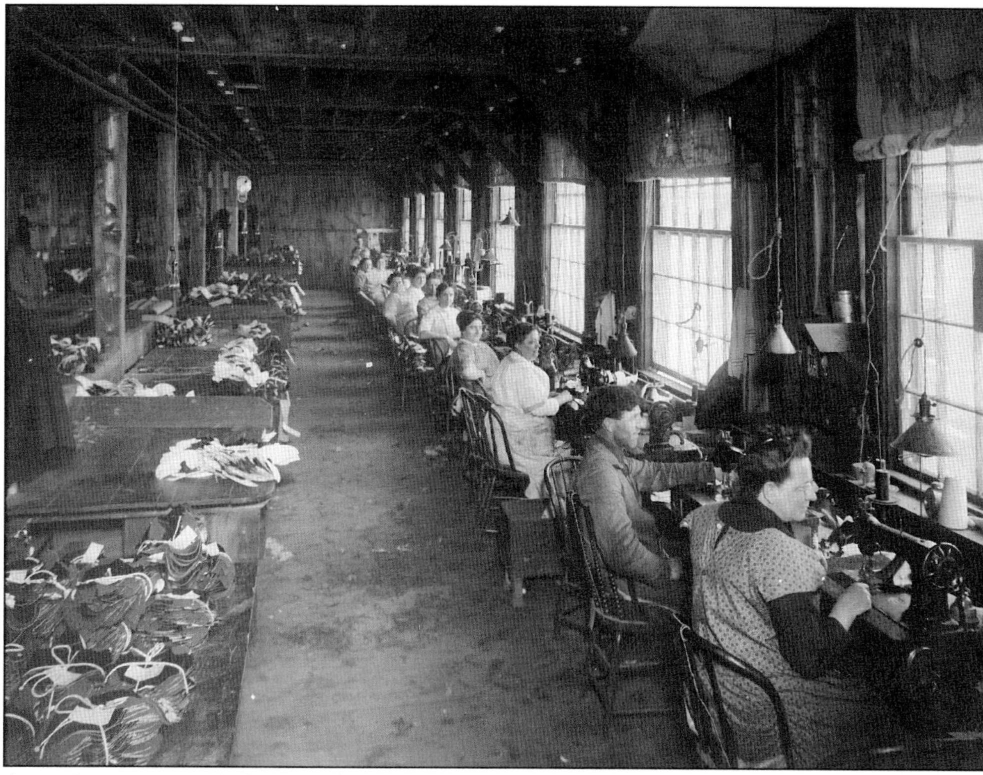

A stitching room at "The Big Shop" in 1916; note that all but one of the thirteen workers in this department were female.

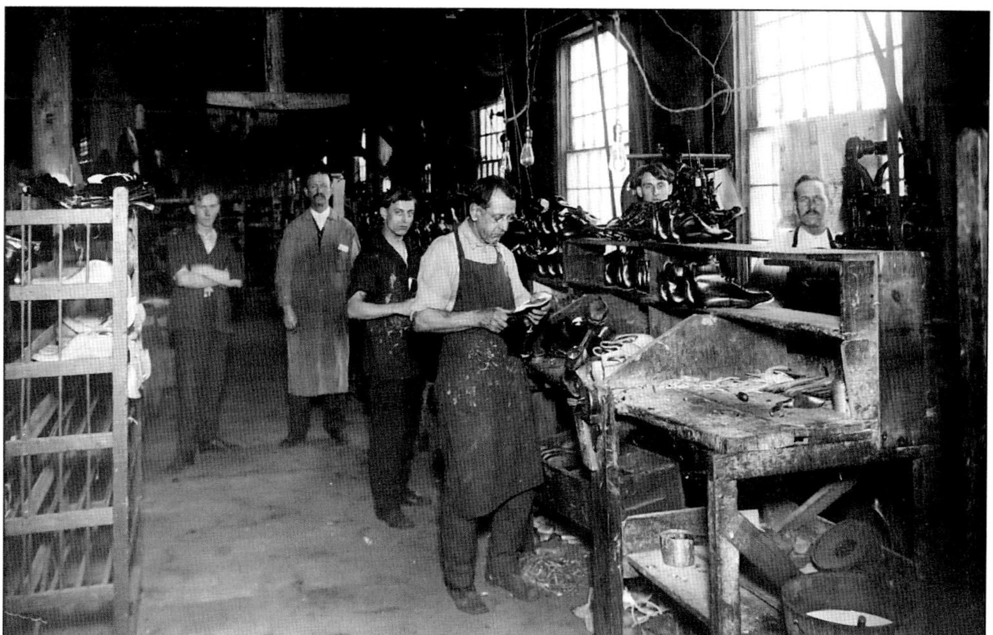

Workers at the Derry Shoe Factory in 1916 are photographed working on "uppers." This seems to have been exclusively a man's job.

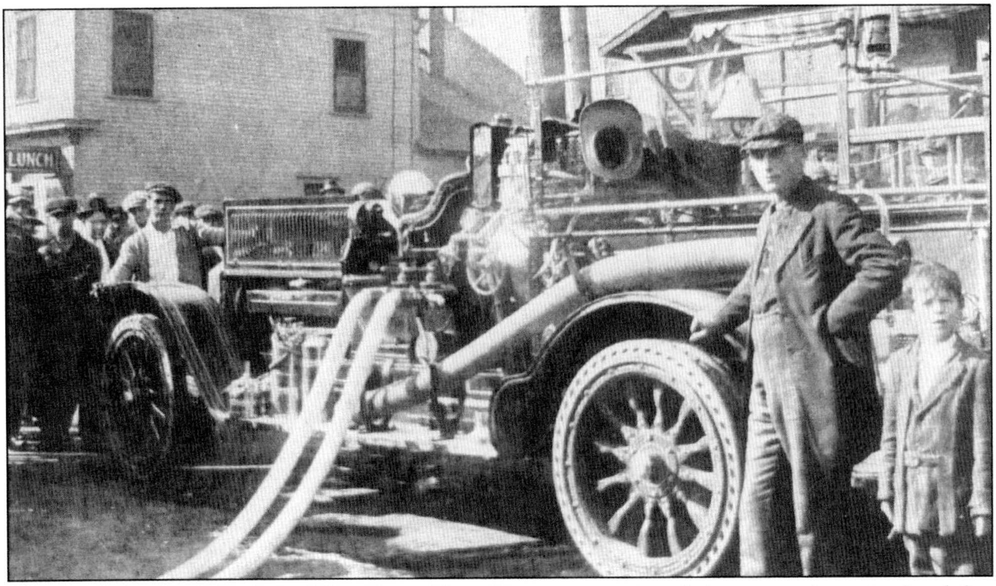

The fiery destruction of the Woodbury Shoe Factory convinced the town that the local fire department needed to be brought out of the horse-drawn era and into the automotive age. This 1915 photograph shows the town's first fire truck.

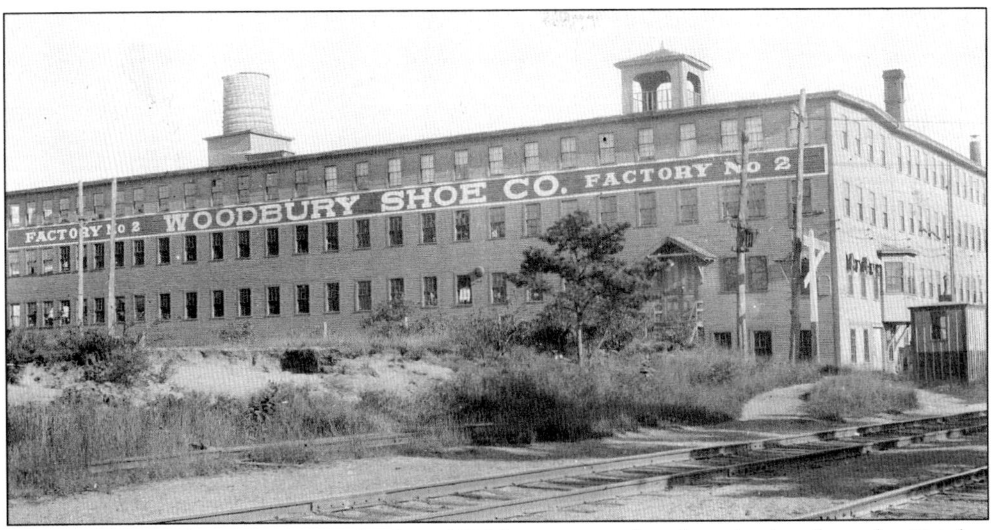

The Woodbury Shoe Factory was built c. 1890 by a group of trade unionists from the Knights of Labor. They had originally worked for Colonel Pillsbury but quit due to a labor-management disagreement. In a few years the new company sold out and it was eventually purchased by the Woodbury Shoe Manufacturing Company.

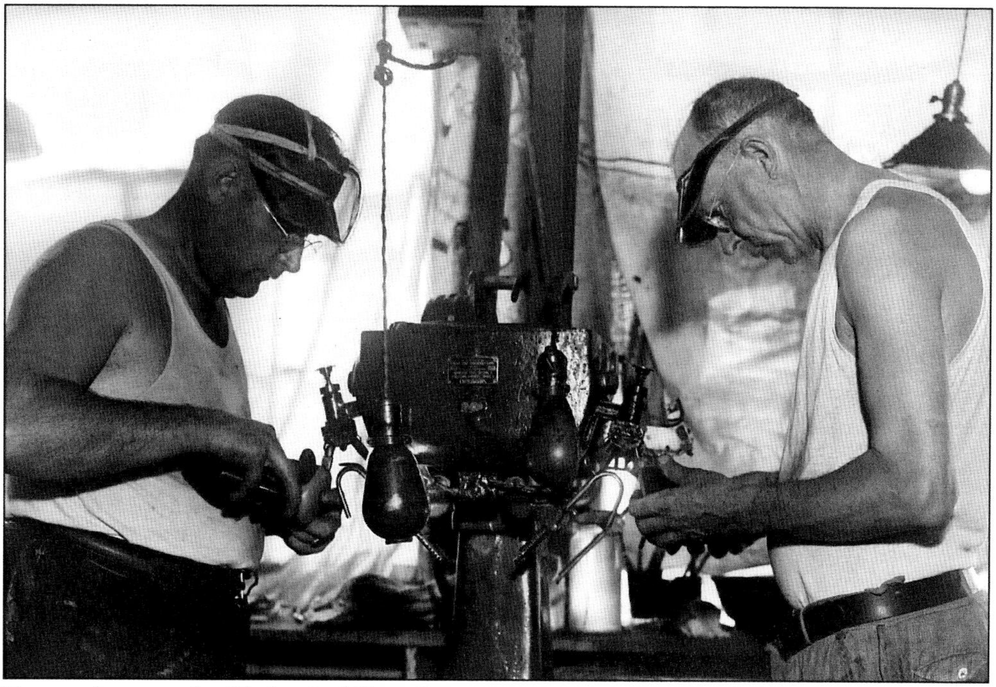

Two workmen at the Chelmsford Shoe Company are seen trimming off the extra leather on the soles of shoes in 1938. Tasks such as edge setting were usually performed by the male workers.

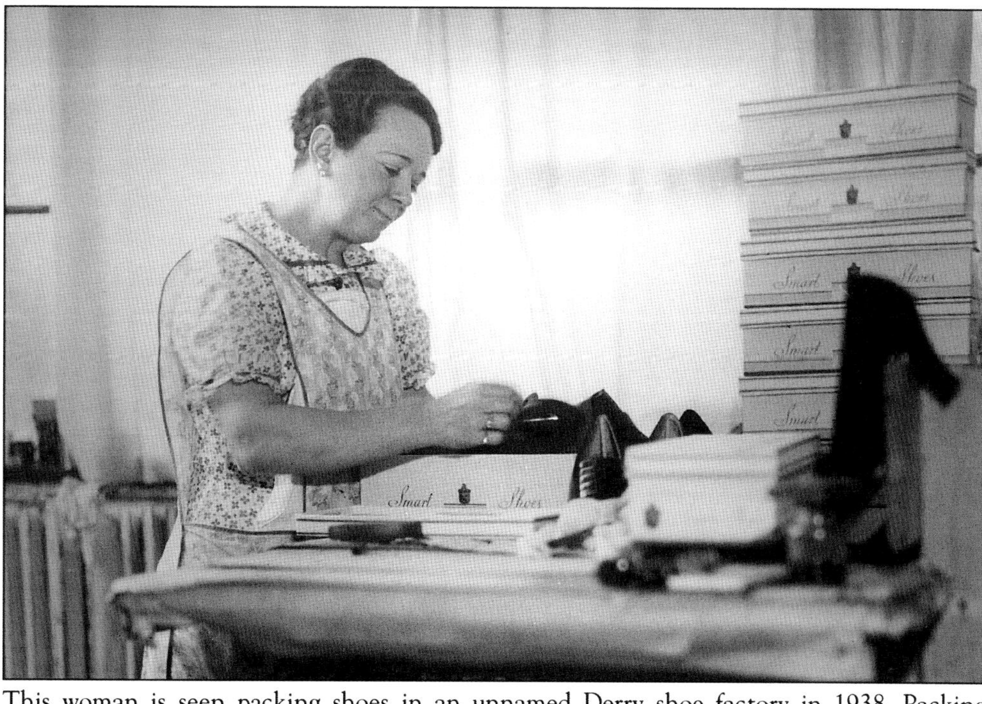

This woman is seen packing shoes in an unnamed Derry shoe factory in 1938. Packing was usually considered a woman's task within the shops. The various local manufacturers made shoes under a large variety of brand names that were distributed to department stores across the nation.

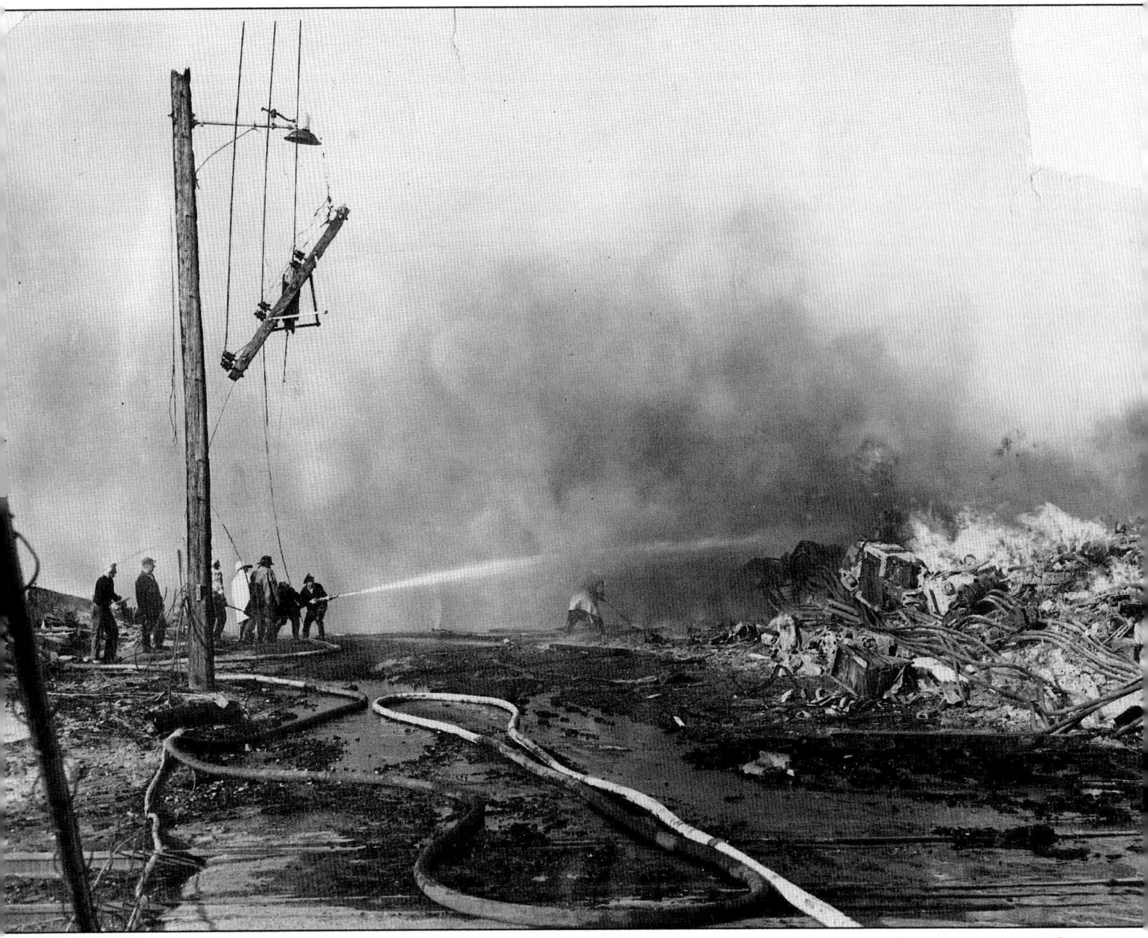

On May 6, 1960, the Chelmsford Shoe Factory on South Avenue erupted in flames. Fire trucks and men from nearly a dozen communities responded immediately, but the fire could not be contained until it had destroyed four large tenements, ten houses, a shoe store, and the huge four-story shoe shop complex. Fifty-seven families were made homeless and four hundred workers unemployed as a result of the fire. In 1915 this shop had burned but had been quickly rebuilt; this time it would not be. The Chelmsford fire, in effect, ended the domination of the shoe industry in West Derry.

West Derry: Commercial

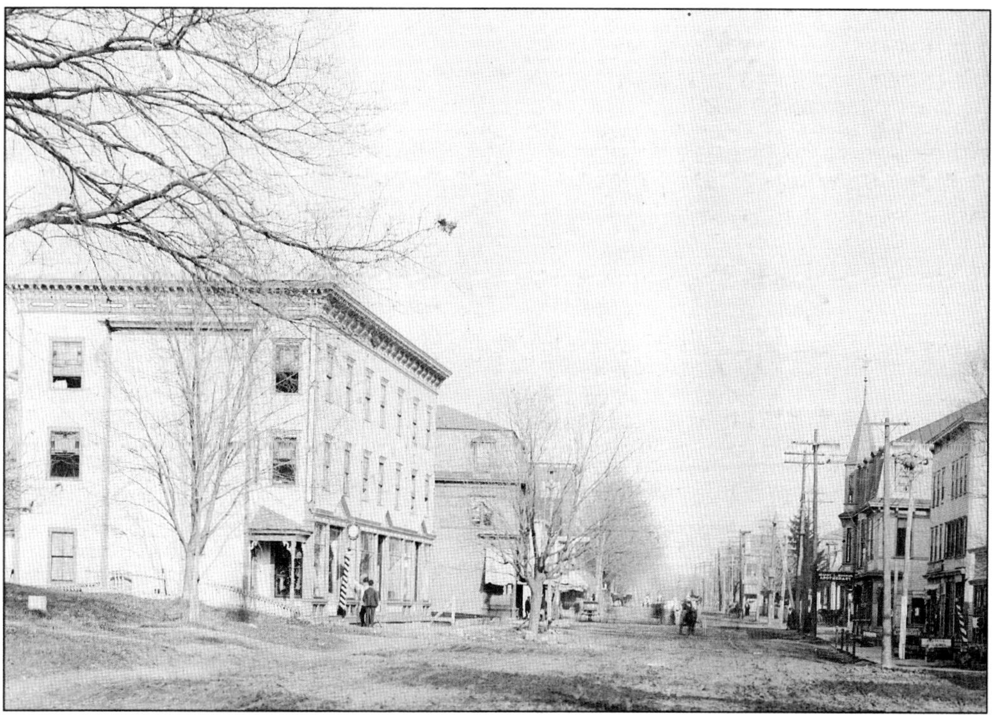

This c. 1895 photograph shows Broadway a great deal quieter than it is today. On the immediate left (past what would be the future site of the Aubuchon block) is the Stearns block. On the right are Charles Young's Laundry and Bensons Apothecary, and barbershops occupy both sides of the road. The railway barrier on the far right was lowered many times each day until it was replaced by a flagman in 1934. Only the Sterns block has survived the one hundred years since this street scene was photographed.

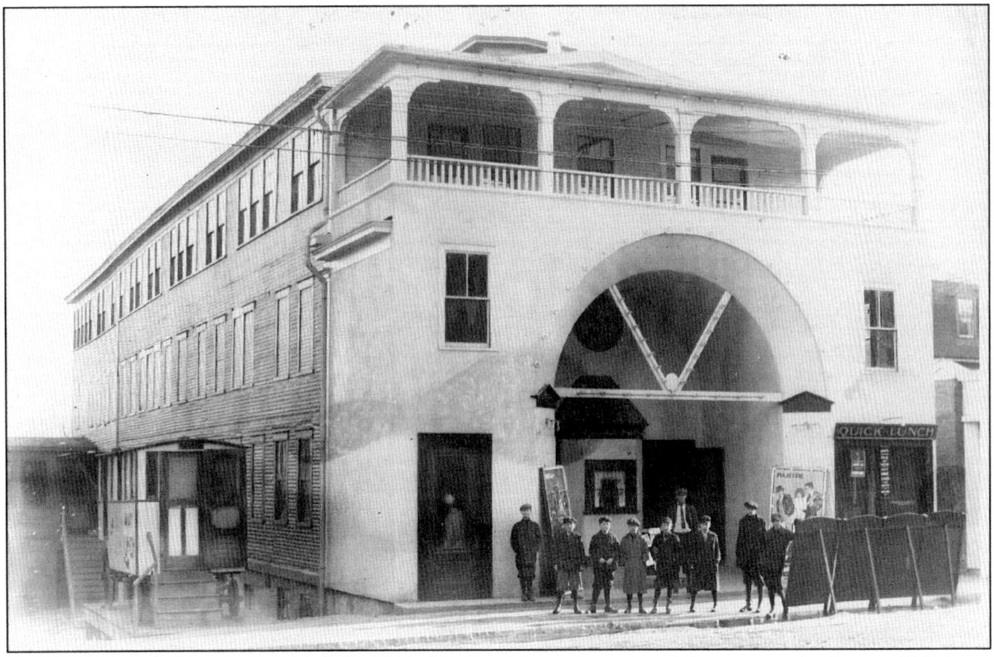

The Broadway Theater was built by Mrs. Minnie Humphrey by adding onto the former Pillsbury Shoe Factory. A bowling alley was in the basement and a dance hall on the second floor. Silent movies were shown here until August 1929, when Jolson's *The Singing Fool* played to turnaway crowds. Note the lunch cart on the left.

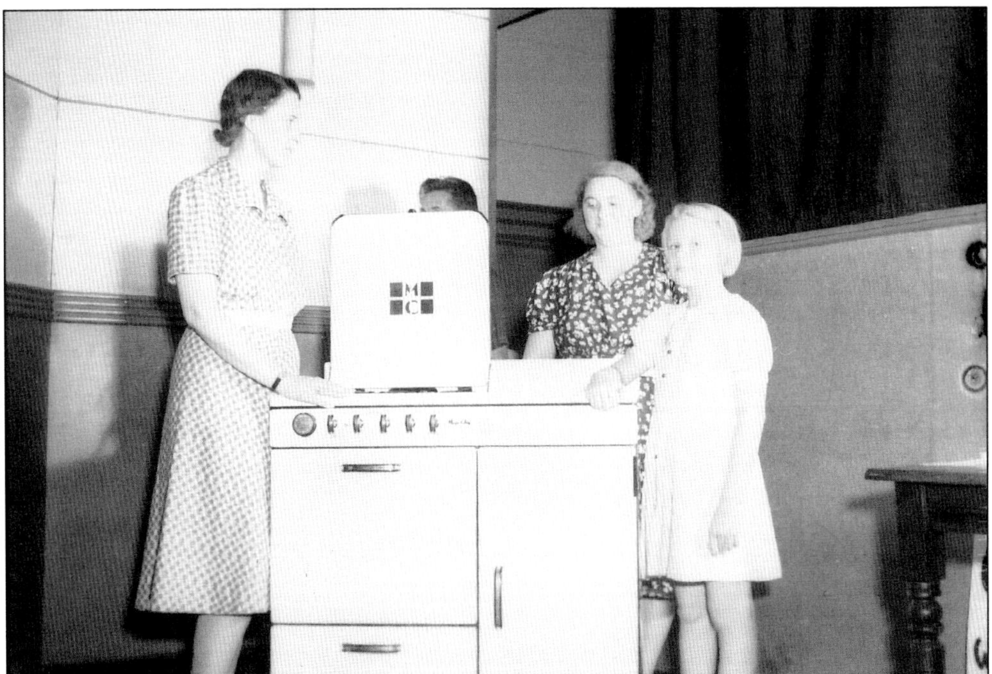

In the summer of 1940 the Plaza Theater hosted a cooking school for the ladies in the area. Miss Barbara Summer was the winner of a Magic Chef gas range donated by Derry's Community Gas Company. (Lear photograph)

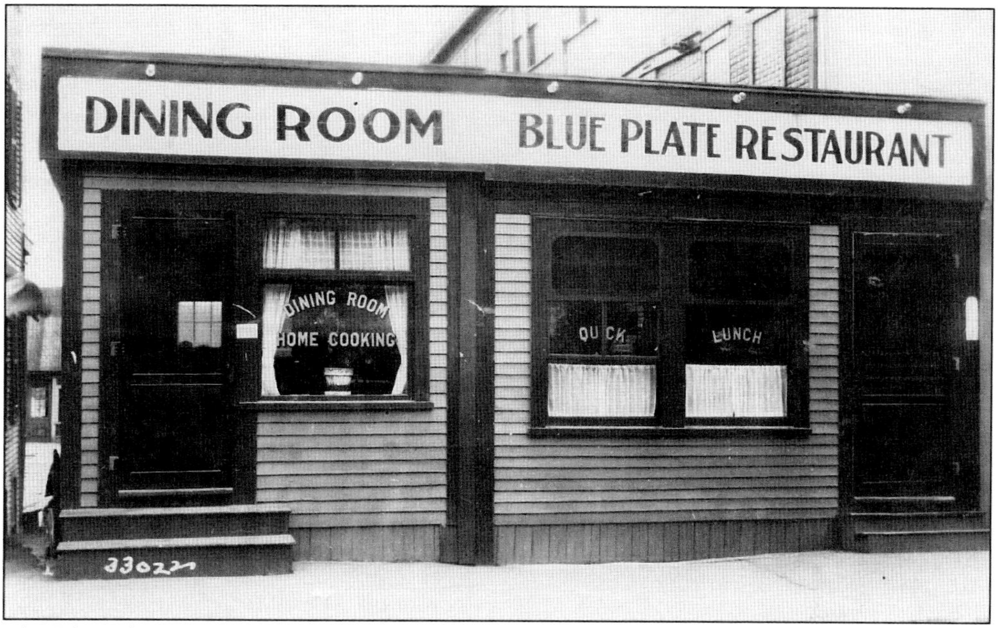

The Blue Plate Restaurant was built next to the Plaza Movie Theater around World War I (previously a lunch wagon had occupied this spot). During the early 1960s it was the site of Robinson's Jewelry Store.

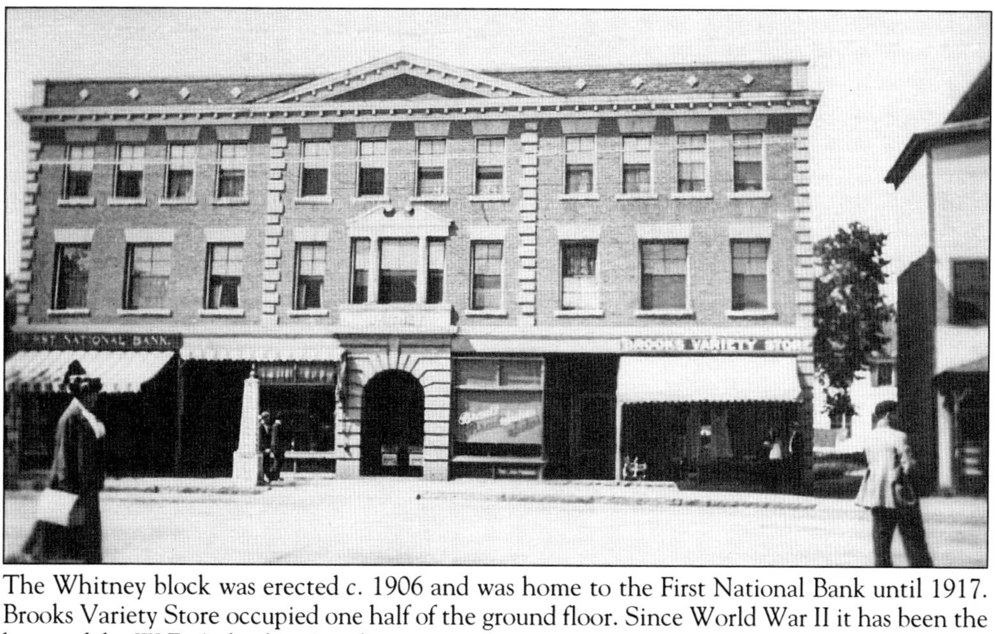

The Whitney block was erected *c.* 1906 and was home to the First National Bank until 1917. Brooks Variety Store occupied one half of the ground floor. Since World War II it has been the home of the W.E. Aubuchon Hardware Store.

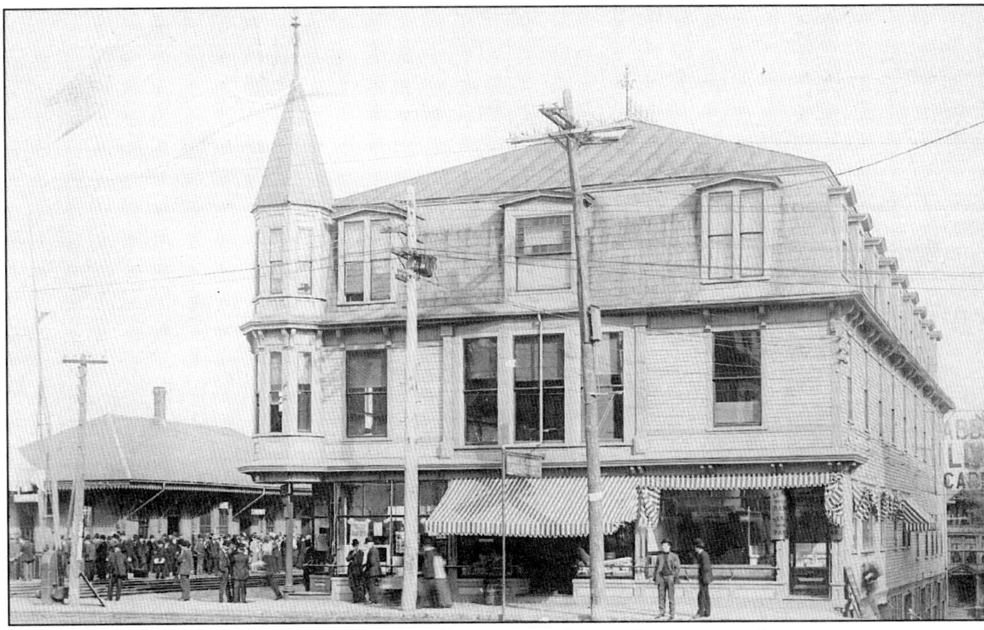

The Shepard block *c.* 1915 next to the depot was a busy place: it was home to a newsstand, drugstore, and bank. The reason for the crowd is unknown—possibly it is Old Home Week. The apartments on the upper floor were long known as the American House. The block was destroyed in a fire in 1979.

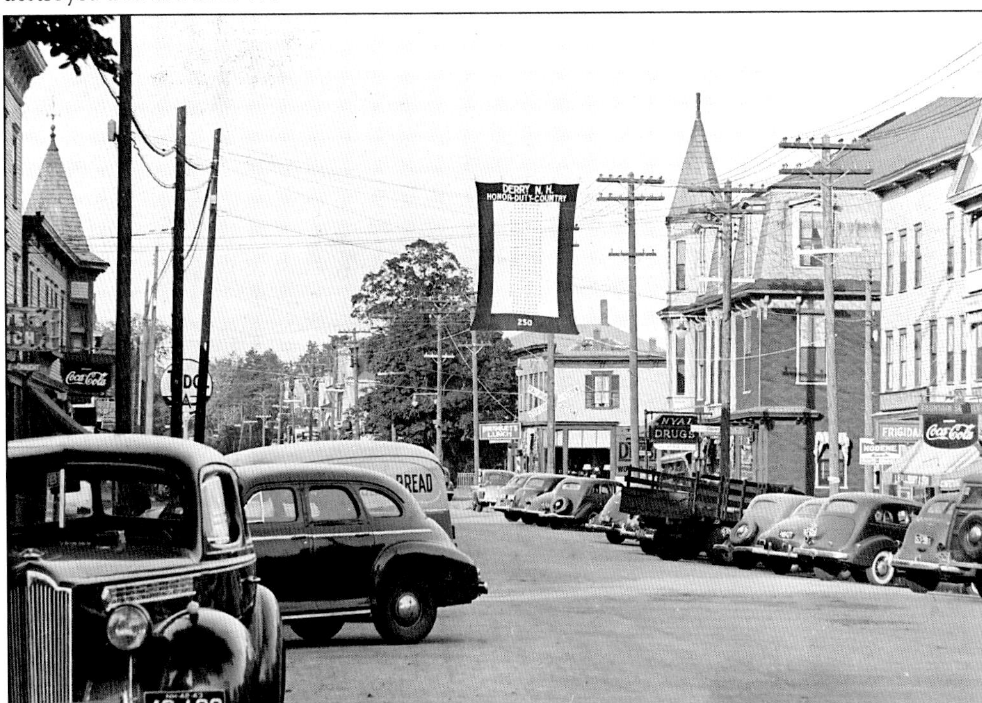

The town's service flag was proudly hung in the middle of Broadway in 1943. Each star stood for one of the 250 men and women who were off fighting in World War II. By war's end the number would climb to 718; 18 lost their lives.

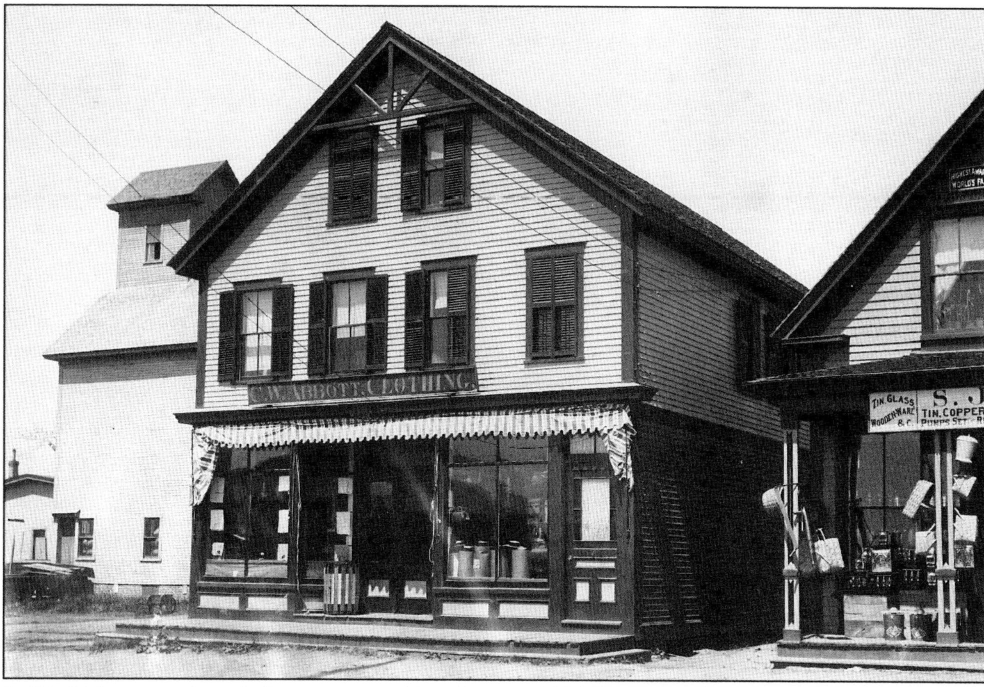

C.W. Abbott ran this clothing store on Broadway *c.* 1895, but since that time it has gone through many owners. Most recently it has been a Cumberland Farms store and Ozzie's Chicken (it is now J.J. Pizza). In the background on the left can be seen Hood's grain elevator and creamery.

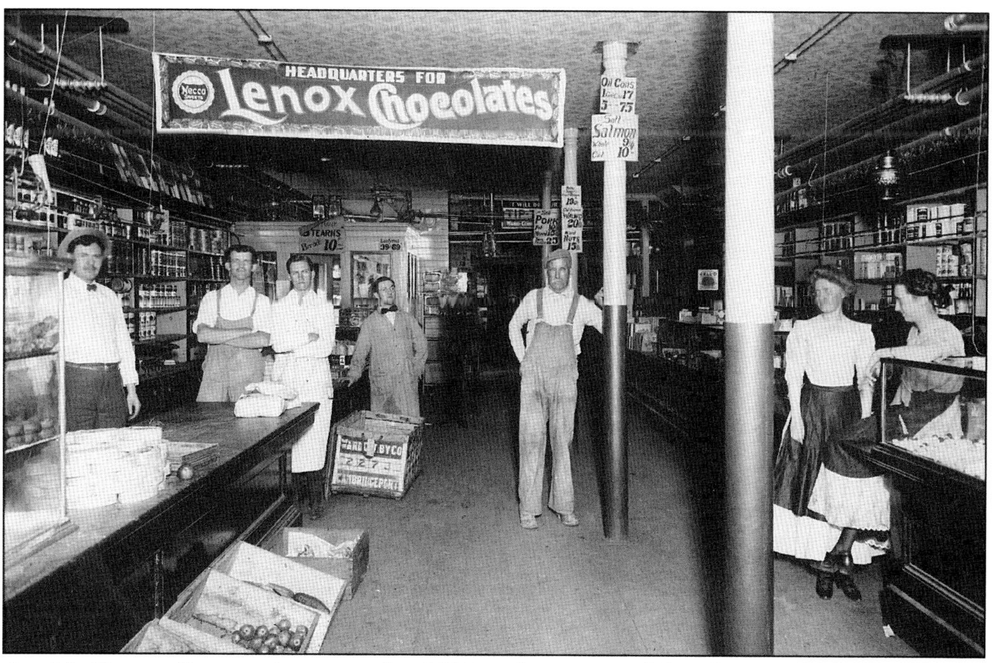

Annis's Grocery Store as it appeared *c.* 1910 at the corner of Broadway and Manning Street. From left to right are Frank Crabb, Frank Berry, Richard Durkee, Joseph P. Lander, James Hunt, Josie Payne George, and Helen Chamberlain.

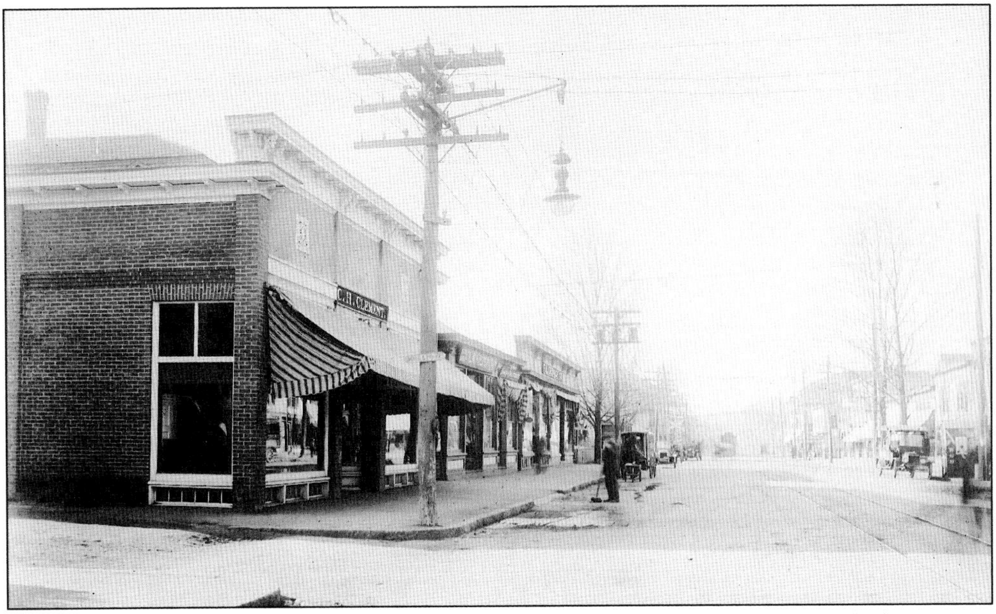

A street sweeper cleans up the pavement in front of the Charles H. Clement Clothing Store to get West Broadway ready for the 1919 parade celebrating Derry's 200th anniversary. (Grinnell collection)

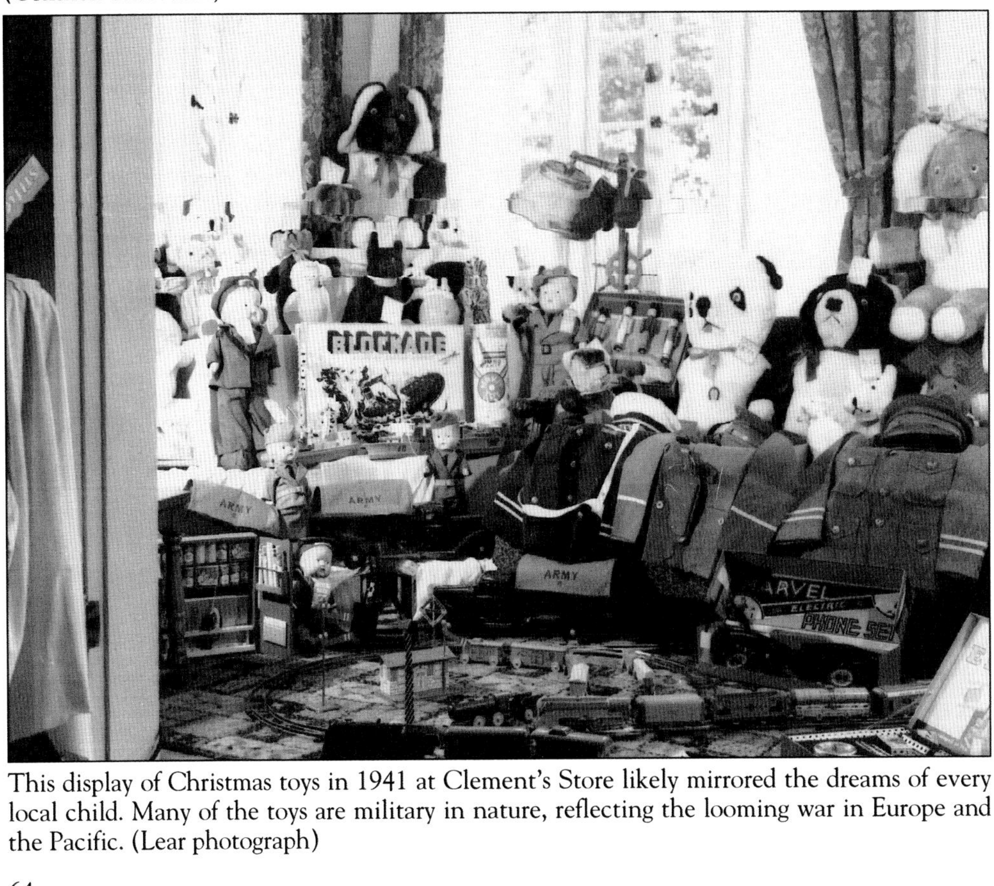

This display of Christmas toys in 1941 at Clement's Store likely mirrored the dreams of every local child. Many of the toys are military in nature, reflecting the looming war in Europe and the Pacific. (Lear photograph)

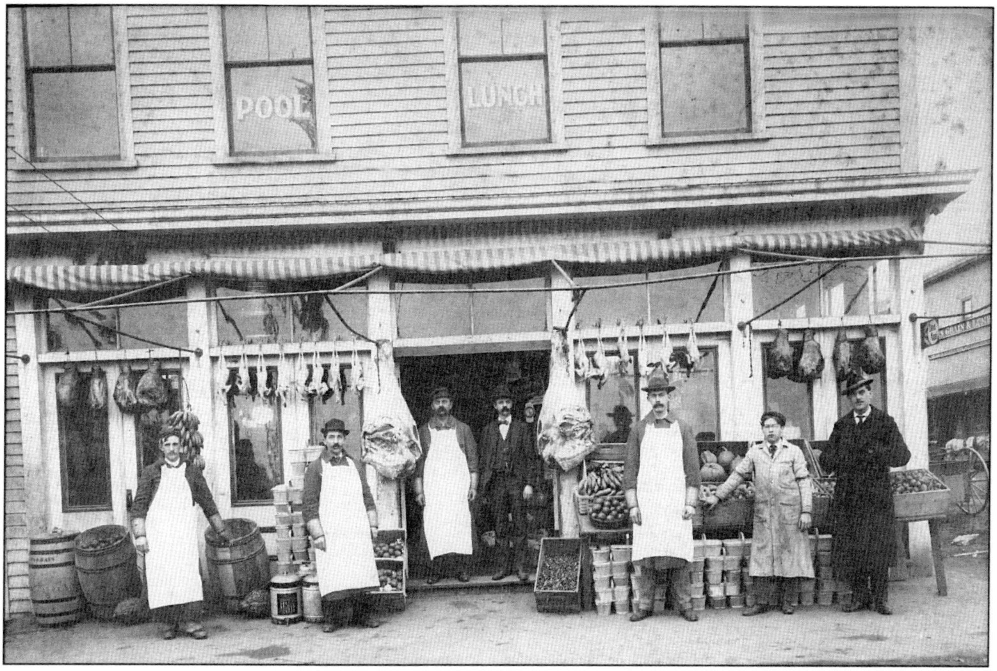

The exterior of Wilson's Market with vegetables, plucked chickens, sides of beef, and hams displayed to tempt the discriminating customer. Guy Chadwick ran a lunch and pool room on the second floor. (Grinnell collection)

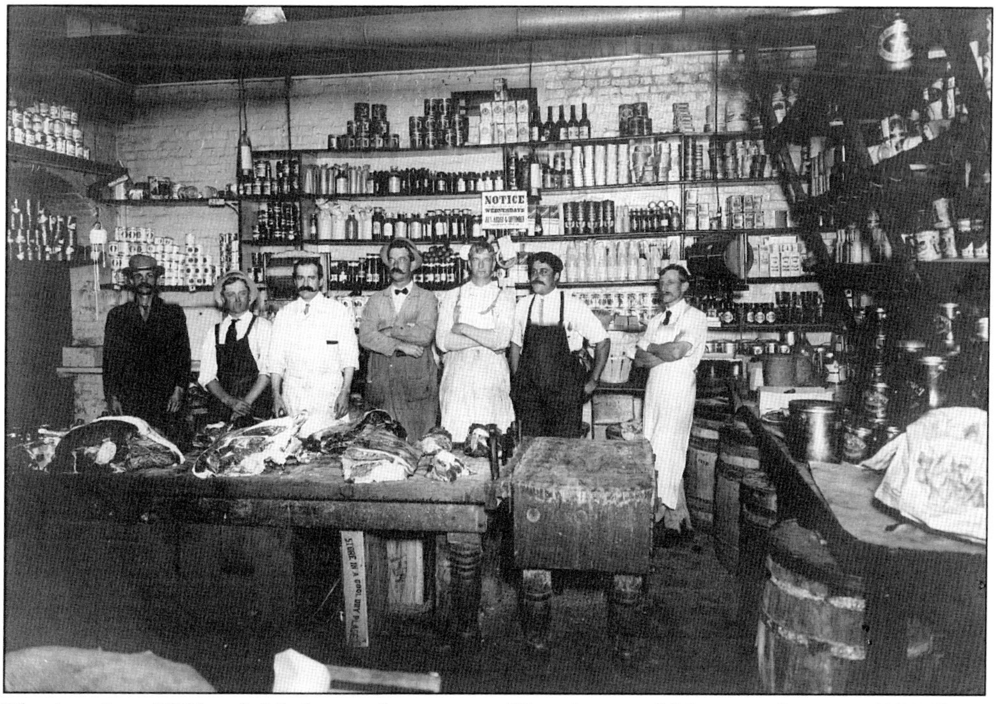

The interior of Wilson's Market at the corner of Broadway and Manning Street *c.* 1900. From left to right are Harry W. Wilson (owner), Allen Noyes, George Guilbeant, Fred Farnham, Walter Farnham, Bill Burbank, and Bert Colby. (Grinnell collection)

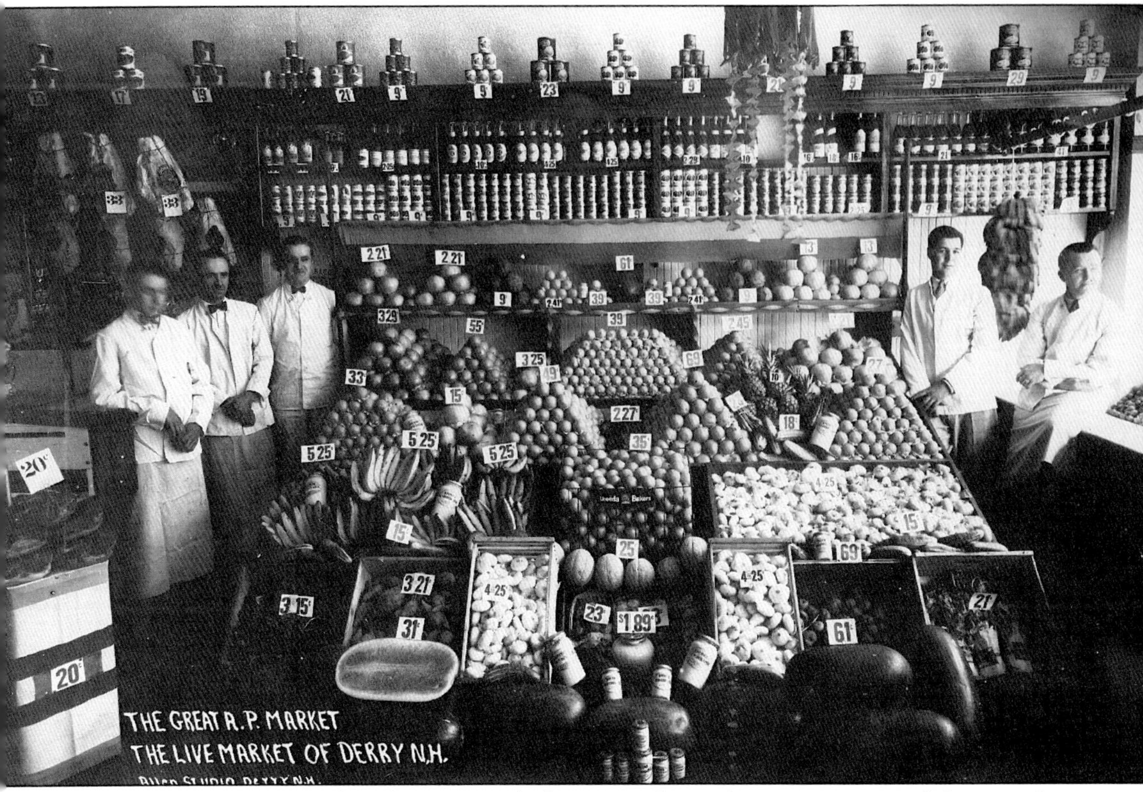

The great A & P Market demonstrated obvious pride in the presentation of their stock at its Broadway and Wall Street location *c.* 1932. In 1958 it would move to upper Crystal Avenue. From left to right are Cy Smith, Charles Audette, Francis Paradis, John Gratton, and Pete Messier.

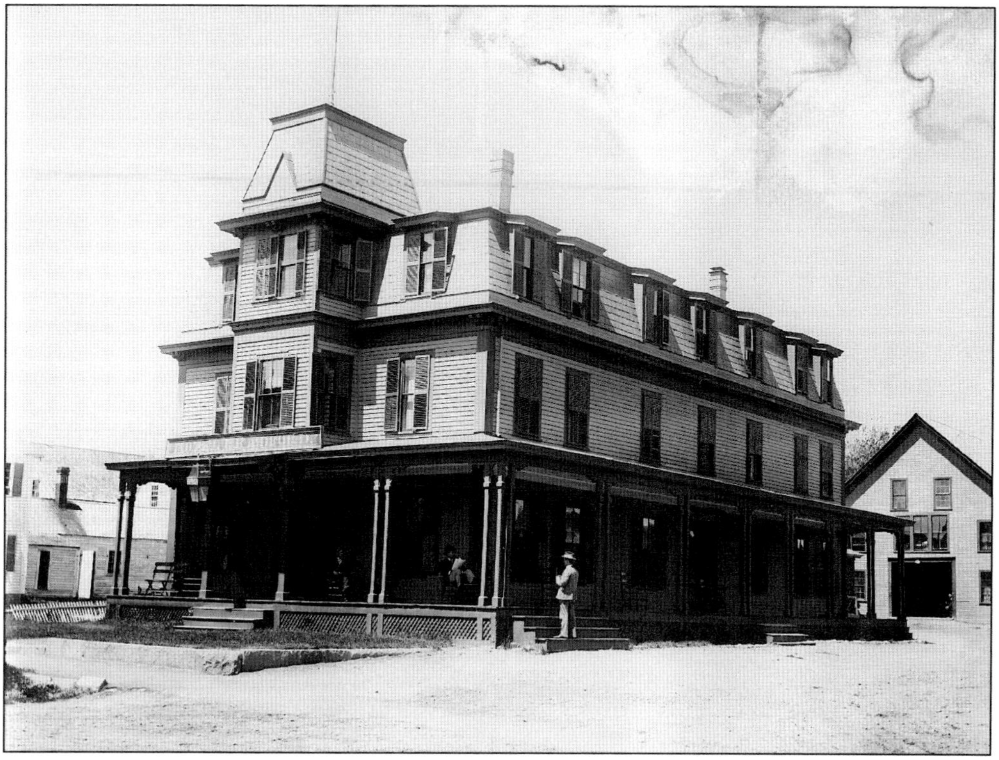

The Hotel Bradford at Broadway and Martin Street was built *c.* 1882. Its clientele was comprised of salesmen and buyers brought in by the nearby railroad, and its large livery stable was run by the Abbott and Davis Carriage Company. The front has since been extended out to the sidewalk, making it scarcely recognizable today.

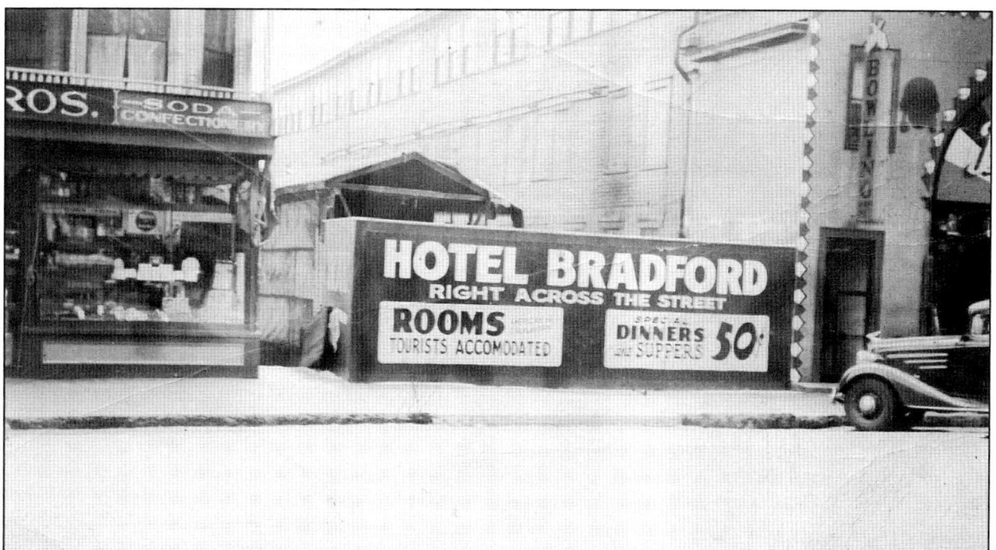

On the right is the entrance to the bowling lanes at the Broadway Movie Theater. The 50¢ price of dinner at the Hotel Bradford across the street is less remarkable when it is realized that $5 a day in the 1920s was considered a very good wage.

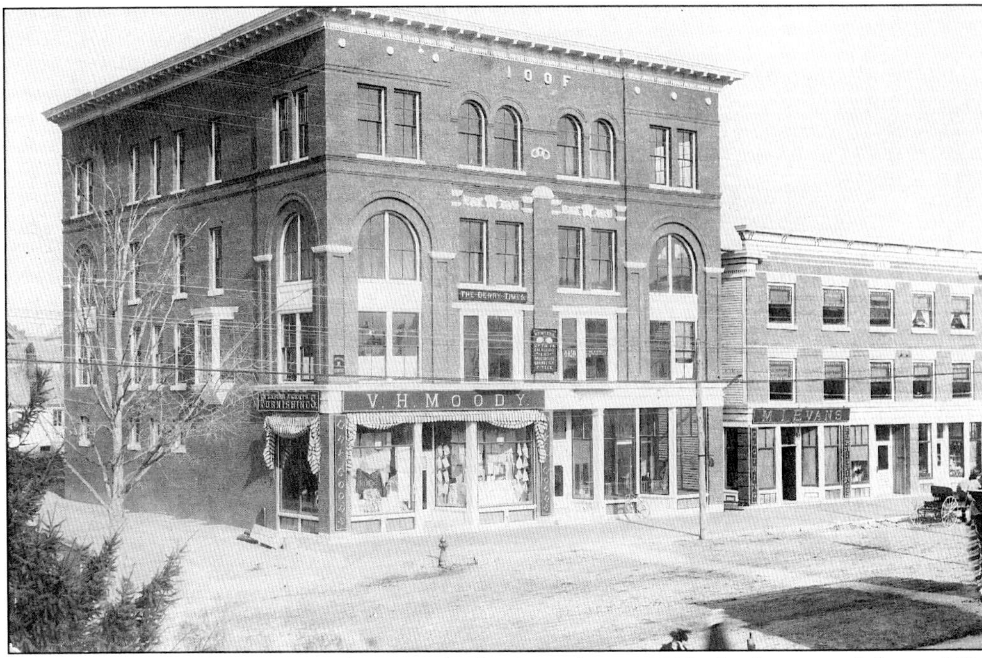

The Odd Fellows block on Broadway was built after a fire in 1897. At the time of this c. 1898 photograph it was the home of the *Derry Times*, one of the approximately thirty newspapers that failed over the years to survive competition with the *Derry News*. The block burned in 1963.

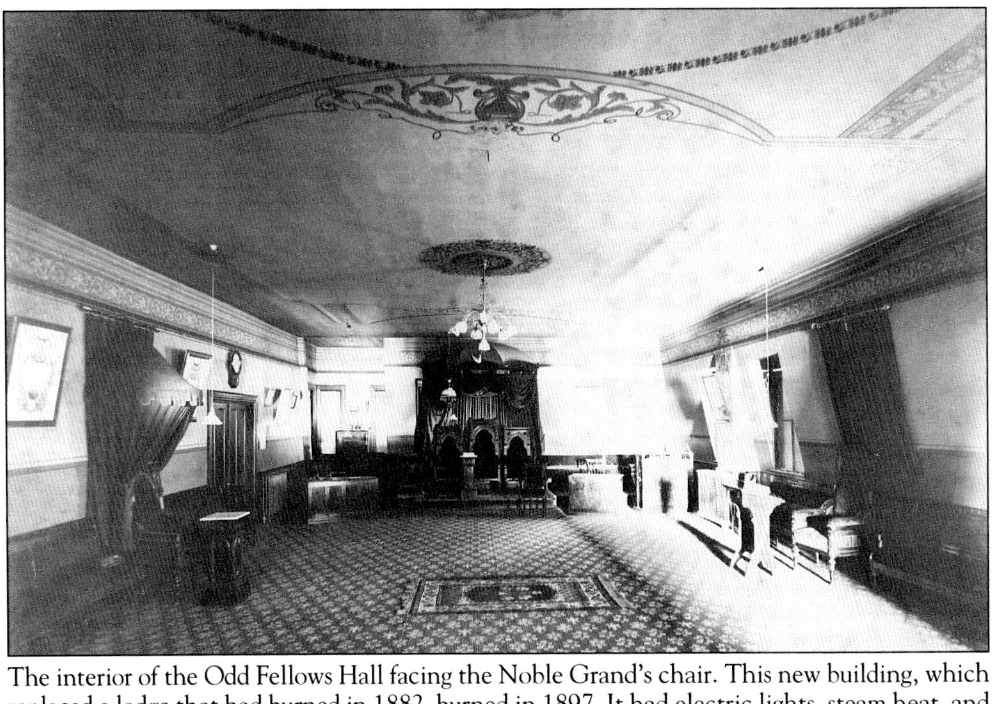

The interior of the Odd Fellows Hall facing the Noble Grand's chair. This new building, which replaced a lodge that had burned in 1882, burned in 1897. It had electric lights, steam heat, and a banquet hall that seated 250 people. The Rebekahs even had their own ritual room.

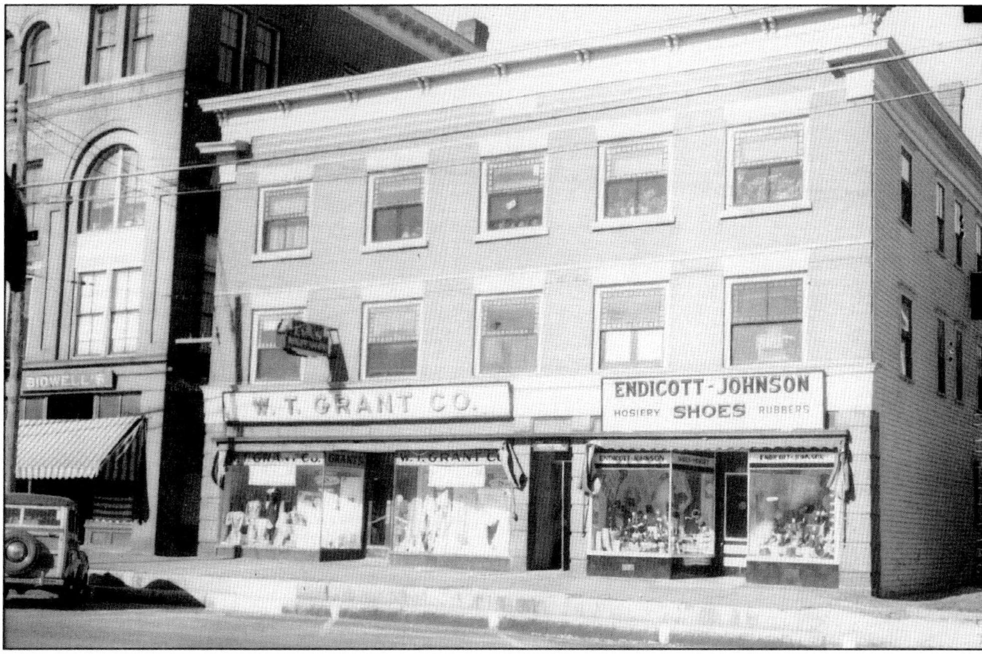

The W.T. Grant Department Store on Broadway in 1944 played an important role in the everyday commercial life in Derry. The sidewalk was originally two steps above the street level to aid in getting in and out of carriages. The Cumberland Farms strip mall now occupies this site. (Lear photograph)

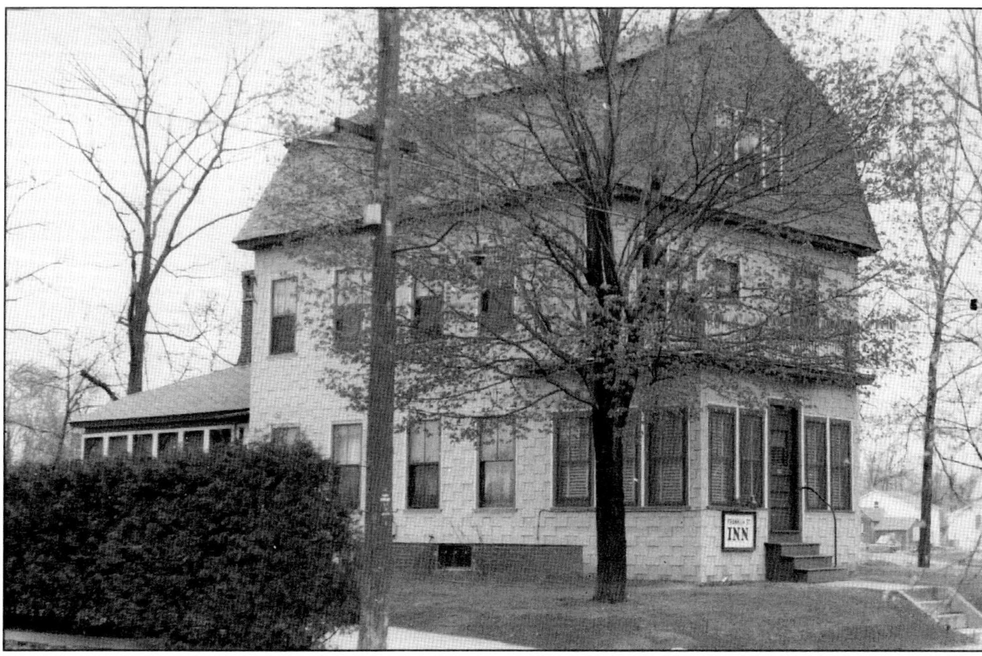

The Franklin Inn on Franklin Street in 1944 was one of many small boarding houses in West Derry. These houses had most of their clientele siphoned away during the last few decades by the tremendous increase of apartment complexes in the area. The Franklin Inn was razed in the 1970s and replaced with an apartment court. (Lear photograph)

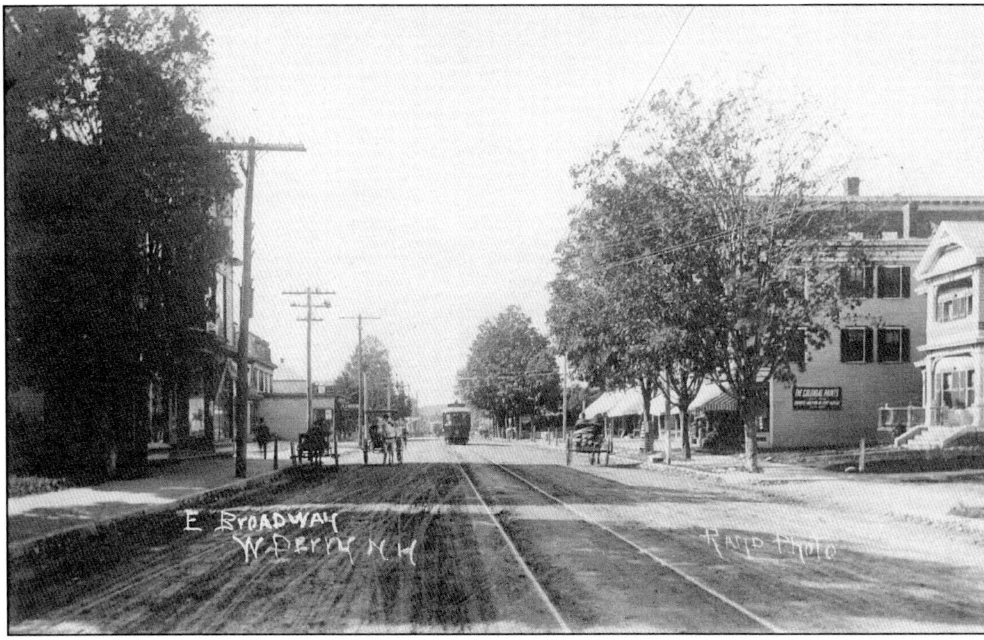

The Chester and Derry Trolley travels down east Broadway *c.* 1905. On the left is Bell's Opera House. This structure was torn down in 1953 and replaced with a one-story, three-store building. Across the street was Frank N. Young's insurance office, which burned in the great 1963 fire.

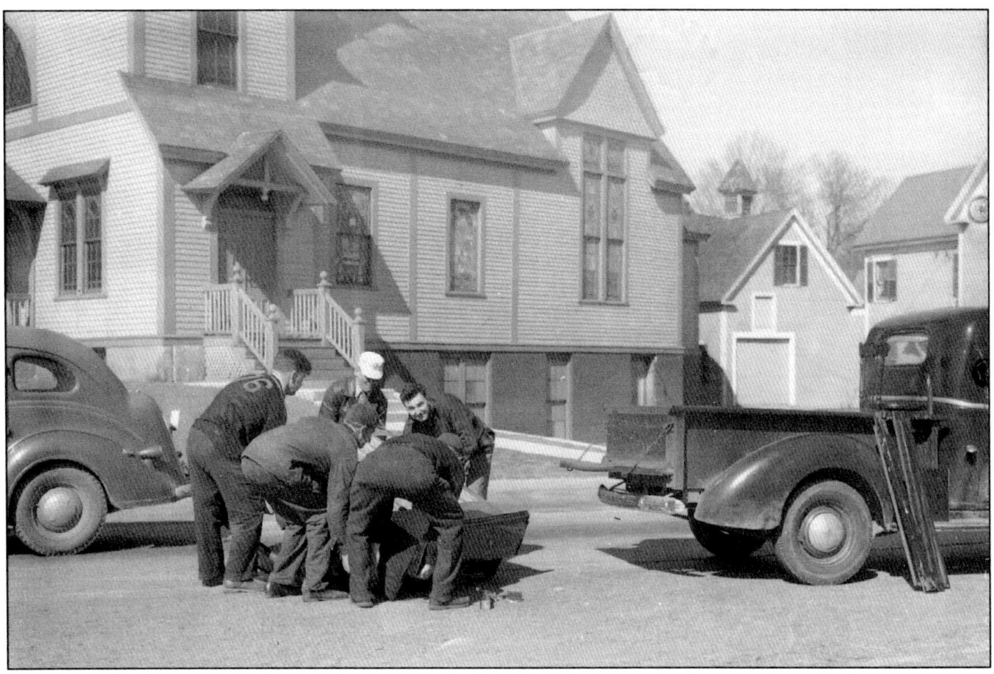

The Broadway and Crystal Avenue intersection has seen a great variety of excitement through the years, such as in 1941 when a piano fell off a delivery truck. In 1933 a mob of five hundred unemployed workers armed with rotten eggs, rocks, and snowballs gathered here to molest shoe shop strikebreakers as they drove through town. (Lear photograph)

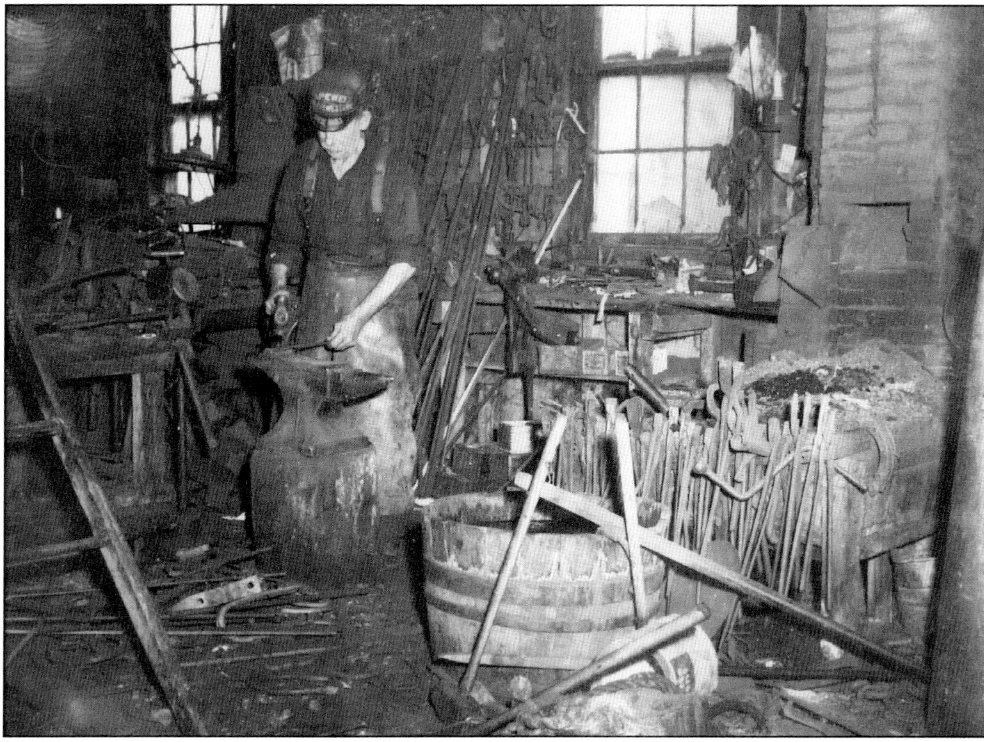

Charles Doherty's Blacksmith Shop on Wall Street in 1942. Mr. Doherty was a nearly legendary figure among the local racing set. He continued his profession well into his 80s. His shop is now a parking lot and the office of the Derry Visiting Nurses. (Lear photograph)

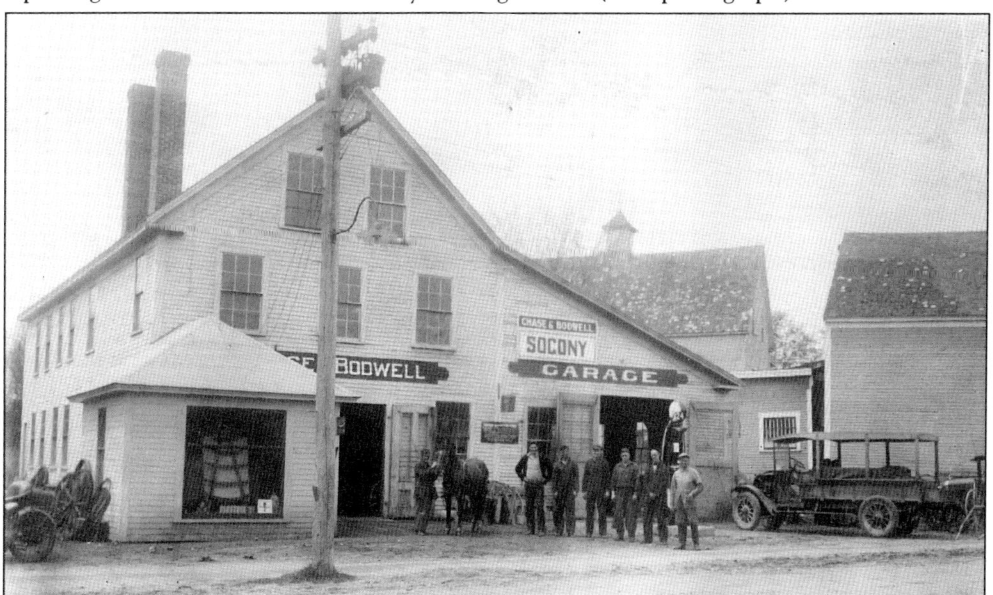

The Chase and Bodwell Garage on Central Street was formally the blacksmith shop of Edmund A. Chase. At the time of this c. 1920 photograph, it was still making the transition from shoeing horses to fixing automobiles.

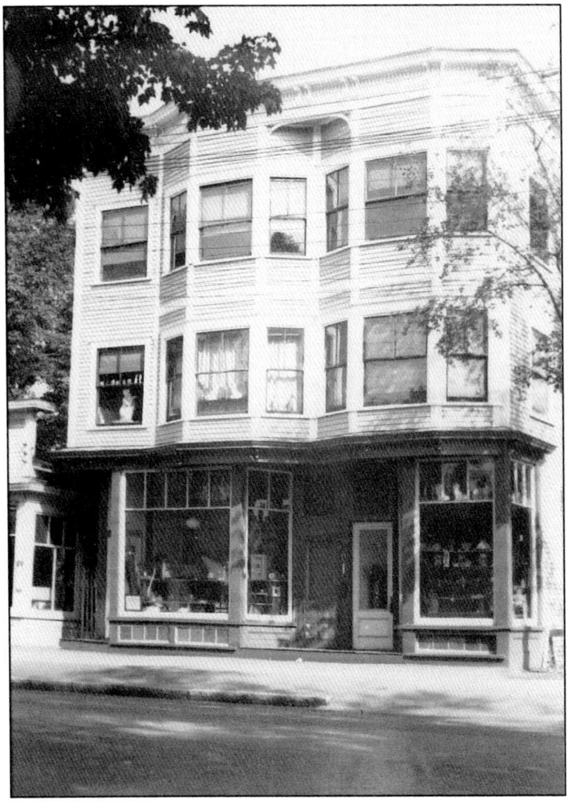

At Allie Davis's Store in the Kimball block in 1940 the sign said "We buy anything." To the left is the Ford Garage that would in 1947 become the Oxen Yoke Restaurant. These East Broadway buildings were razed in the 1970s to make room for a three-store mall. (Lear photograph)

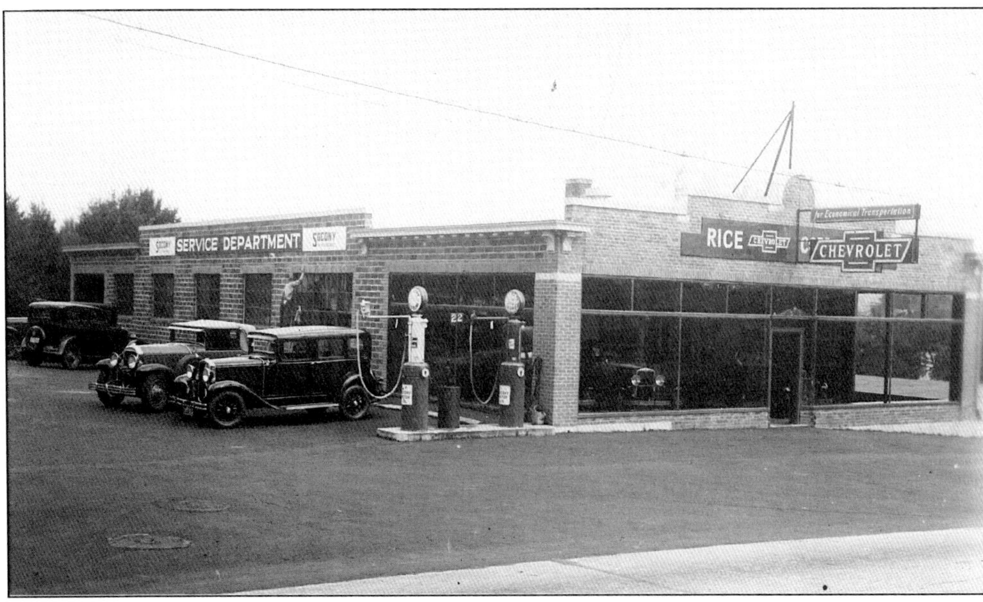

Harold Rice's Chevrolet Garage on Crystal Avenue was one of the first automotive dealership shops in Derry, and it sold gasoline at 22¢ per gallon. In 1941 it would be purchased by the Derry Egg Auction (a later addition on the right side of the building is now the Copy Shop).

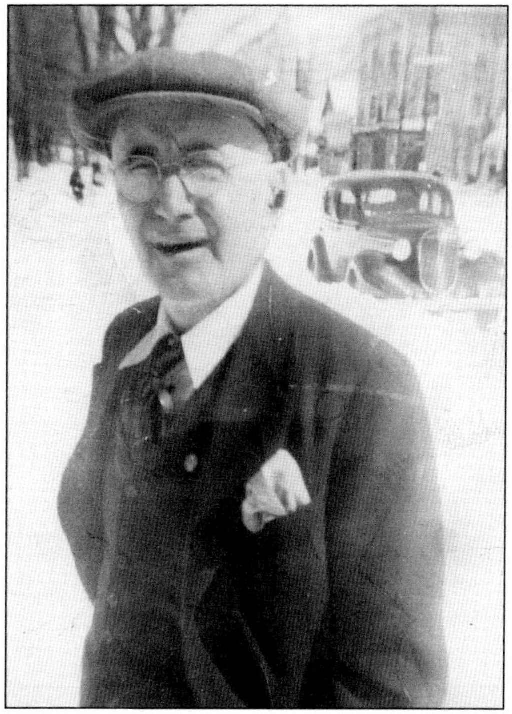

Dennis Casey ran a barbershop on East Broadway for nearly fifty years. In 1943 at age seventy-two his patrons presented him with a silver boxing trophy after he was found guilty of public brawling on the sidewalk with neighboring storekeeper Hyman Gross.

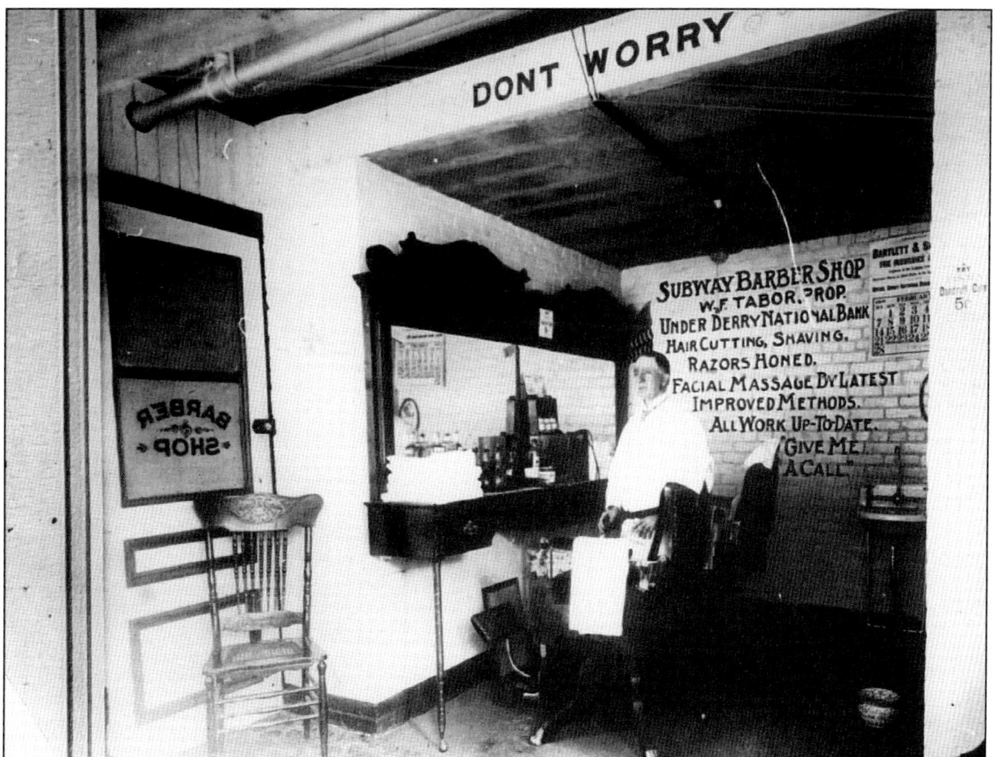

W.F. Tabor's Subway Barbershop occupied space in the basement of the Shepard block next to the railroad depot c. 1900.

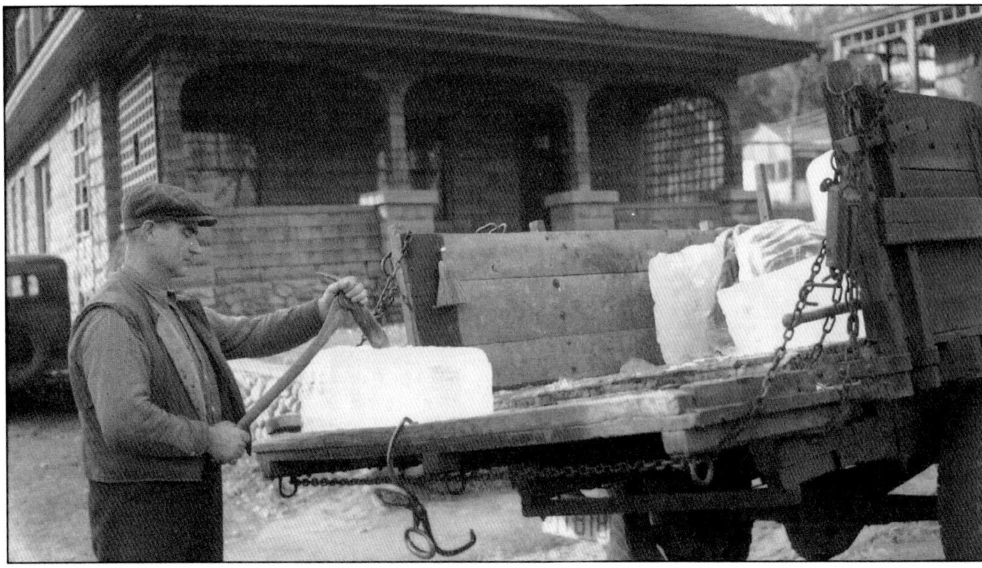

Iceman Joe Sullivan is photographed making a delivery on Franklin Street in December 1939. (Lear photograph)

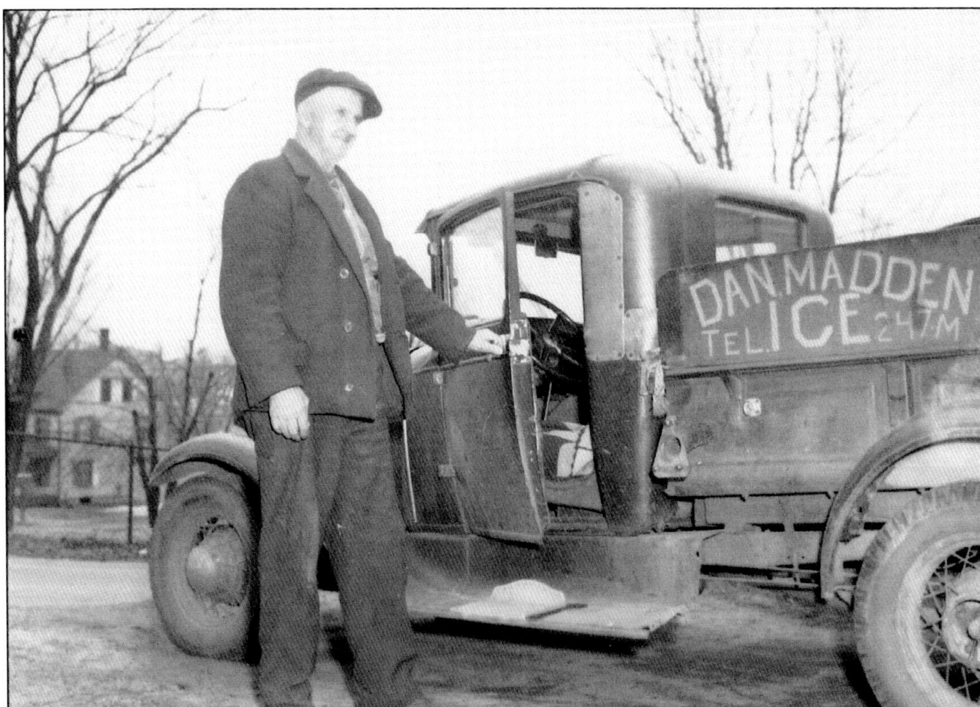

Joseph and Edward Madden cut ice on Beaver Lake from 1907 to1924. They were succeeded by William Madden, pictured here in 1940, and later by his three sons, Dan, John, and Theodore, who cut ice each winter through 1948. (Lear photograph)

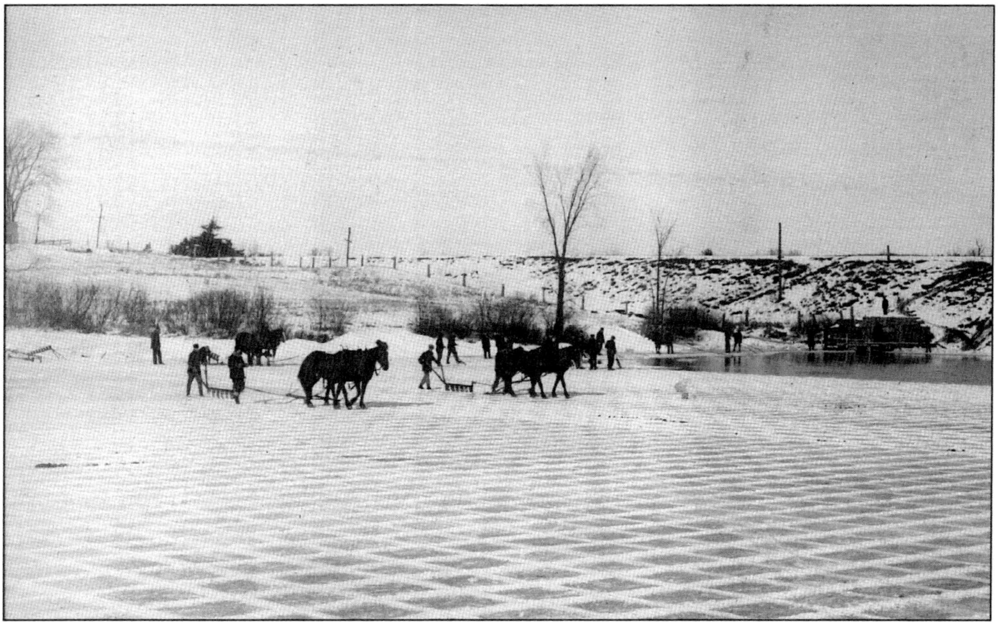

Ice cutting on Horne's Pond, now Hood Park, c. 1912. Ice from this pond was considered to be of poor quality as cinders from passing trains were often found in the blocks of ice. Beaver Lake ice was considered much more desirable.

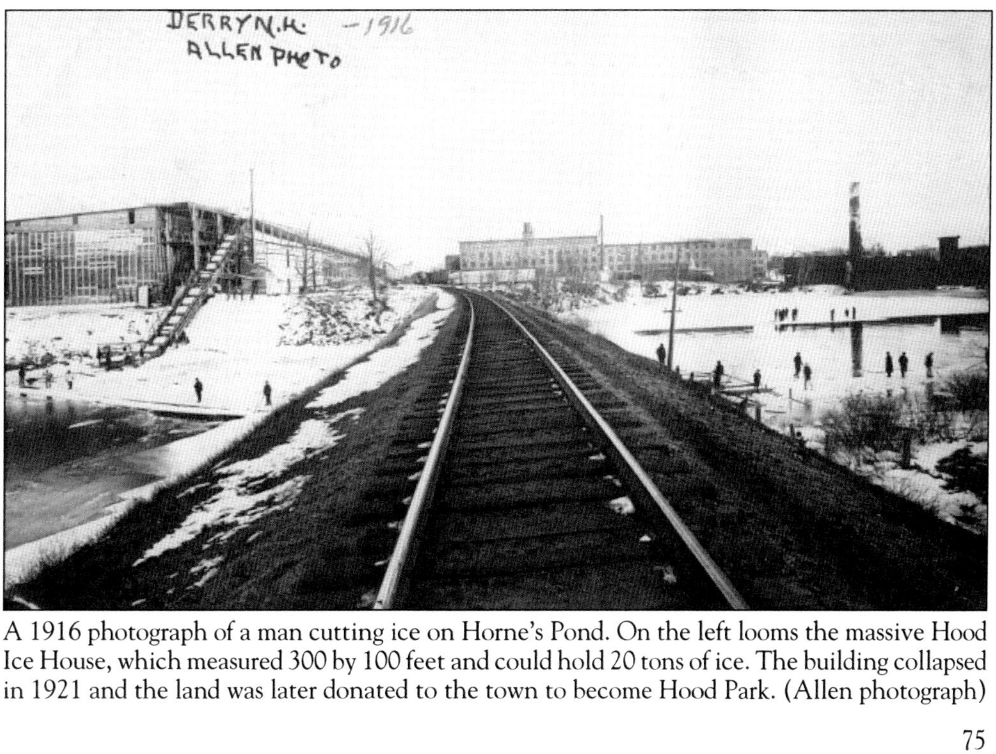

A 1916 photograph of a man cutting ice on Horne's Pond. On the left looms the massive Hood Ice House, which measured 300 by 100 feet and could hold 20 tons of ice. The building collapsed in 1921 and the land was later donated to the town to become Hood Park. (Allen photograph)

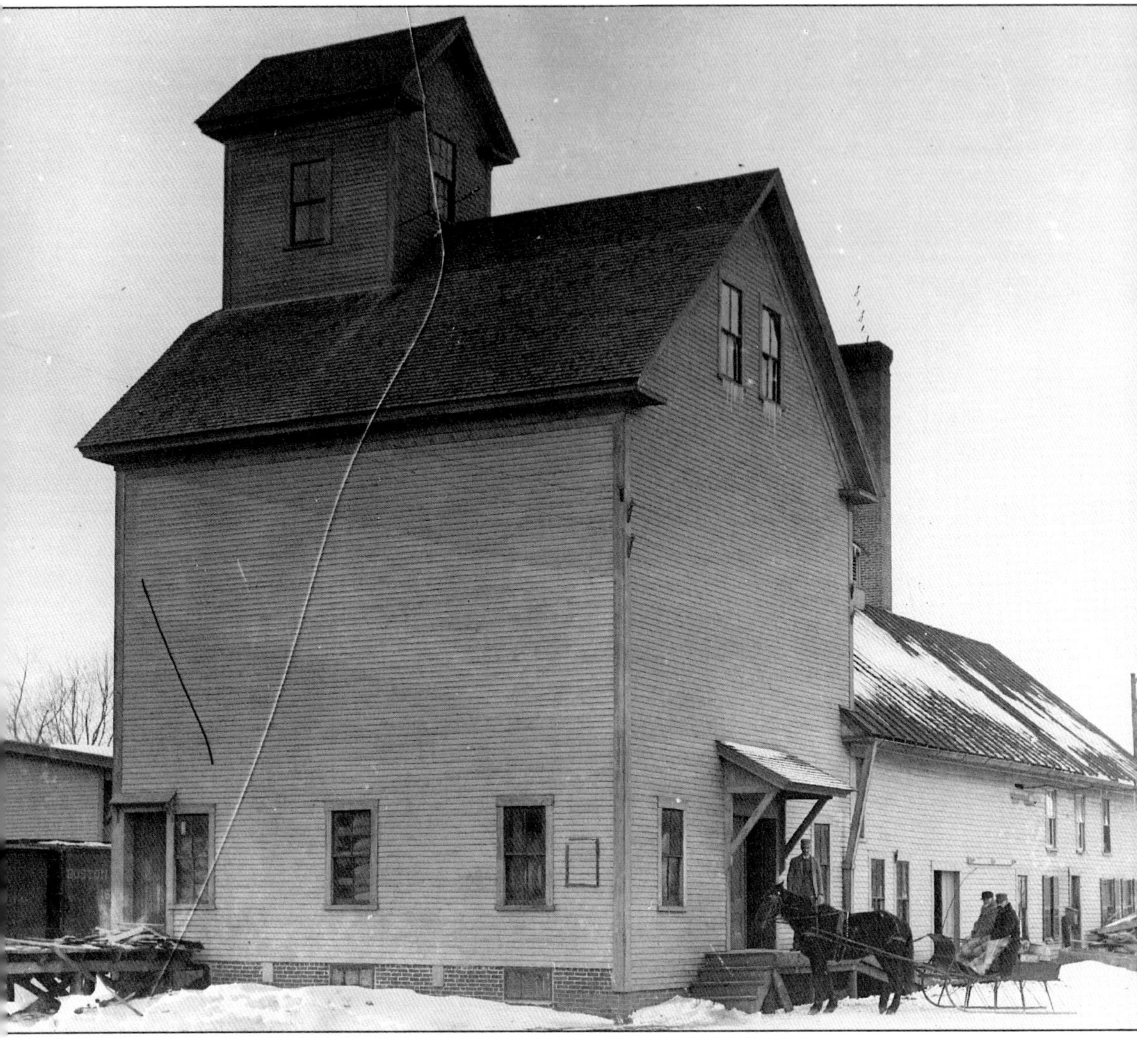

The creamery on Manning Street was the heart of the H.P. Hood Company's early success. Milk was separated from its cream on the first floor and then poured into 1,000-gallon vats in the basement. After churning, Hood's Gold Medal butter and cheese were rushed on railroad cars to satisfy the Boston market. The building was built in 1882 and torn down in 1963 to make way for a fifty-car parking lot.

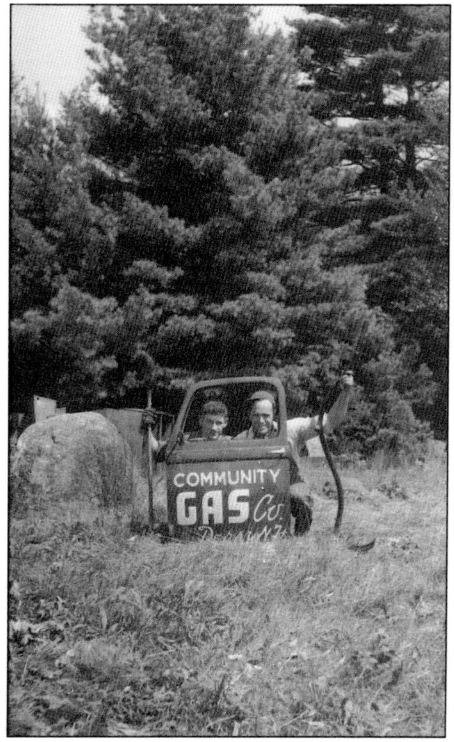

Why Don Tyler and Edward Joyce are posing like this in October 1941 is not known today. The Community Gas Company was owned by Norman Bangs and operated from a building at Crystal Avenue that had been built in 1935 (the site is now occupied by Wendy's). (Lear photograph)

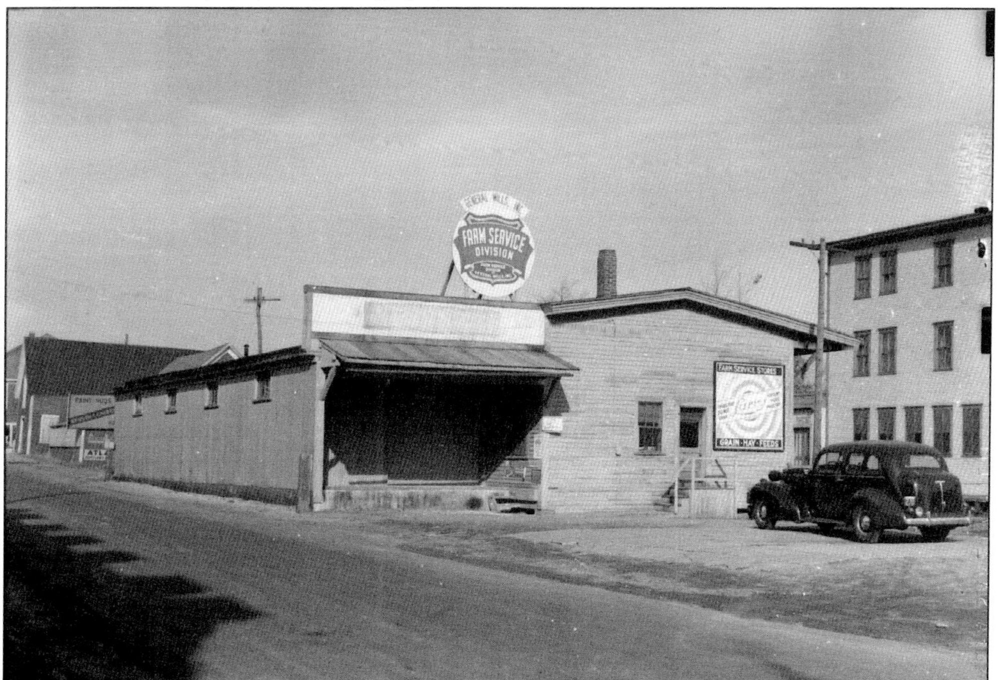

Ned Reynolds managed a farmer's supply store on Martin Street in 1944. Half the building was occupied by the freight depot for the Boston and Maine Railroad. It is now the Derry Feed and Supply Store. (Lear photograph)

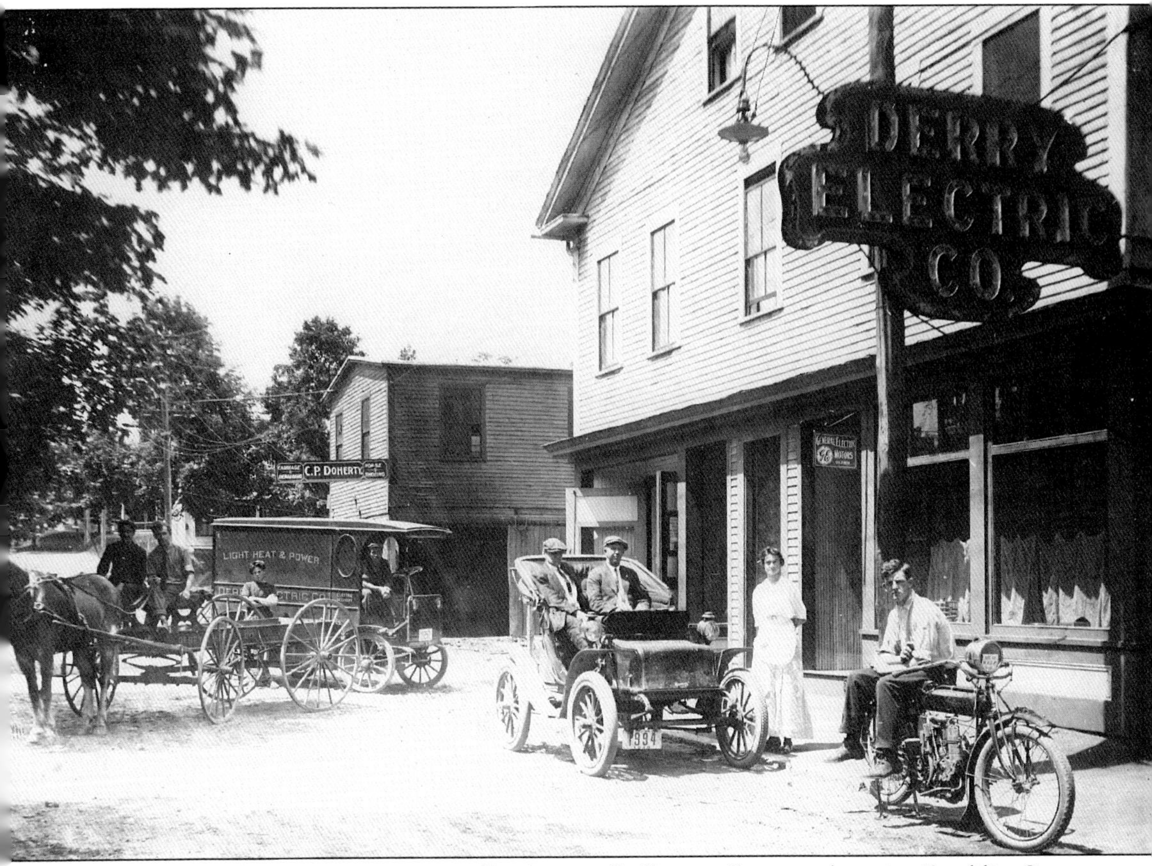

The Derry Electric Company proudly shows off all its rolling stock at its Franklin Street headquarters in 1915. The company was incorporated in 1891 and moved to this location in 1906. The employers in this picture are David M. Griffiths, Frank A. Low, Walter A. Angell, Robert Gilman, Hugh E. Webb, R.H. Moore, and Walter J. Pomith (the women are unidentified). In the background can be seen Charles Doherty's blacksmith shop; he would move to Wall Street later that year and remain there until 1956.

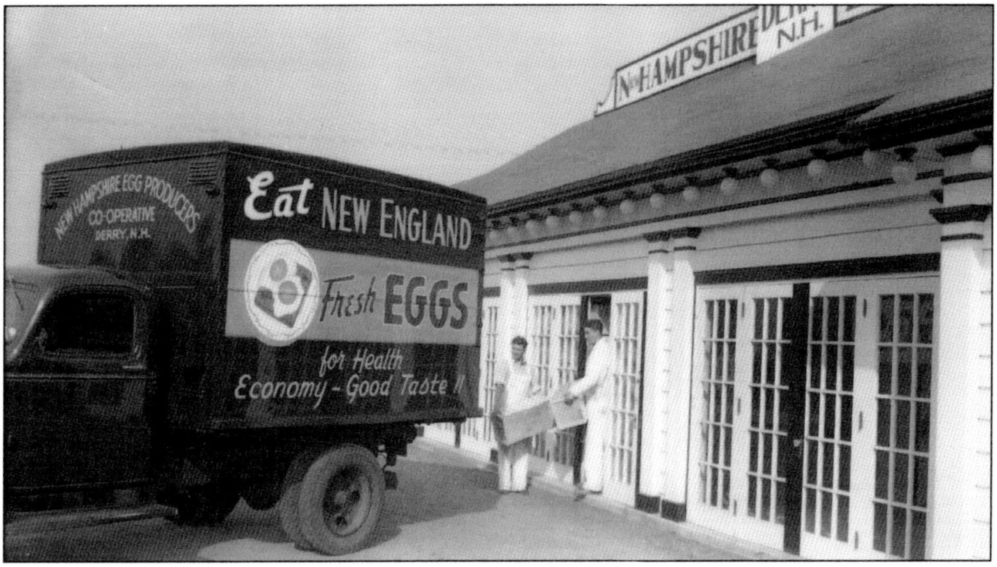

Fresh eggs from all over northern New England were delivered to the Derry Egg Auction, which graded and auctioned the eggs in their Crystal Avenue building. In 1959 (as a division of Agway) they set a record for grading 1,113,000 eggs in a single week. (Lear photograph)

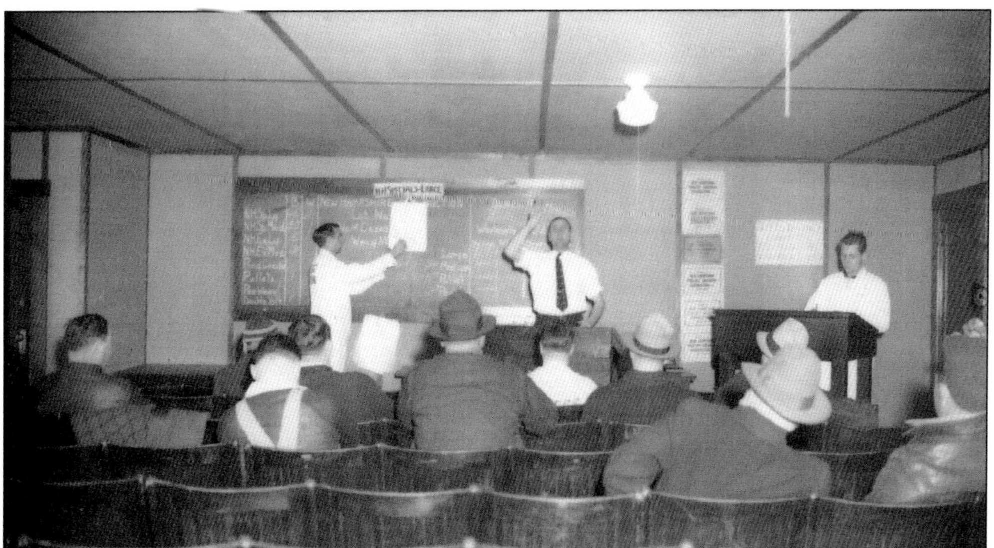

The New Hampshire Egg Auction occupied the former Farmer's Market building on Crystal Avenue from 1930 until 1941, when it moved south to the corner of Lenox Road. In 1934, after sorting 90,000,000 eggs, a candler, Roger Beliveau, found the company's first four-yoke eggs. (Lear photograph)

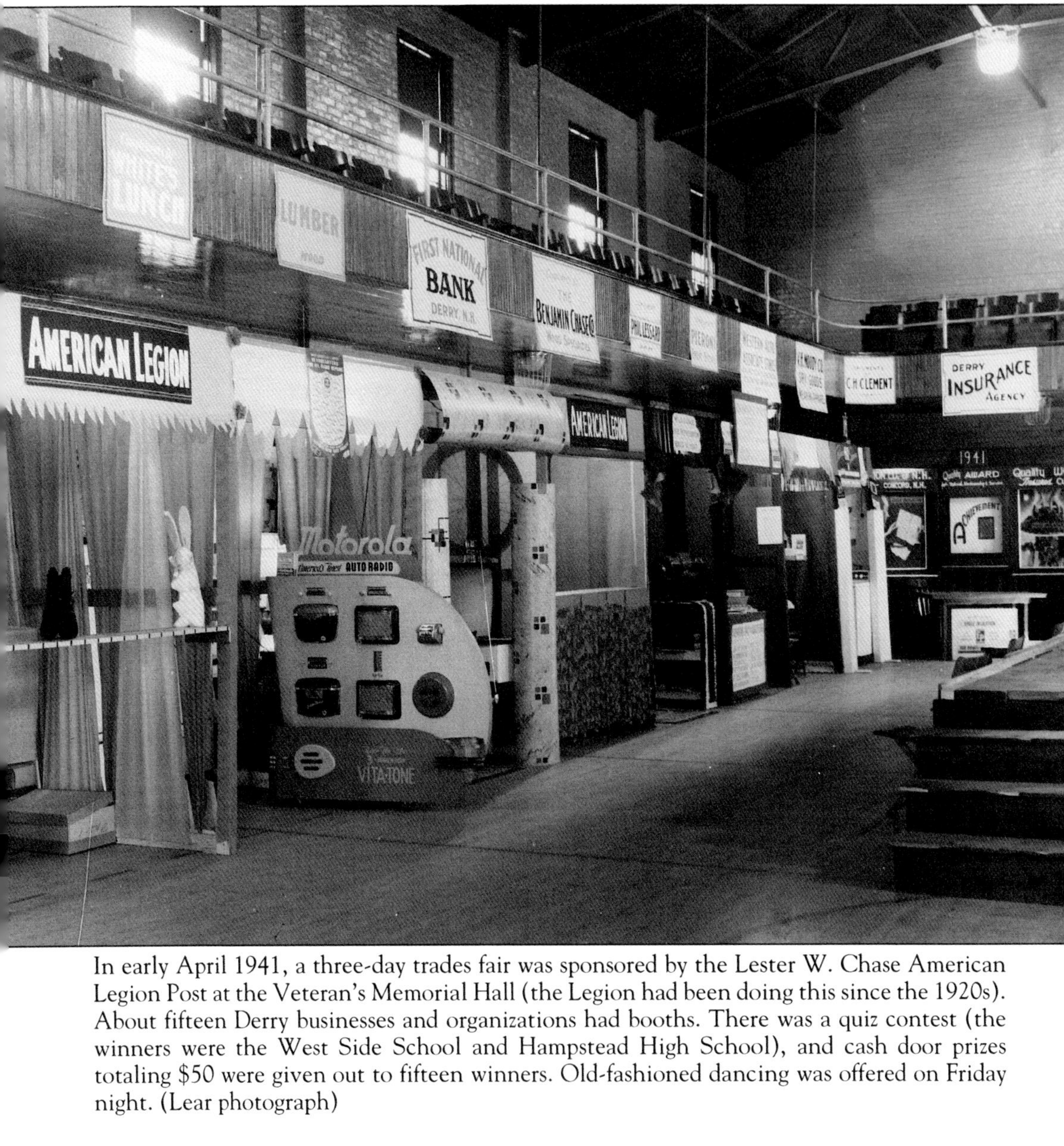

In early April 1941, a three-day trades fair was sponsored by the Lester W. Chase American Legion Post at the Veteran's Memorial Hall (the Legion had been doing this since the 1920s). About fifteen Derry businesses and organizations had booths. There was a quiz contest (the winners were the West Side School and Hampstead High School), and cash door prizes totaling $50 were given out to fifteen winners. Old-fashioned dancing was offered on Friday night. (Lear photograph)

Five

Institutions

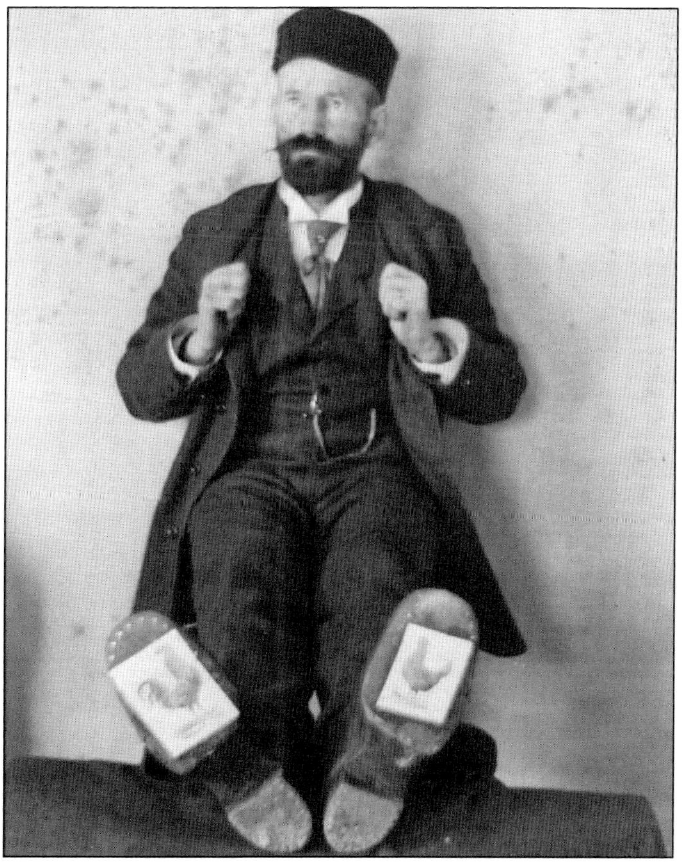

Derry News editor Charles Bartlett wants the passing world to know that he is rooting for Grover Cleveland for president. On his shoes he has pasted the strutting nineteenth-century symbol of the Democratic Party—the Rooster. Or is he saying he wants to stomp on the Democrats? Or is there another explanation which we are as yet unable to interpret?

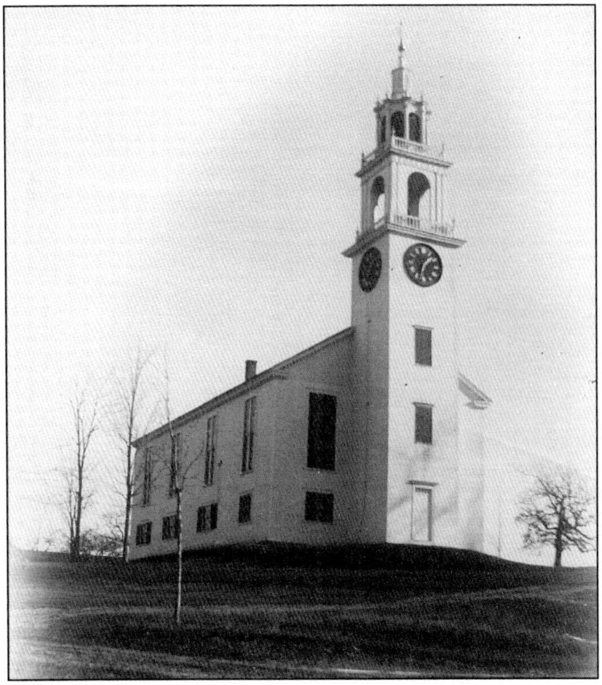

In 1722 the town's first church was built near this site, but it was replaced by the present First Parish Church in 1769. Many changes have been made over the years: a 24-foot section was added to the middle in 1822; the clock was added in 1880; the Christian Education Wing was put on in 1973; and the carillon was installed in 1973.

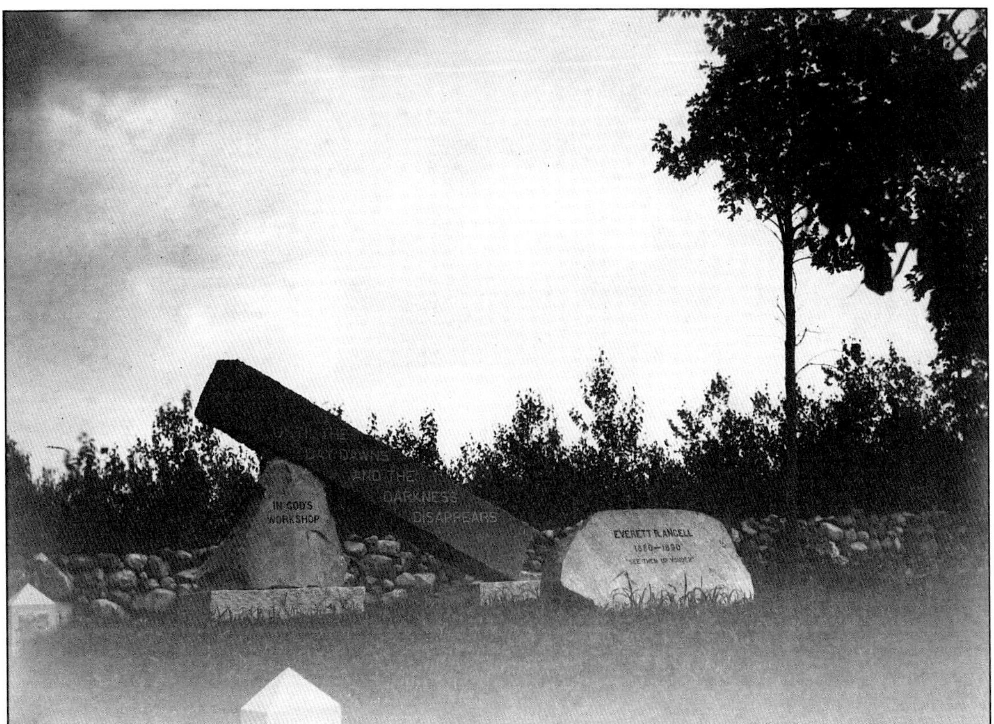

The most famous gravestone at the Forest Hills Cemetery is that of ten-year-old Everett R. Angell. As he laid dying he saw visions of angels coming into his room. His father put on his stone the boy's last words, "see them up yonder." On Everett's mother's stone is carved her last words, "I don't know how to die."

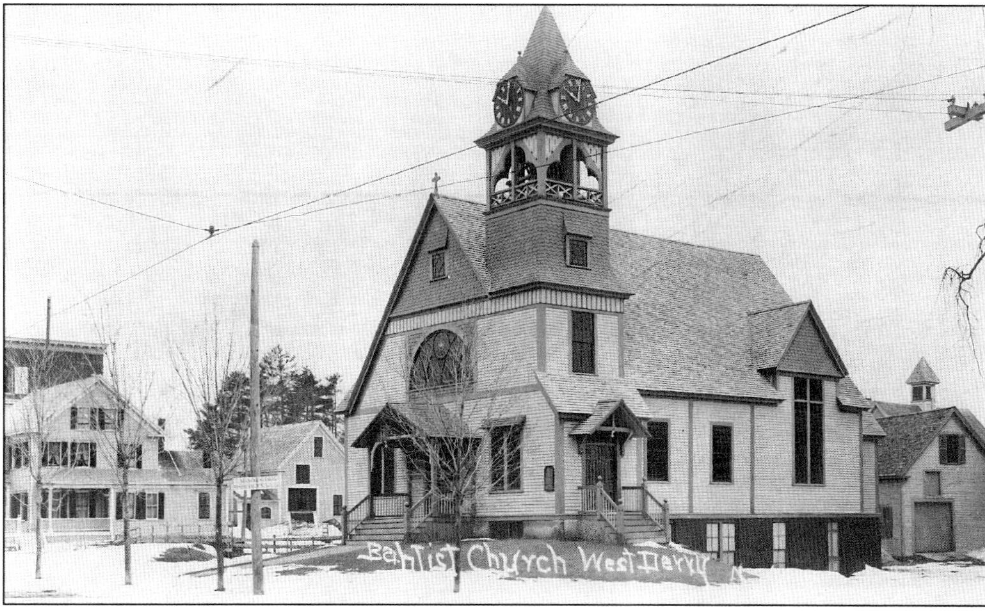

The First Baptist Church was built in 1884 and the parsonage added in 1890. The original steeple clock was bought by public subscription and not by the church itself. In 1921 the congregation voted not to set the clock an hour ahead at the start of daylight savings time, because they said it caused disruptions in home plans, mealtimes, and the sleeping hours of the children of the town.

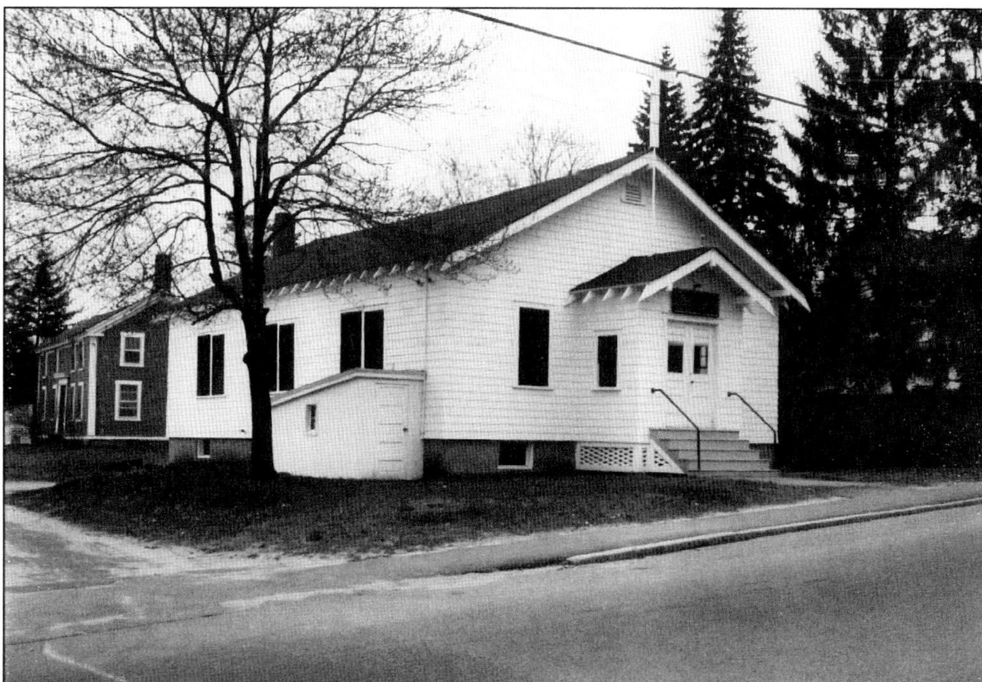

The Nazarene Church was built in 1926 under the pastorate of Reverend H.A. Park. Its membership, while never large, was always enthusiastic. The building was sold in the 1980s to be a day care center.

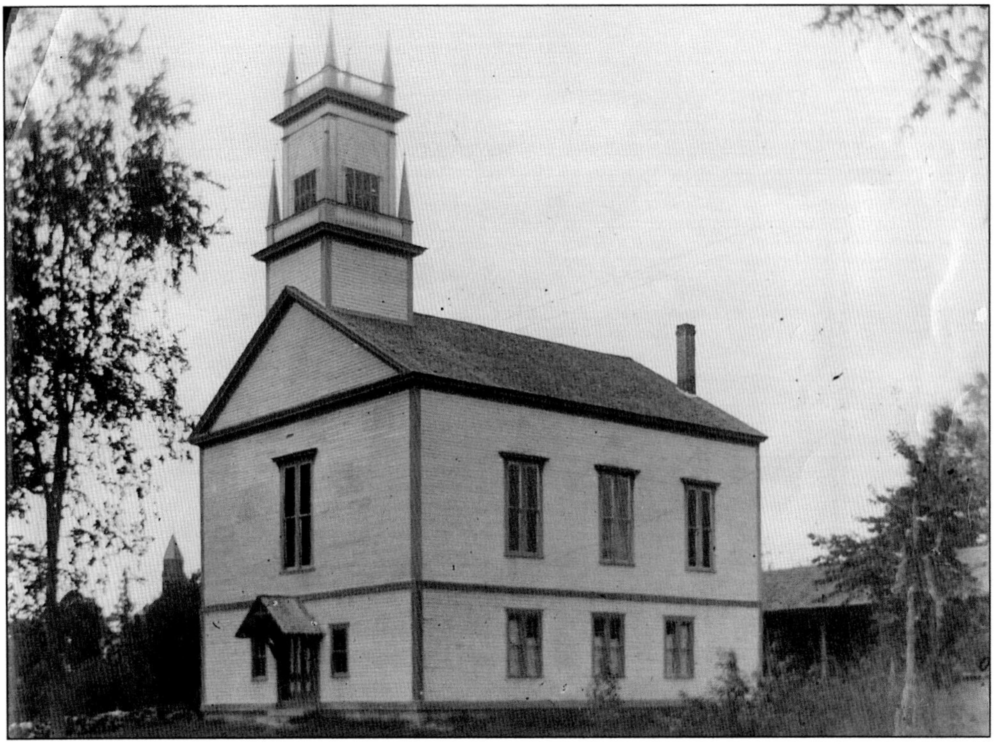

The First Methodist Church on Nesmith Street was built in 1836. The mission church it started in West Derry would in time overshadow the parent church. The building was sold in 1925 to the Knights of Malta and torn down during the Depression.

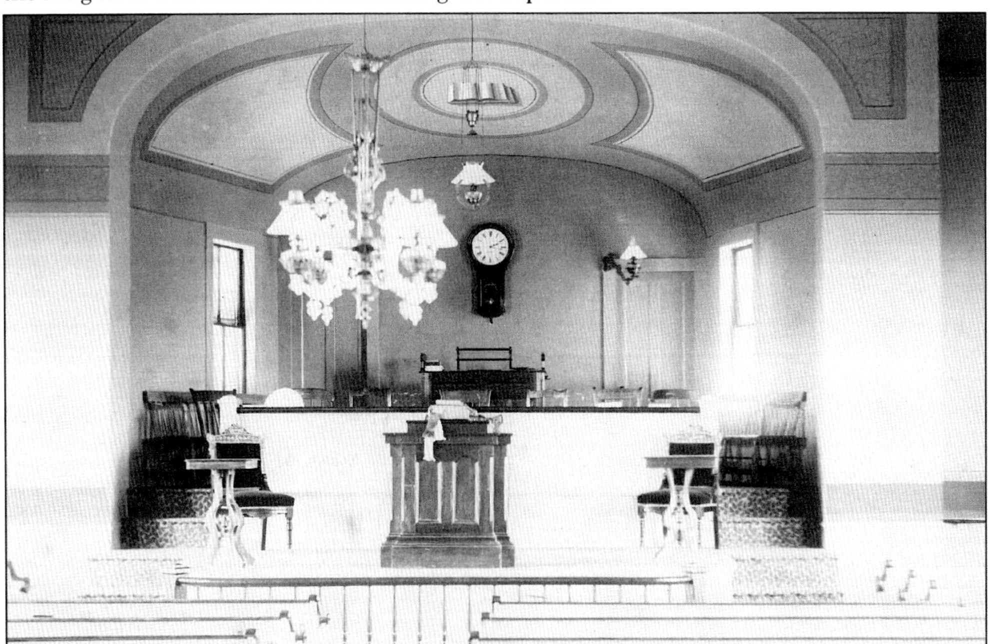

The interior of the First Methodist Church of Derry Village *c.* 1900. Note the trompe l'oeil bible painted on the ceiling. The sanctuary was lit by an elaborate kerosene chandelier.

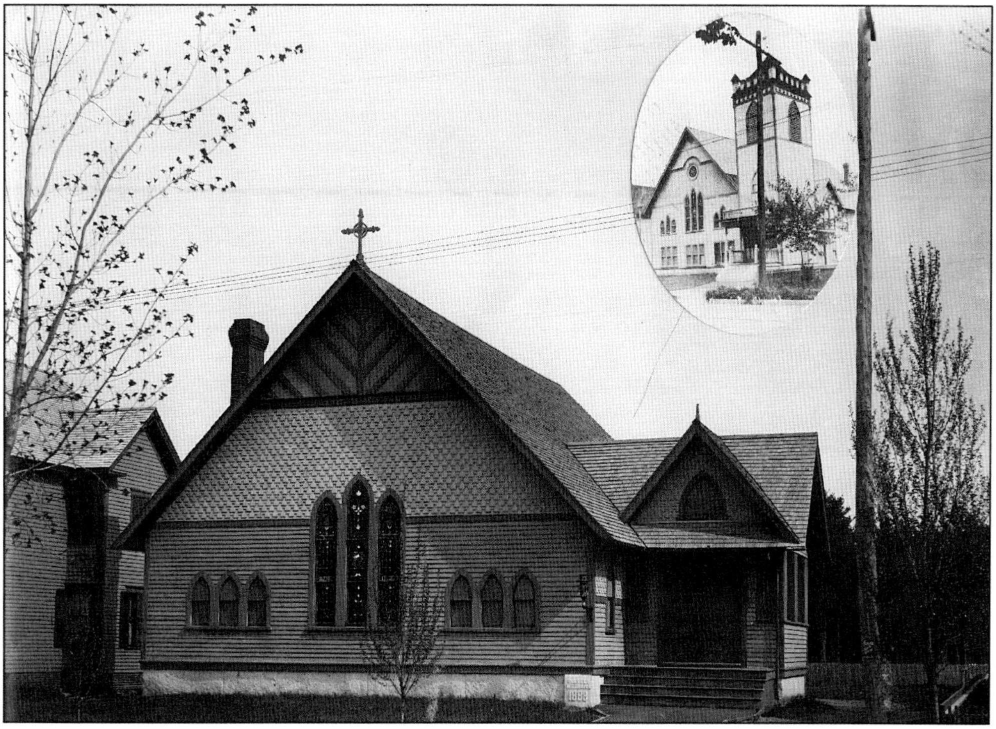

St. Luke's Methodist Church on Broadway was built in 1889. The church grew rapidly and soon needed more space. In 1894 the whole structure was raised and a vestry built underneath. A steeple was added at the same time (see insert).

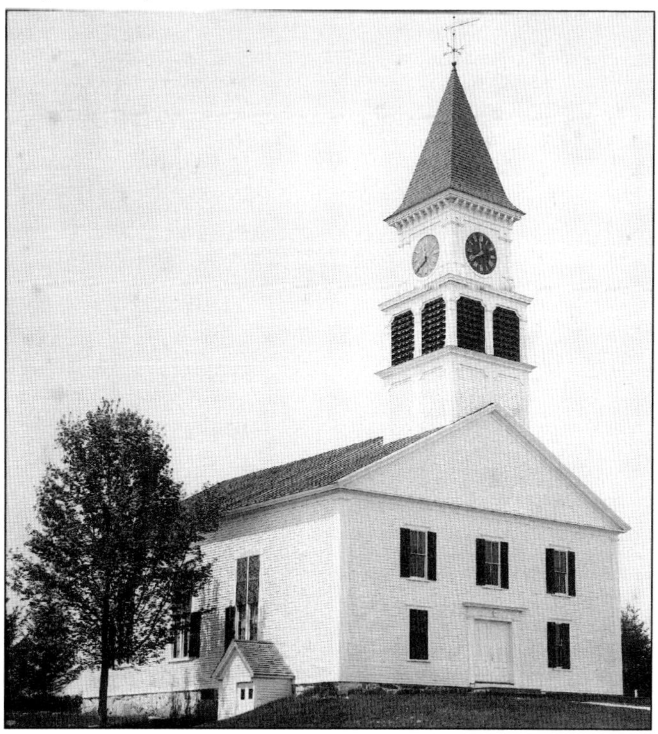

Central Congregational Church (built in 1837) as it appeared in 1887. In 1916 a pillared portico was added. In 1970 the church built a Christian Education Wing on the left side of the structure close to the site of the former horse sheds.

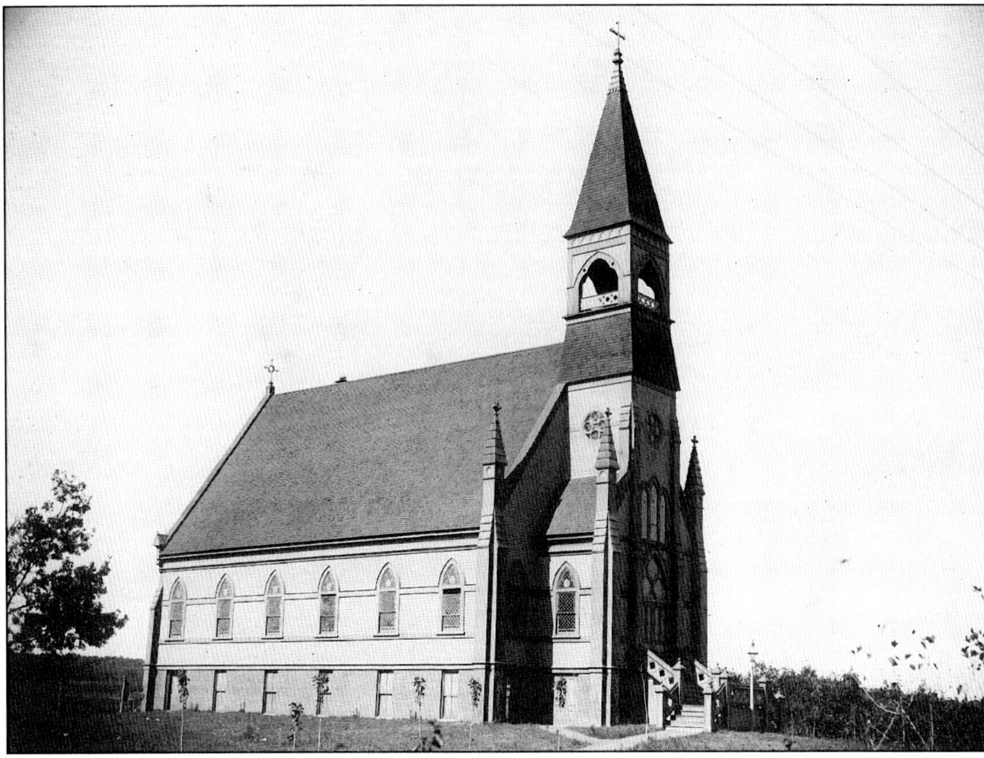

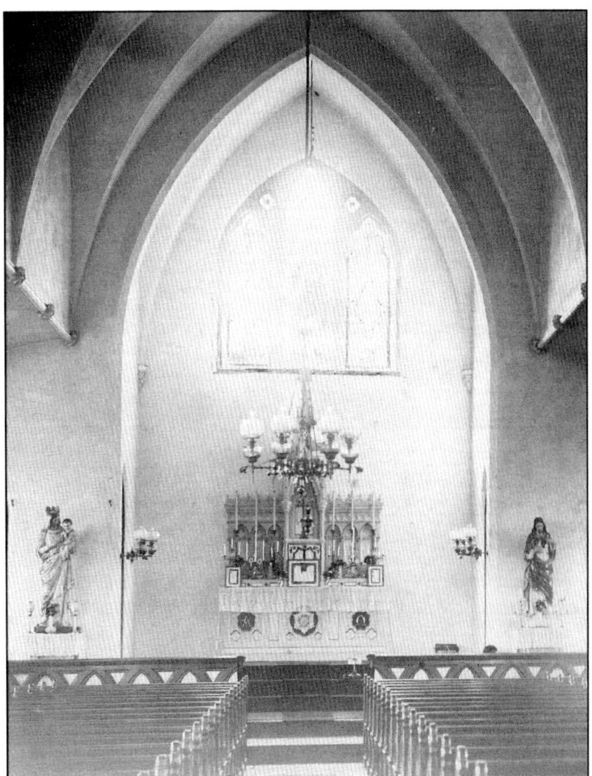

St. Thomas Aquinas Catholic Church was built in 1889 under the pastorate of Father William O'Brien. A parochial school building housing students from the first through the eighth grades was built in 1952.

The interior of the original St. Thomas Aquinas Catholic Church as it appeared prior to the 1914 fire.

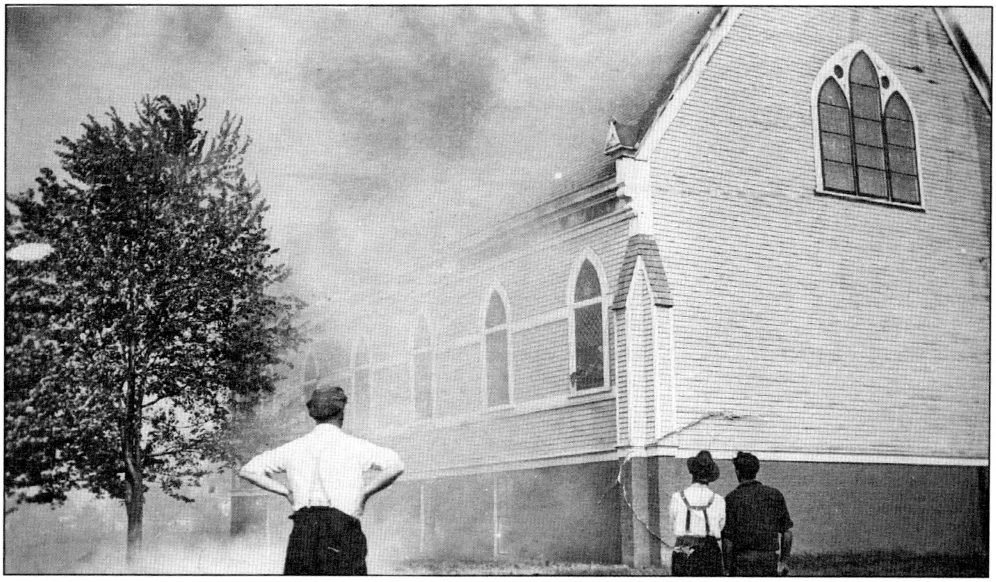

In August 1914 a fire destroyed the twenty-six-year-old St. Thomas Aquinas Church. It would be three years before a new chapel was built on the site of the old church. During those years the congregation met in the former Scenic Movie Theater on Railroad Avenue.

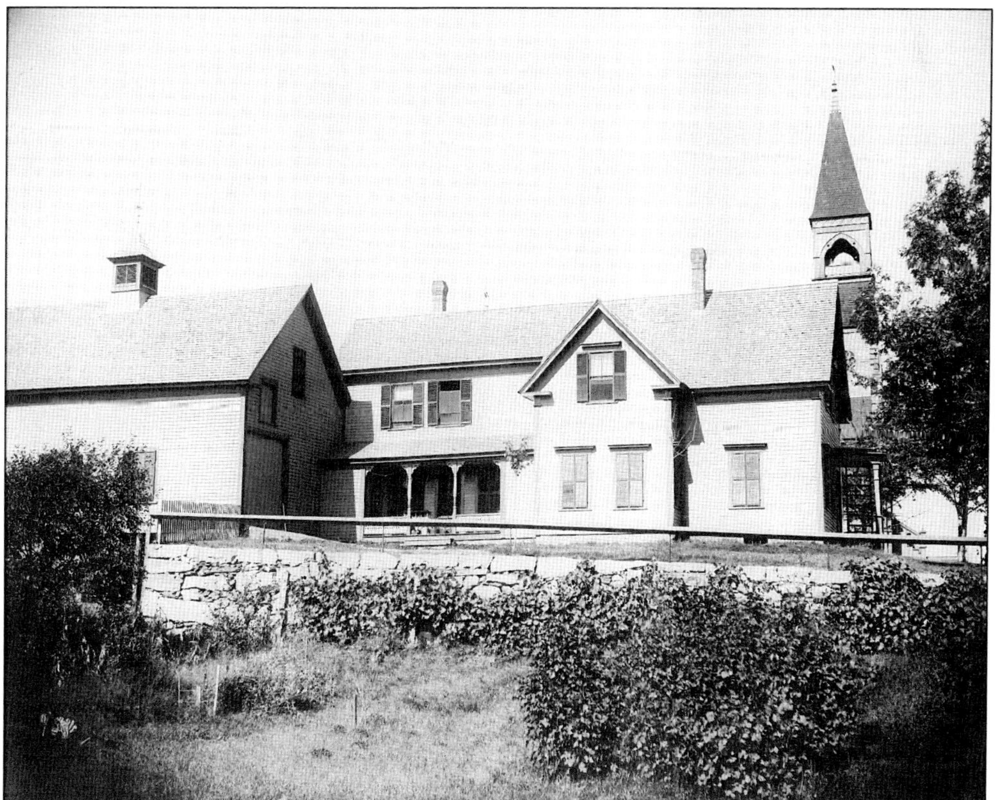

George S. Rollins built this house in 1885. Two years later it was sold to the St. Thomas Aquinas Catholic Church to be their rectory.

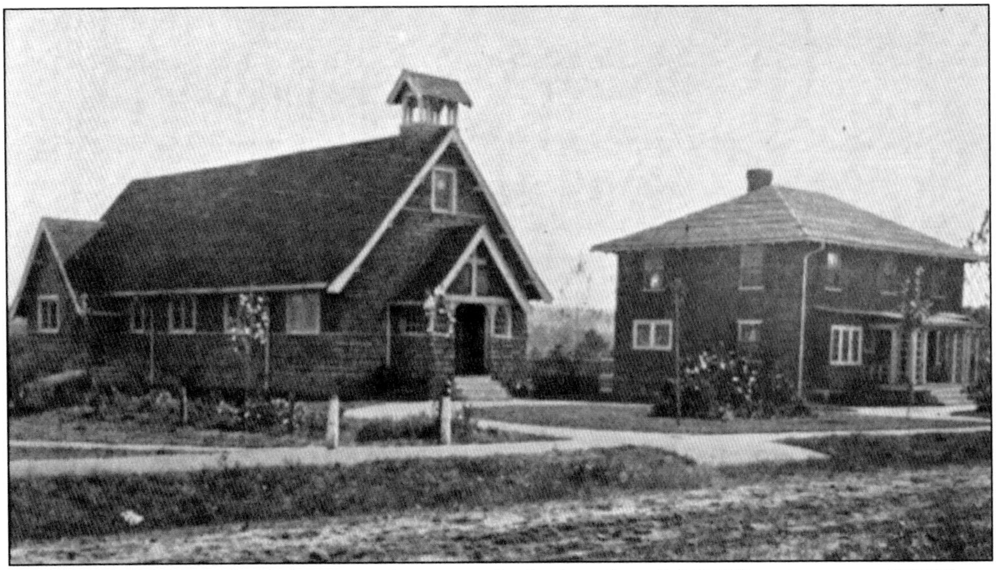

The Episcopal Church of the Transfiguration built this chapel (1905) and rectory (1907) on Oak Street. In 1960 it was decided to build a new facility on Hood Road. The old church was sold to the Odd Fellows.

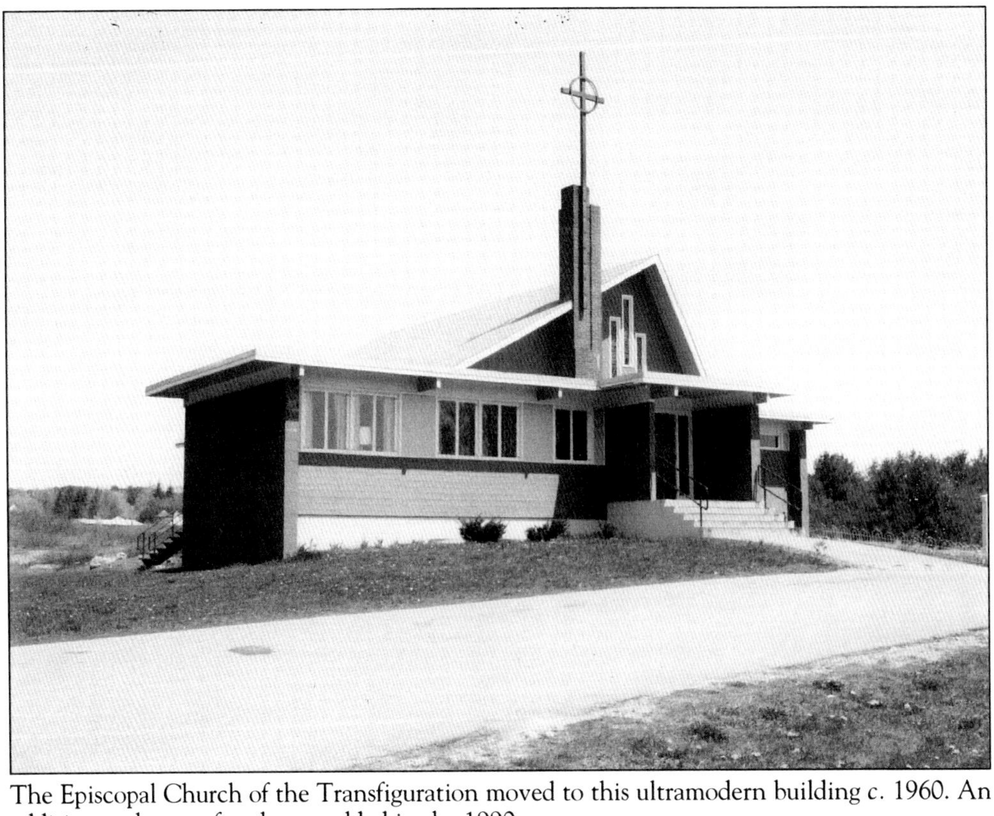

The Episcopal Church of the Transfiguration moved to this ultramodern building c. 1960. An addition and a new facade was added in the 1990s.

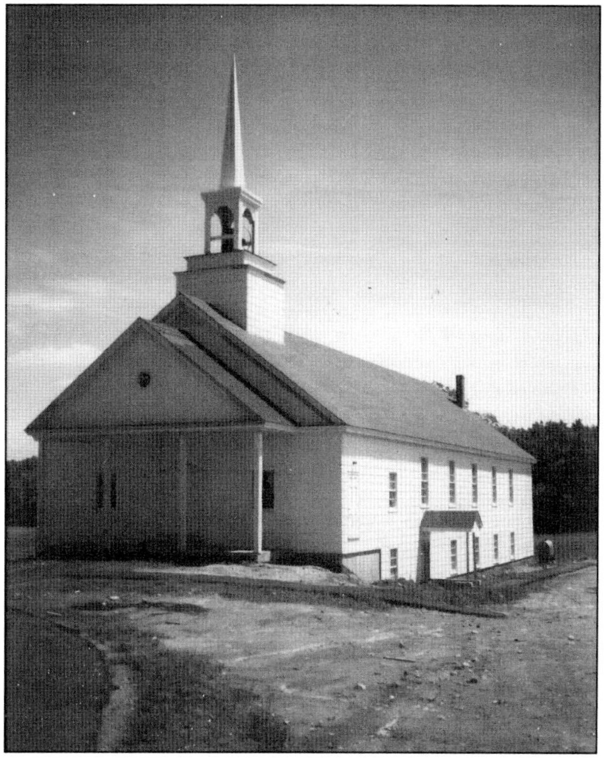

The Calvary Baptist Church erected this building in 1969 under the dynamic leadership of Reverend Ivan Smith and Reverend Dan Courter. It would later become a non-denominational evangelical church. The education wing was added 1975 and a private day school started shortly afterwards.

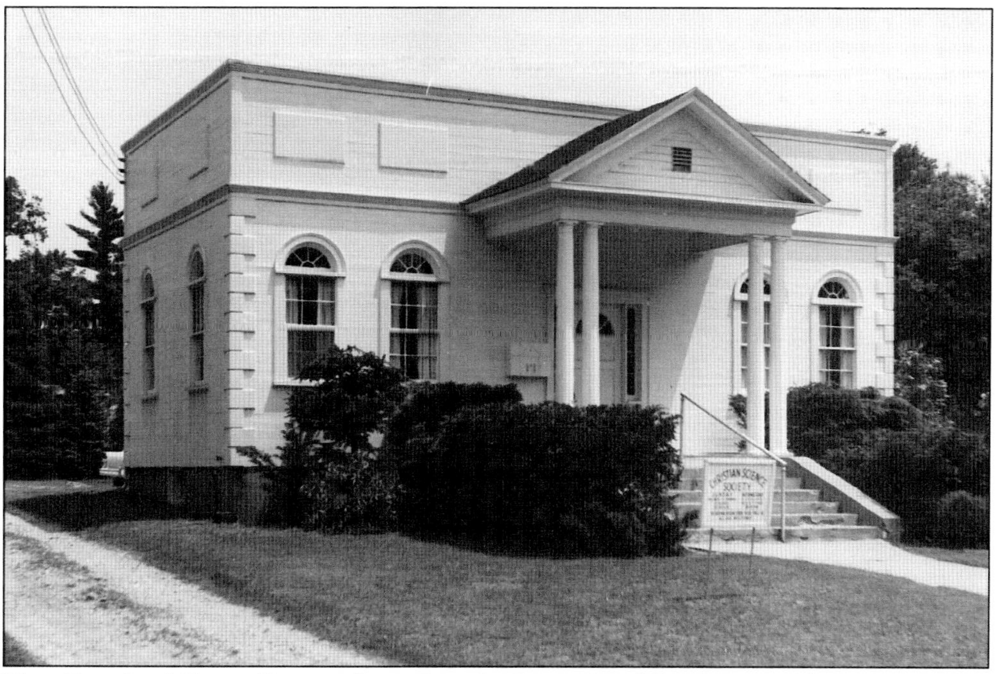

The Church of Christ (Scientist) purchased a lot on Boyd Road in 1925 but continued to meet at the Knight of Pythias Hall until it built this gleaming white church in 1940. The new church with its neo-classic design could hold about one hundred people in its 12-by-22-foot reading room.

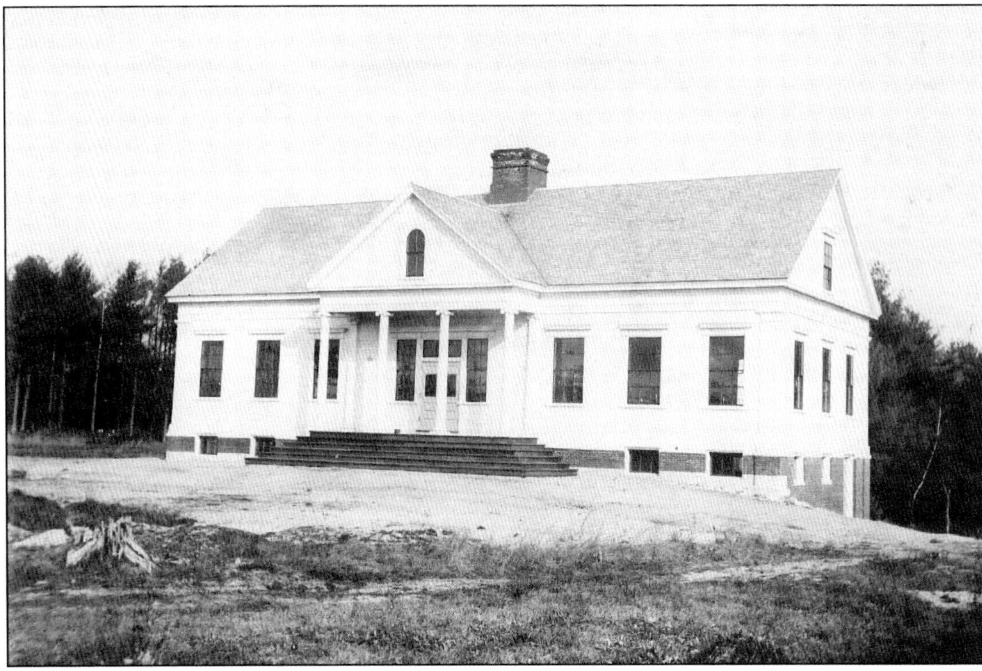

The East Side or Oak Street School was built in 1892. It was later enlarged by raising the building and adding a new ground floor. With the building of the Hood School in 1952, the Oak Street School was sold to the H.E. Harris Stamp Company (it is now an apartment building).

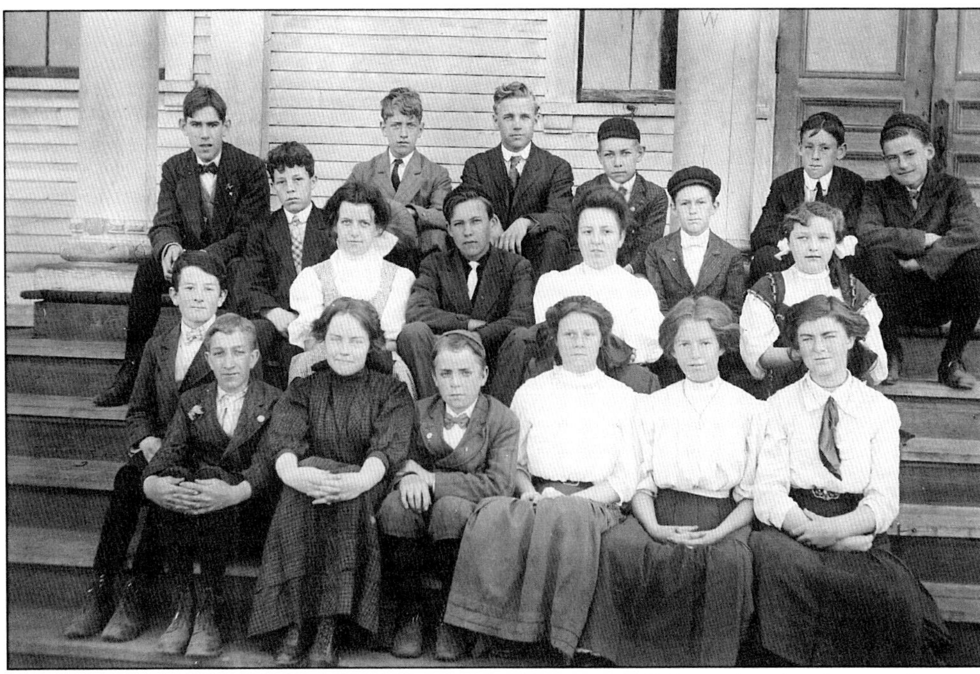

The Oak Street School's Class of 1909 sits on the front steps all dressed up for their graduation. At the closing exercises these eighth graders sang "Come, Where the Fields are Beaming." Their farewell gift to the school was a framed picture of Sir Galahad.

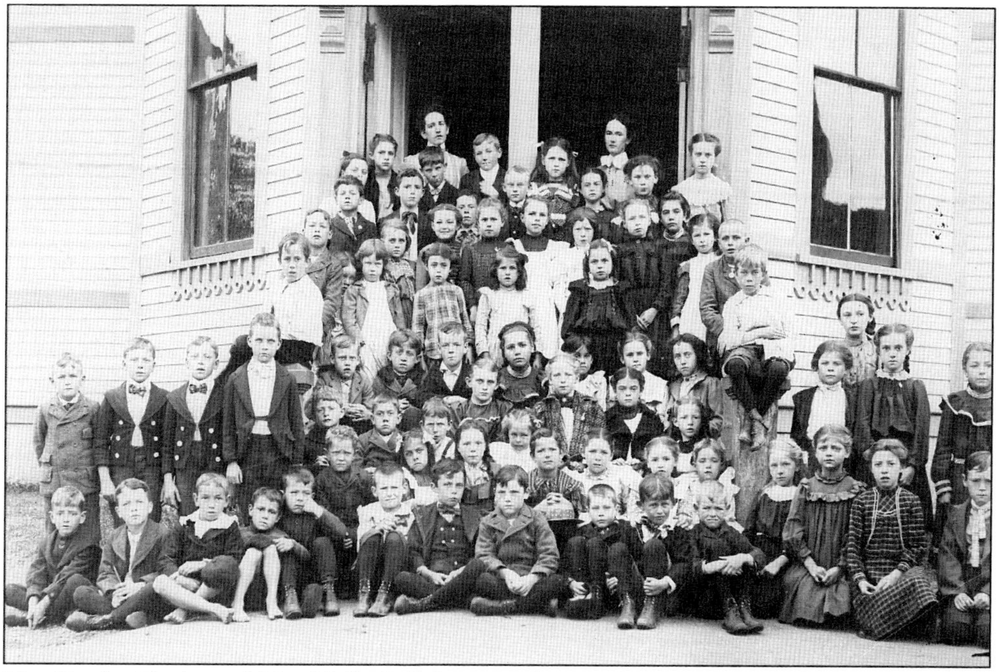

Miss Bertha Clarke and Miss Nella Callahan watch over their young unsmiling charges at the West Side School in 1902. Note the bare feet of several of the boys in the front row.

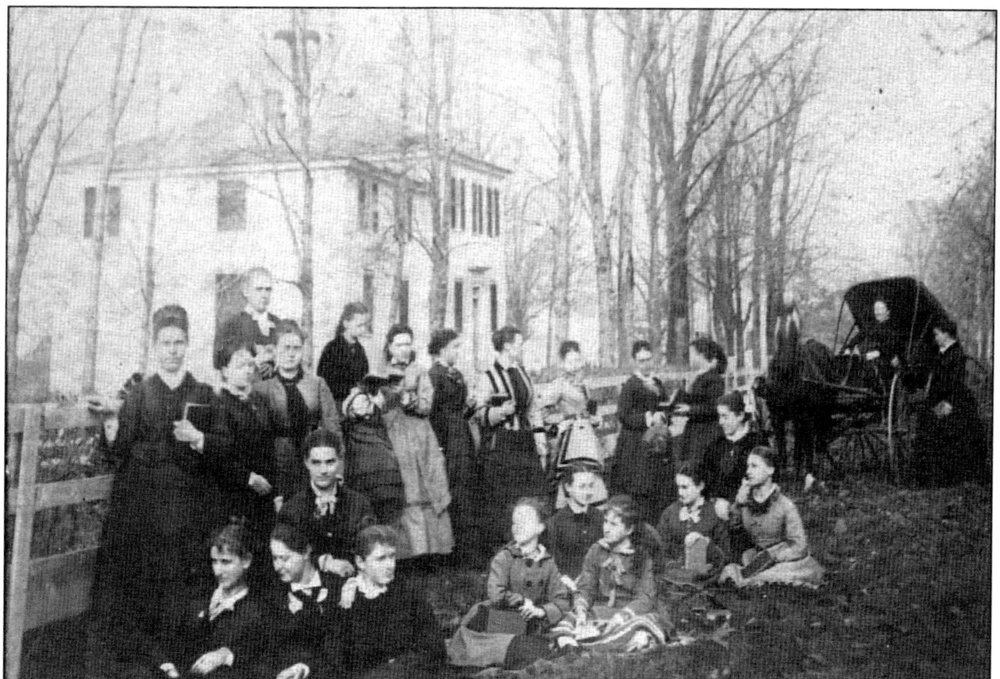

The Adams Female Academy on Lane Road was established in 1823. One of its first teachers was Mary Lyon who later founded Mount Holyoke College. Lafayette visited the school in 1825. The academy merged with the public school district in 1887 and its alumna have included New Hampshire Governor Charles M. Floyd and astronaut Alan B. Shepard, Jr.

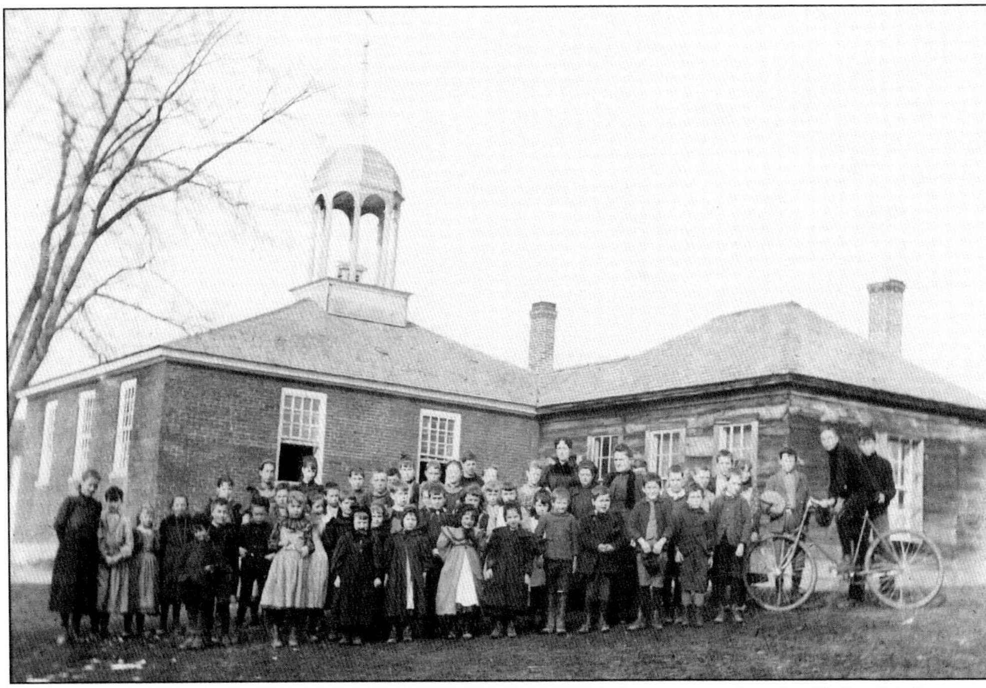

The brick one-room Village School was erected in 1824. It measured only 29 by 36 feet and had two fireplaces. A wooden recitation room was added in 1881. The building was torn down in 1901 and a new brick multi-room school was erected. This is now the office of the Derry superintendent of schools.

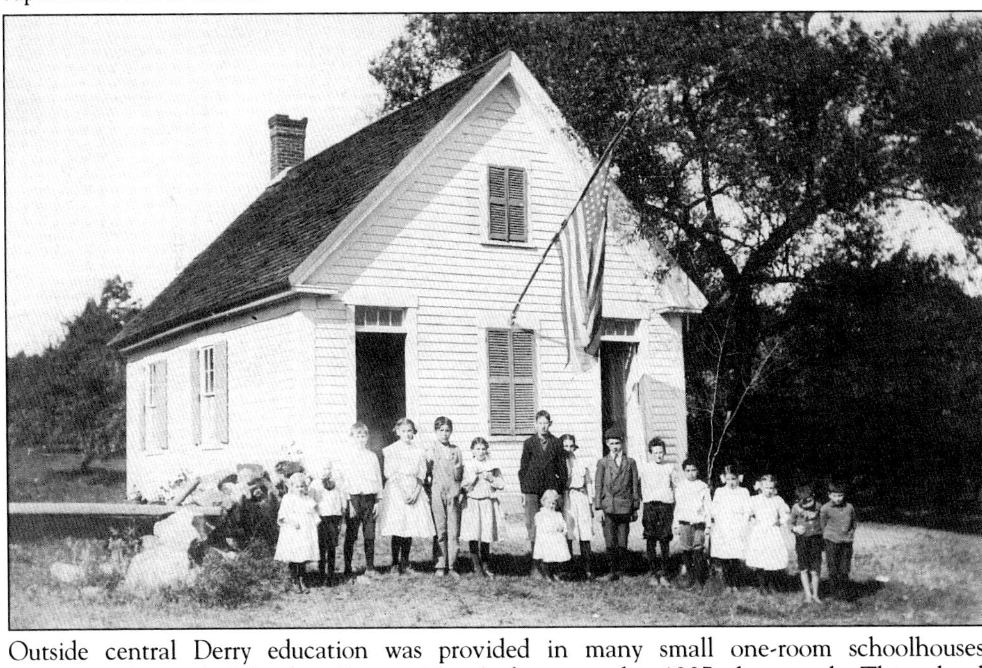

Outside central Derry education was provided in many small one-room schoolhouses. Typical is the Peak School in District No. 6, shown in this 1907 photograph. This school, built in 1856 on Hampstead Road, was closed in 1936 and torn down by the town c. 1990. (McEvers photograph)

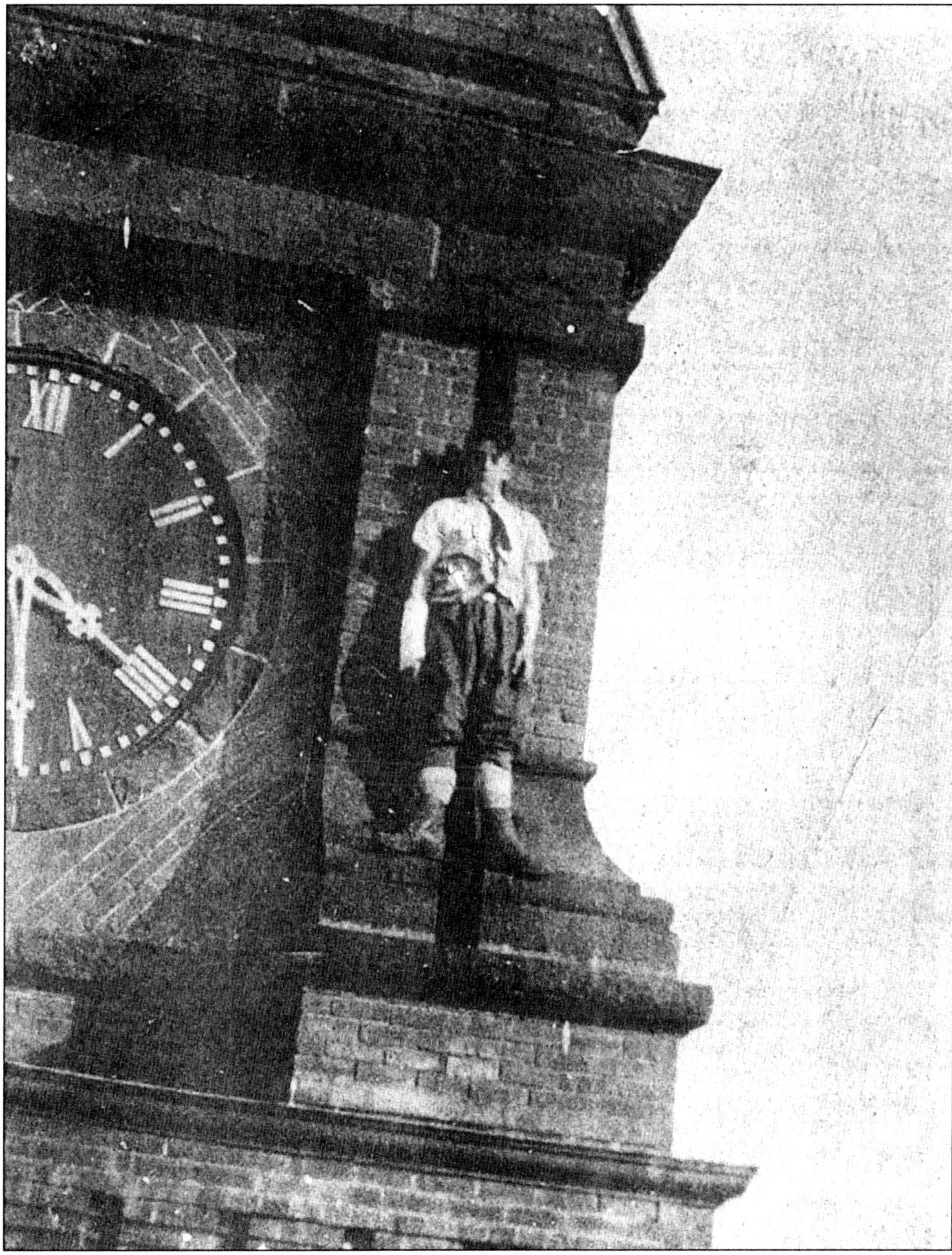

The roaring twenties were famed for their daredevils. Here young George Grinnell poses on the 128-foot-high clock tower at Pinkerton Academy while his friend, Ben Bartlett, takes the picture. The future judge's arm is in a cast as a result of a crank kicking back while starting an automobile. (Grinnell collection)

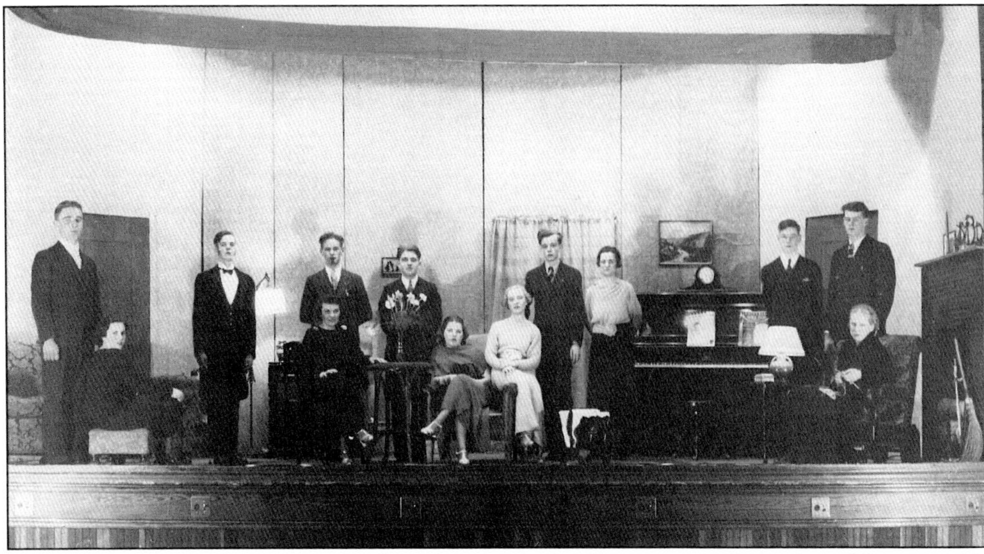

The Pinkerton Academy's senior class play *Green Stockings* was performed in February 1936 and was considered a smash hit. The entire cast and crew were later treated to a trip to see a professional show at the Metropolitan Theater in Boston. From left to right are: (standing) Norman Watts, Wilfred Normandeau, Winston Ramsden, Alvin Johnson, Philip Bartlett, Lurlene Gorgon, Frederick Manning, and Robert Morrison; (seated) Katherine O'Neal, Evelyn DesMarais, Ruth Harlow, Miss Marion Billings, and Mary Peart. (Sunset studios)

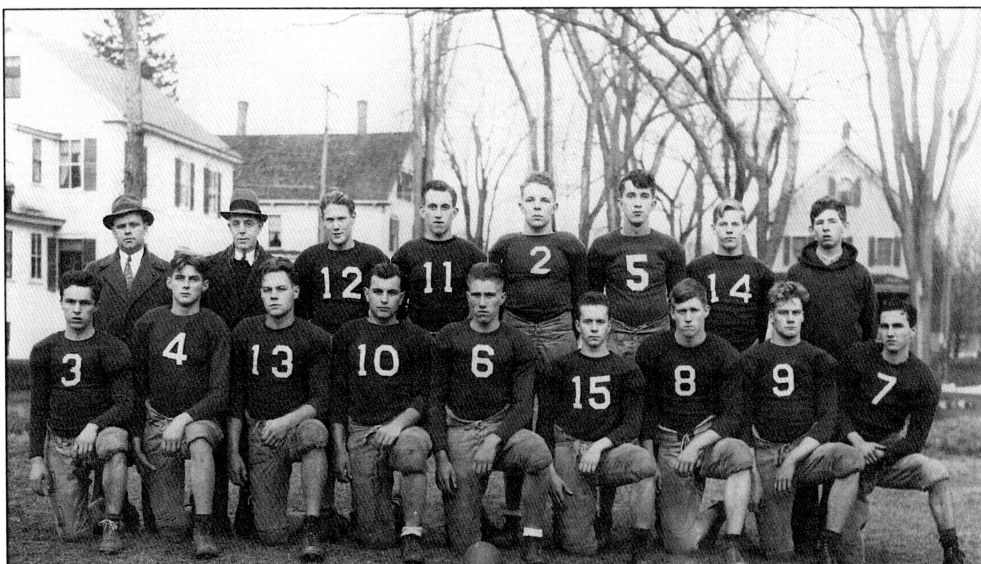

During the Depression Pinkerton Academy turned out some remarkable sports teams, and among the best was the 1936 football team coached by Thomas Clark. His team had undefeated seasons in 1936, 1937, and 1939. Within a very short time thirteen members of this 1936 team would be fighting in World War II. From left to right are: (front) T. Clark (coach), H. McKenney (trainer), L. Latulippe, L. Wells, W. Fay, R. Provencher (captain), F. Ball, and R. Stevens (manager); (back) J. Byrne, C. Perkins, R. Durkee, C. Kachavos, H. Campbell, H. Hilberg, DiPietro, C. Ackerman, and L. Pieroni.

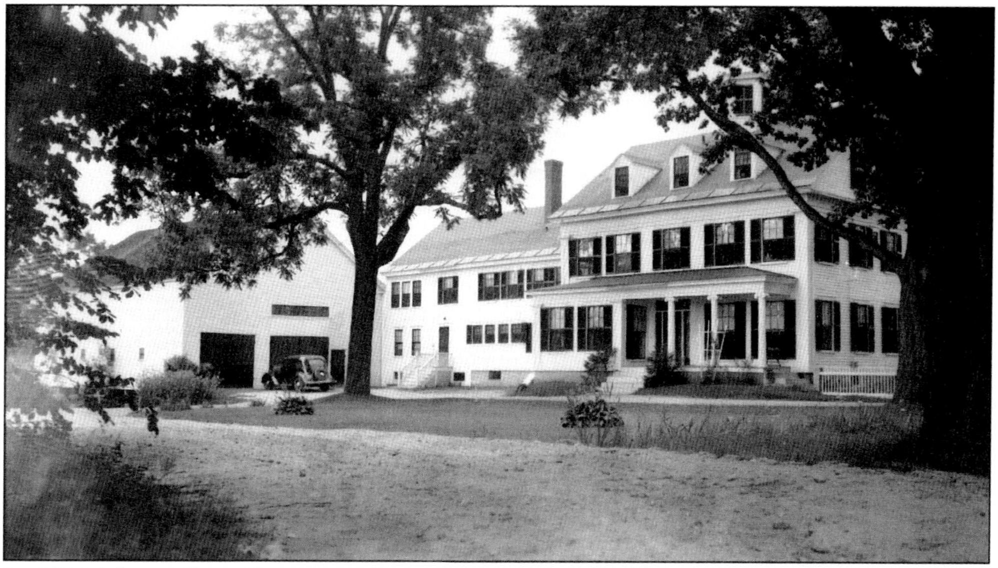

In 1933 Mrs. Gilbert Hood gave her twenty-room colonial home in East Derry to be the Alexander-Eastman Hospital. After thirty years of operation it was replaced by a modern fireproof building on Crystal Avenue. The old hospital was then sold and became an apartment building. (Lear photograph)

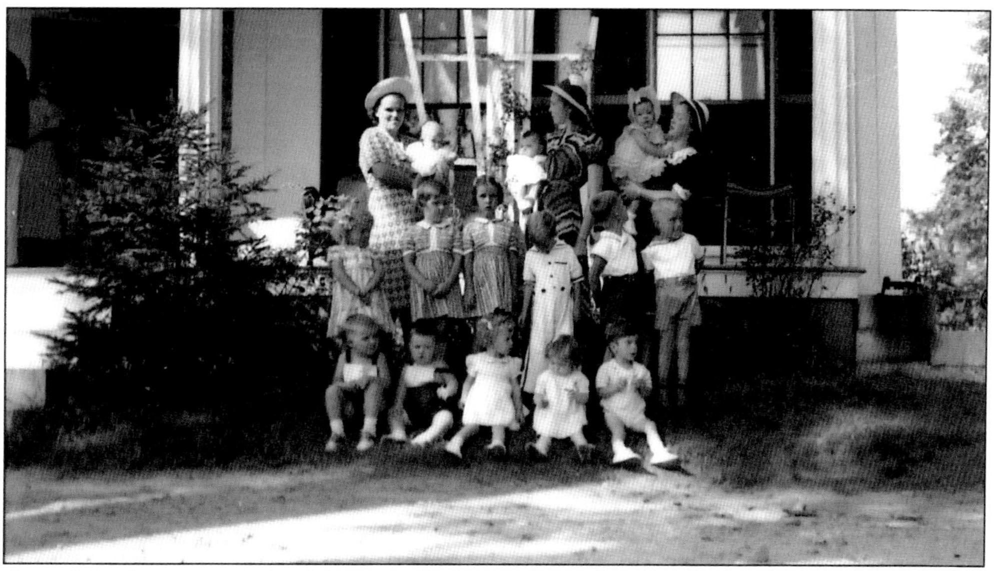

One of the functions of the Alexander-Eastman Hospital was to serve as a community health care provider. The staff and Visiting Nurses annually sponsored a children's clinic such as this one in 1939. Mrs. Helen Hood donated a new automobile in the 1930s to aid the Visiting Nurses in making home visits. (Lear photograph)

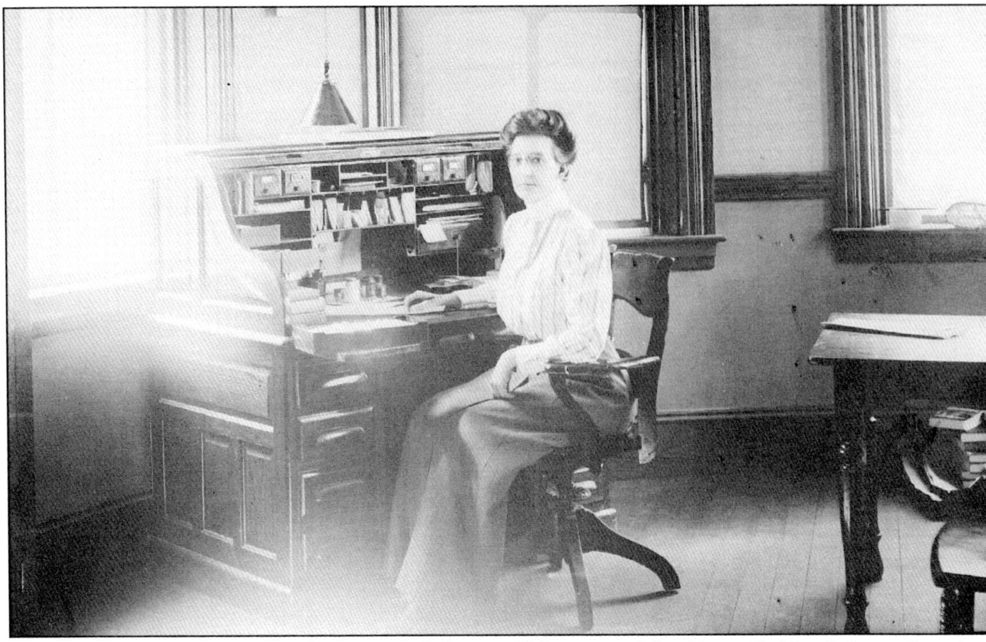

Miss Elsie Gaskin took over the responsibilities of librarian of the Derry Public Library from her father Reverend W.E. Gaskin in 1906. She would remain at her post until her retirement in 1940. (Library collection)

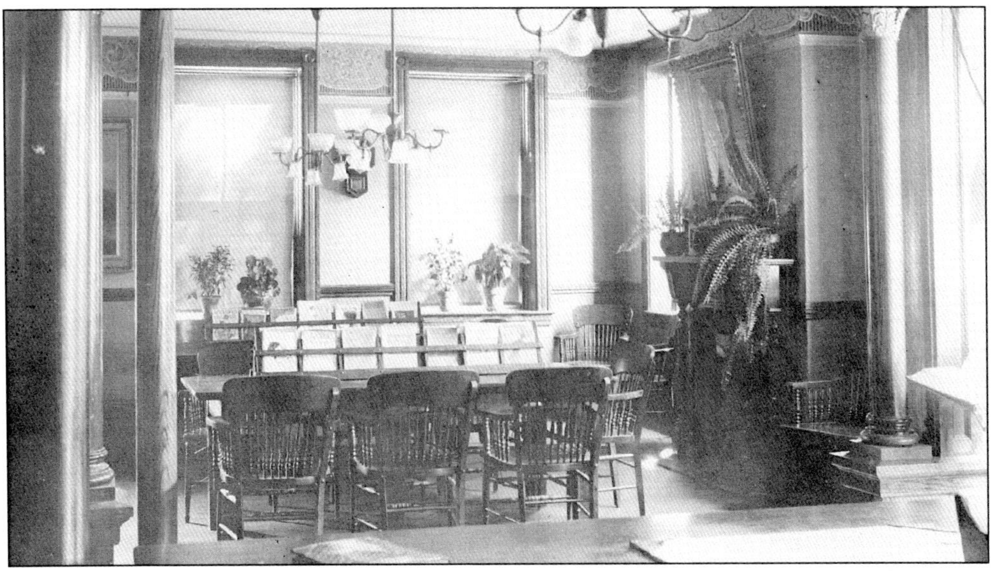

Derry's first public library was in a front room of the Adams Memorial Building from 1905 until 1927. It started with only 1,229 volumes. Many of these were damaged in a fire in 1914. (Library collection)

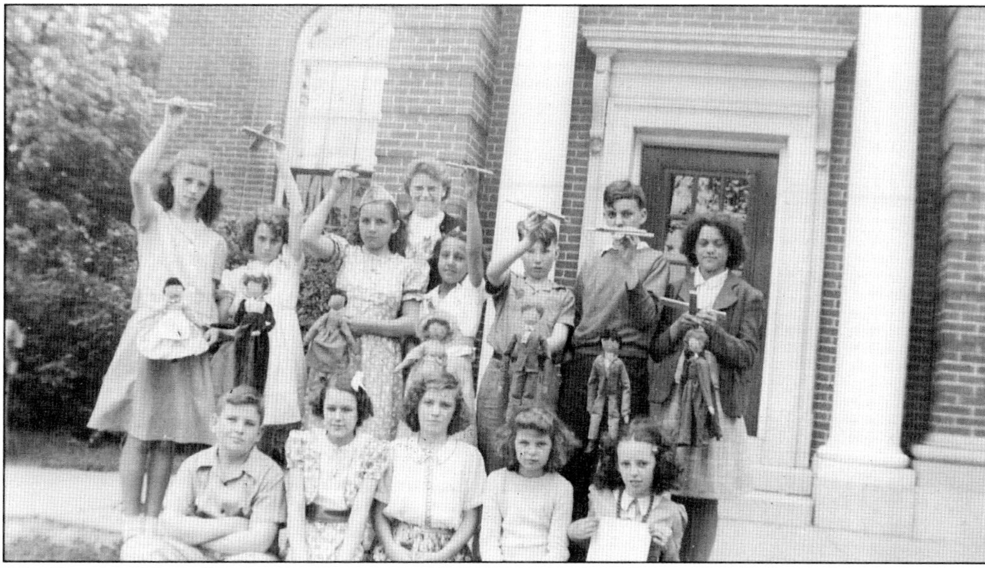

The Derry Public Library in 1943 sponsored the puppet play *Blue Berry Corner*. The cast included, from left to right: (front row) Glenn McDonald, Irene Muzzy, Elaine Rand, Patricia Butterfield, and Joanne Merrill; (back row) Virginia Verge, Faye Gordon, Patricia Boles, Dorothy Poison, Miss Merill, Edith Hall, Ernest Keith, and Arlene Kinsbury. (Library collection)

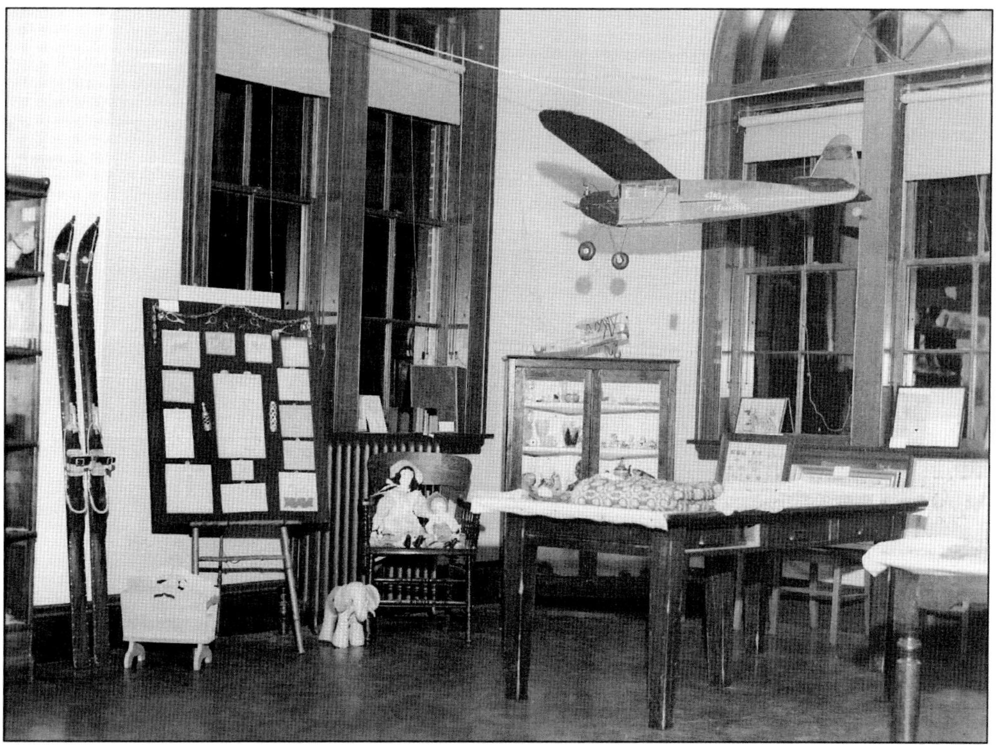

In 1941 many area adults and children presented their treasures at a hobby show held at the Derry Public Library. (Library collection)

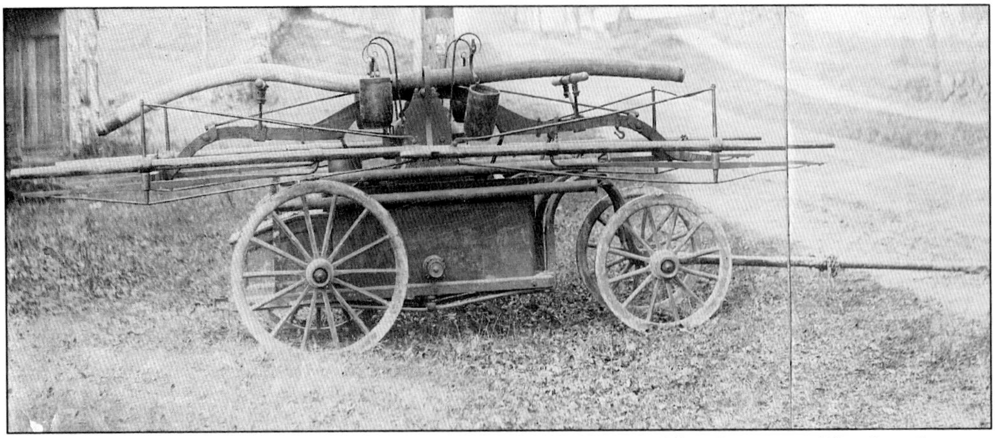

Old Niagra was one of the first pieces of fire equipment owned by the town. This hand pump was purchased in 1889 by the Derry Village fire department and stored in the basement of the Association Hall. The central fire station in Derry Village was built in 1974.

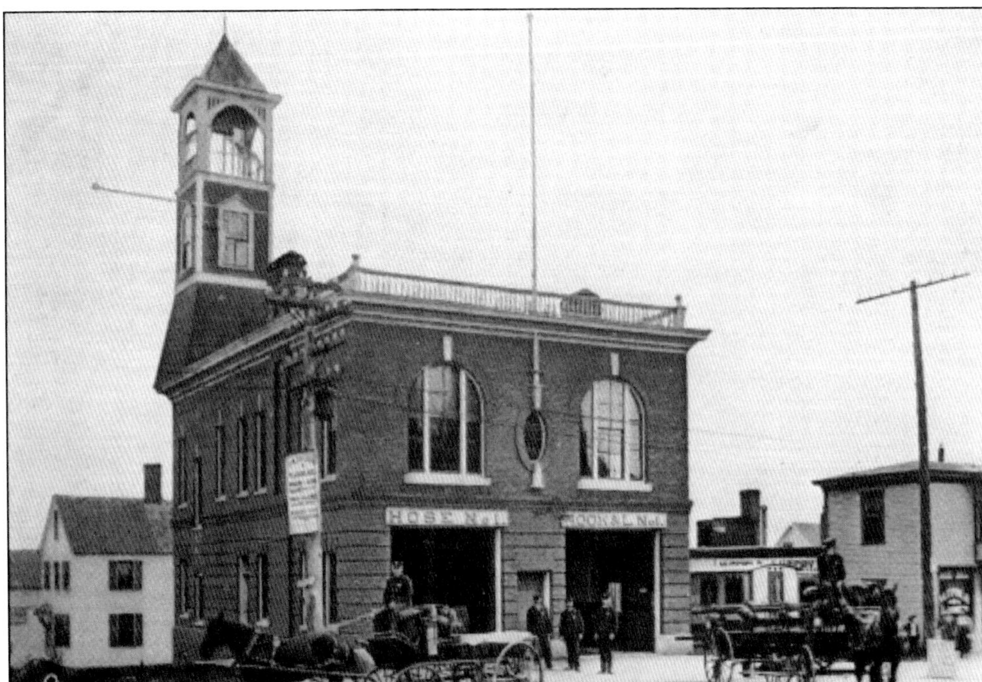

In 1898 the fire station in West Derry was erected. Its horse-drawn equipment is seen here proudly displayed out front. The tower with its signal bell is now gone. Since 1974 this building has been reduced to the status of substation. It is also the home of the Derry Historical Society's Bicentennial and Fireman's Museum.

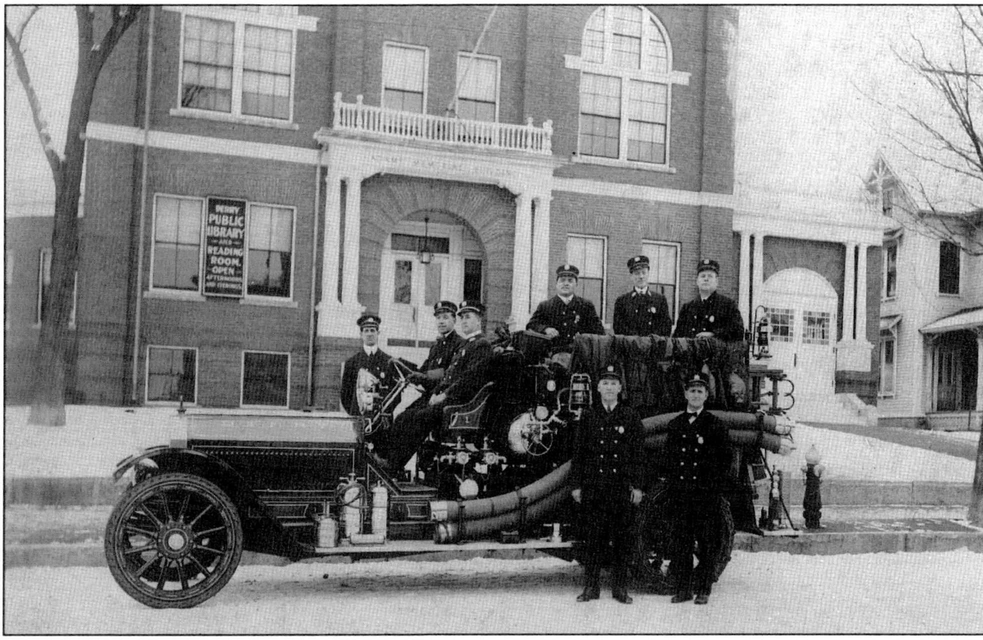

In 1915 the fire department went roaring into the twentieth century with its first mechanized truck. This 100 hp, 6-cylinder LaFrance triple-combination pumping engine cost $9,000 and could carry 800 gallons of water. In the background is the Adams Memorial Building when it also housed the town's library. (Armstrong photograph)

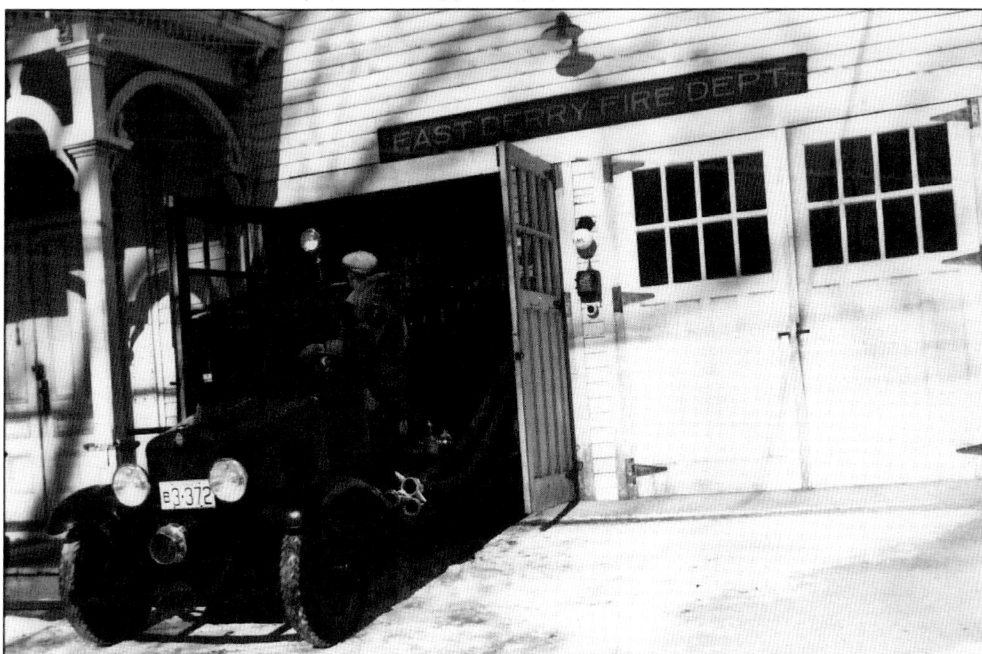

In 1934 an addition to the old town hall in East Derry was brought into service as the fire station. Paul Brickett is shown in 1940 carefully backing in the fire truck. This vehicle was a 1929 Chevrolet truck that had been converted into a combination pumper. The present East Derry station was built in 1970.

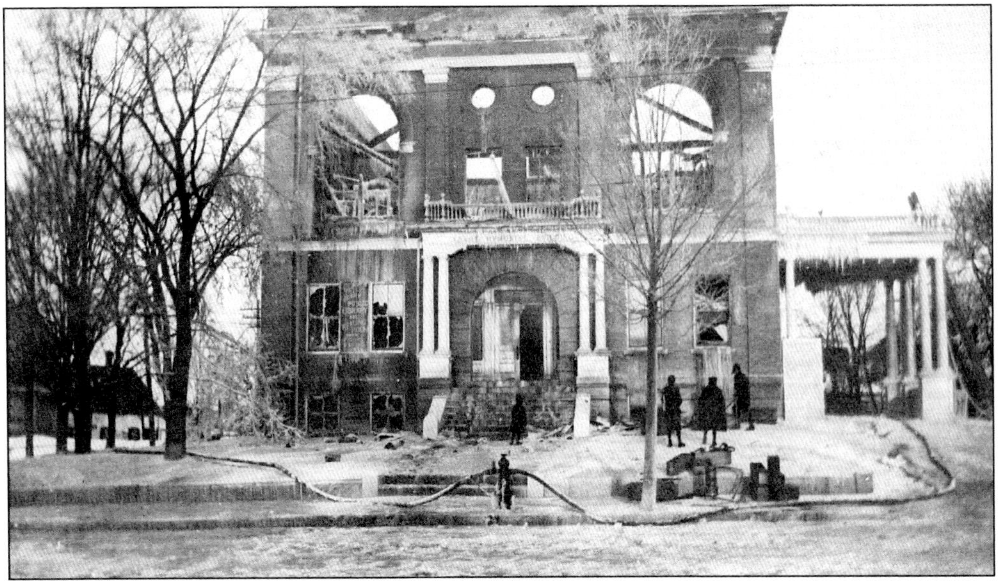

At midnight on January 13, 1914, fire gutted the eleven-year-old Adams Memorial Building. The town papers survived in a basement safe but many of the 5,000 books in the library were damaged. The town offices and library were temporarily moved to the Knights of Pythias building. The portrait of Benjamin Adams, the donator of the building, was rescued and is still on display in the building.

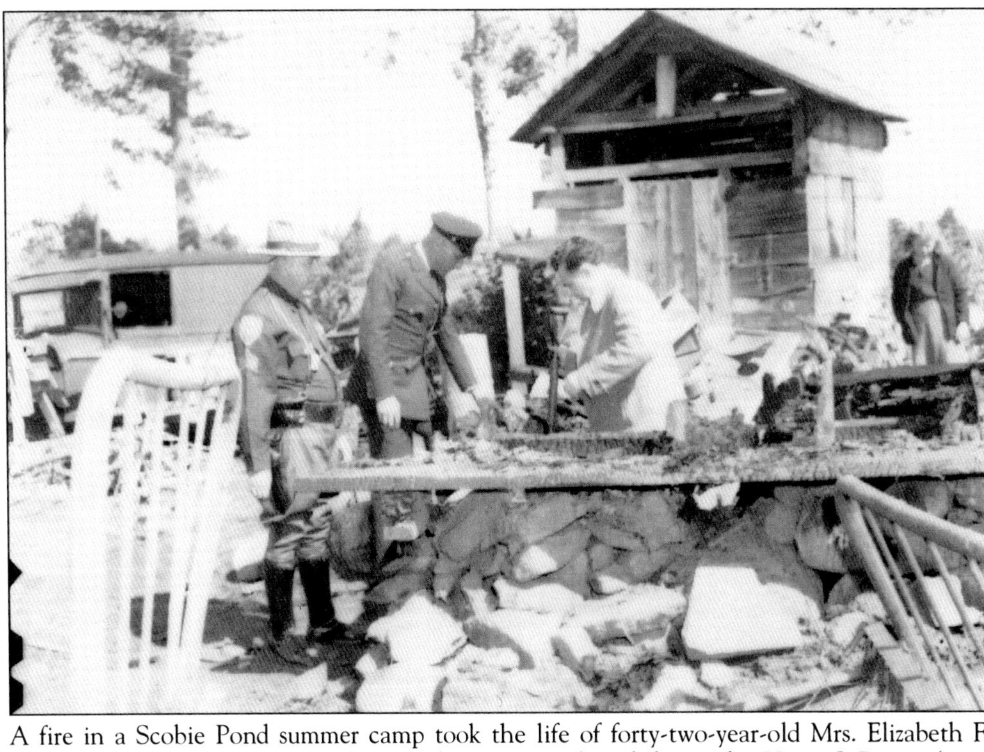

A fire in a Scobie Pond summer camp took the life of forty-two-year-old Mrs. Elizabeth F. Merrithew. Shown here sorting through the ruins are, from left to right, Henry J. Parent (state police), Howard W. Campbell (Derry police), and Dr. William J. Wilson (medical referee).

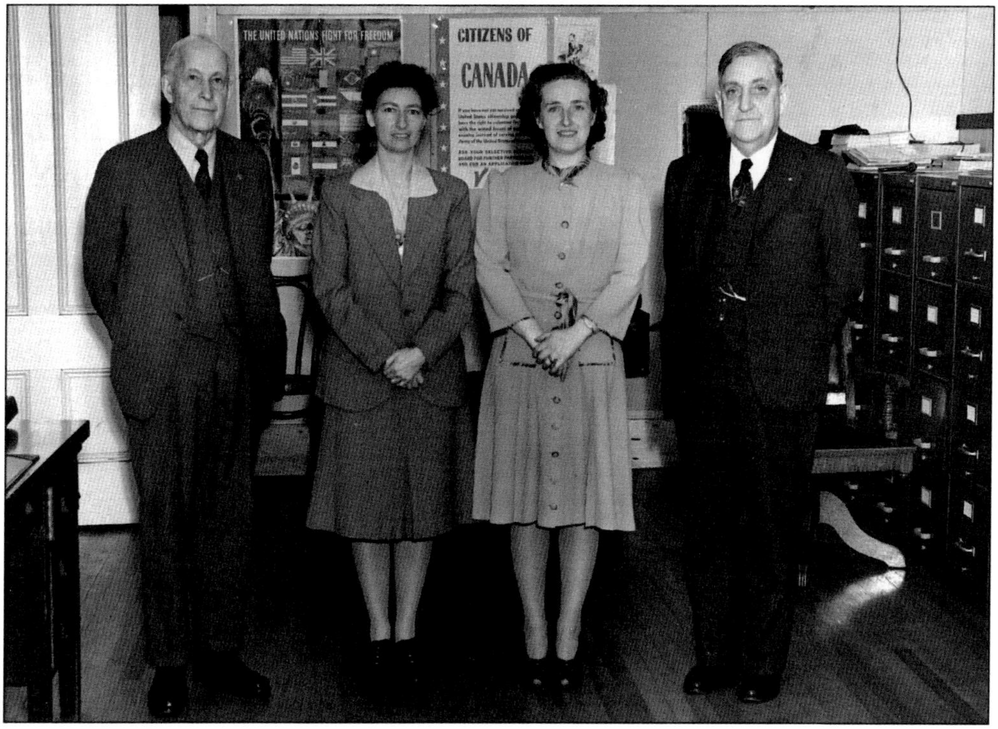

During World War II the county draft board held a virtual life and death grip over the area's men. Judge Herbert H. Grinnell, Jr., at right, served on the board during both world wars. (Grinnell collection)

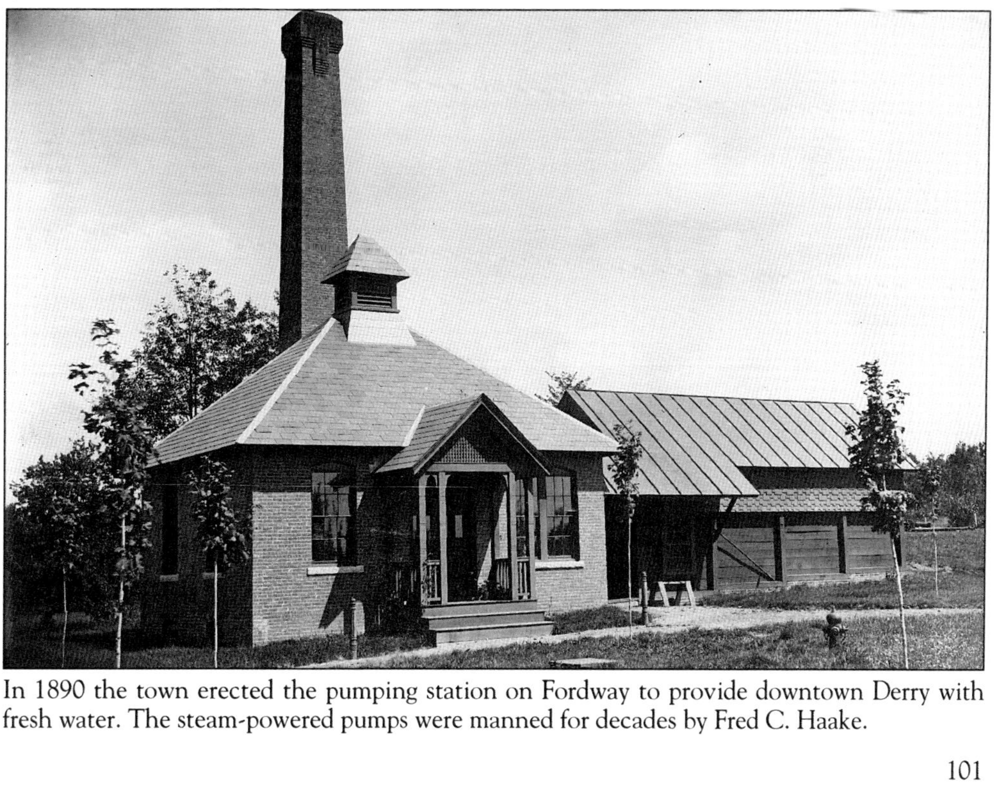

In 1890 the town erected the pumping station on Fordway to provide downtown Derry with fresh water. The steam-powered pumps were manned for decades by Fred C. Haake.

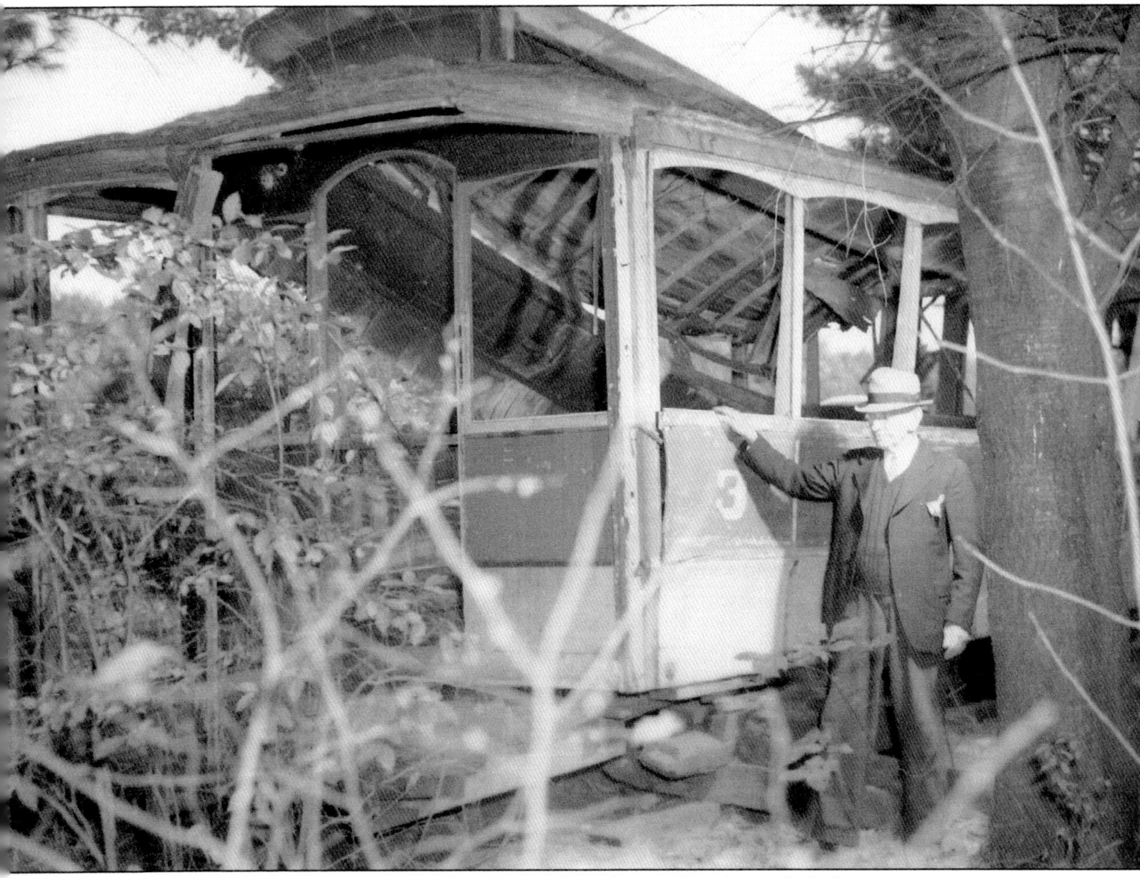

The Chester and Derry Street Railroad was closed in 1928 after it failed to survive competition with the automobile. The once proud trolley car No. 3 was parked in a pine grove off Route 102 near Lake Shore Road, where it was left to rust. In this October 1941 photograph, William West is seen surveying its ruins. (Lear photograph)

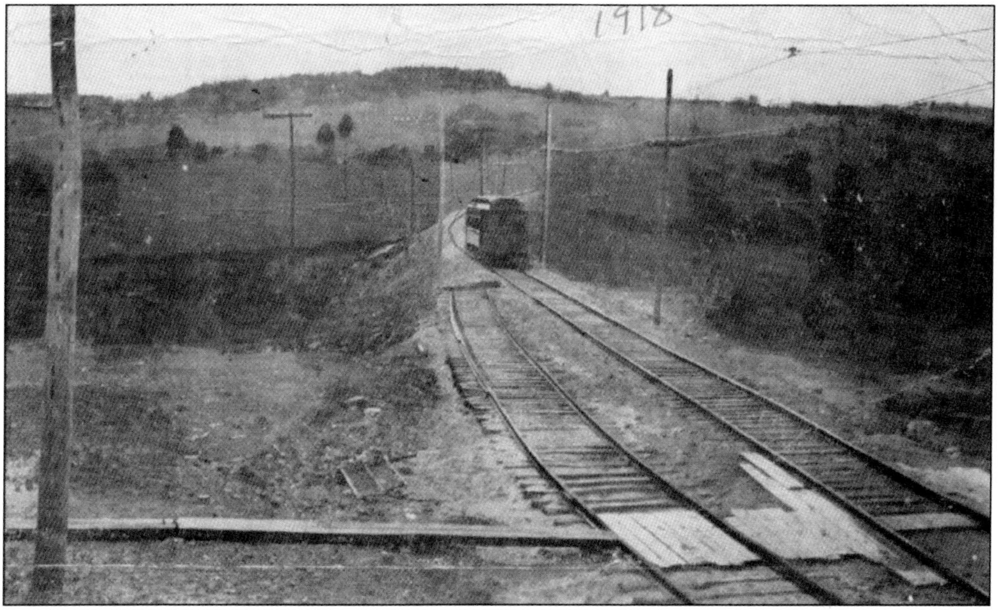

The Derry and Goffes Falls Street Railroad passed through a lot of fields and forests along its 8-mile right of way in 1918.

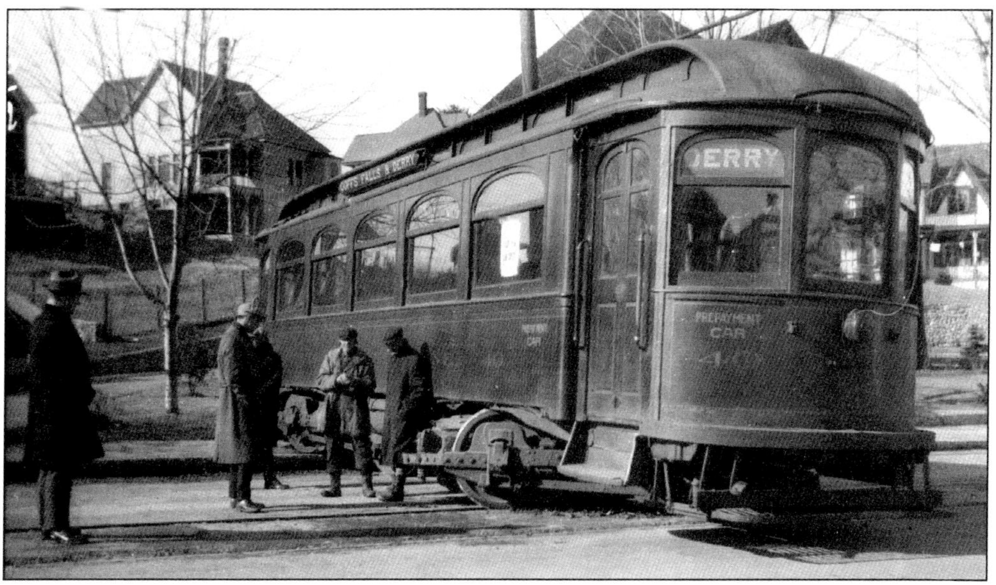

Rapid car No. 40 of the Derry and Goffes Falls Street Railway had jumped its track in this 1919 photograph. The car had a 29-foot body and could carry forty passengers. A ticket for the fifty-minute trip to downtown Manchester cost 10¢. The line operated from 1907 to 1926. (Lear photograph)

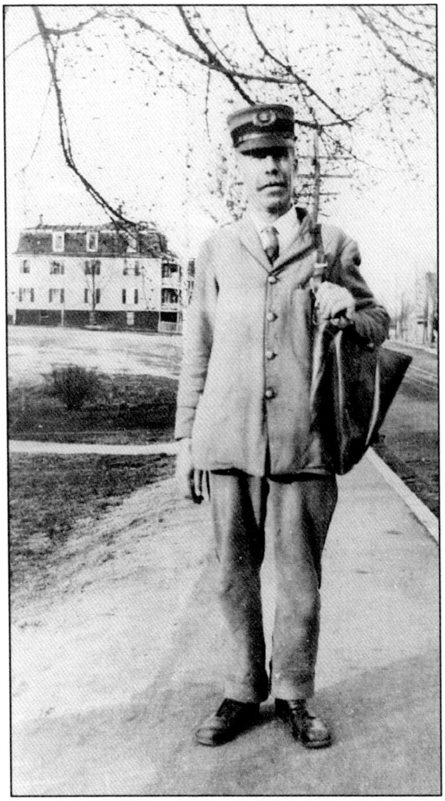

Mailman William C. Floyd (1865–1941) is shown on his route on West Broadway c. 1913. His son Carl became postmaster in 1958.

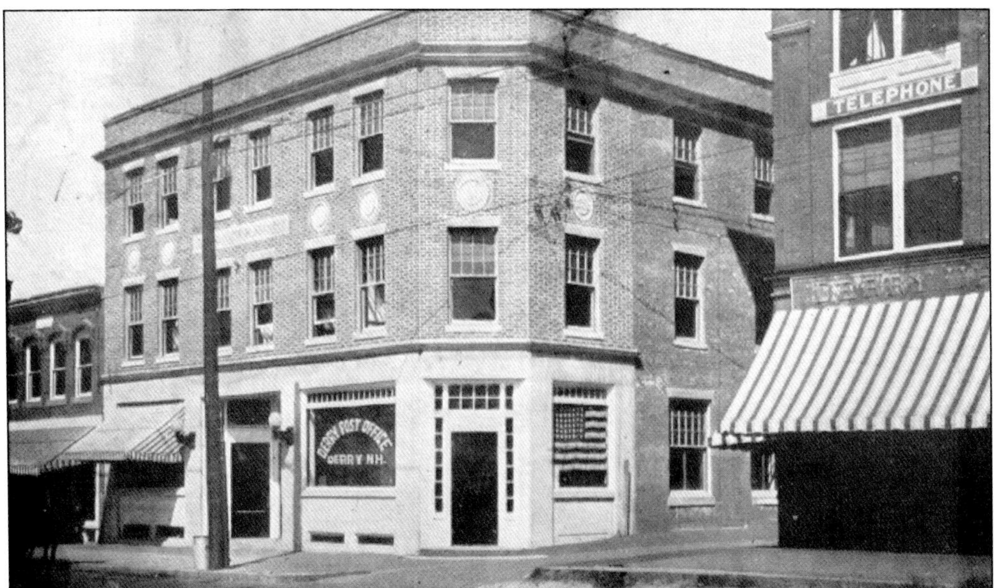

The present Fleet Bank building was built in 1917. At the time of this 1922 photograph it was the West Derry Post Office. After the construction of a new postal station in 1937 the entire ground floor was taken over by the bank.

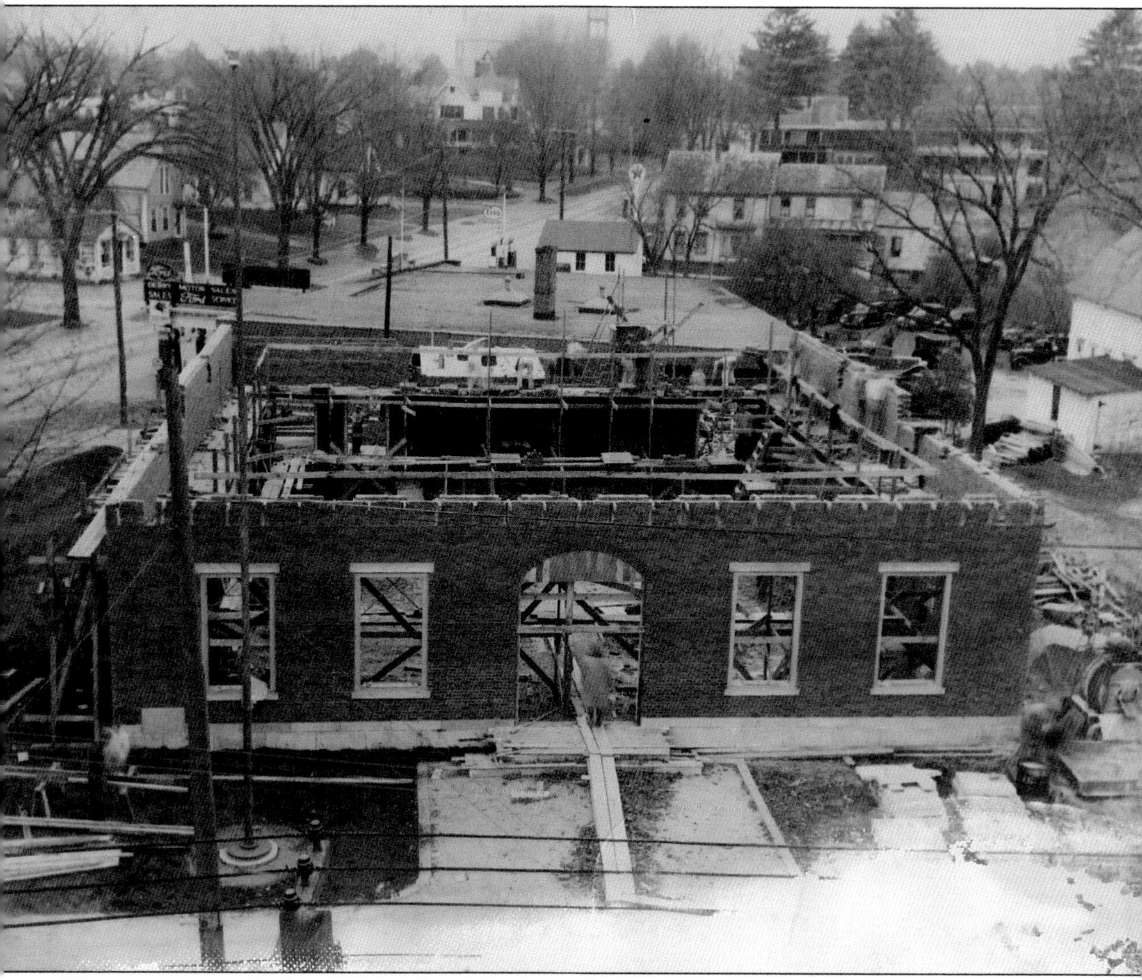

The present town hall was originally built in 1937/8 by the WPA as a post office, and the inside walls were covered with murals illustrating the town's history. When the post office moved to Crystal Avenue in 1972 the town took over the building. The murals have since disappeared, but they may still exist under sheets of wall panelling.

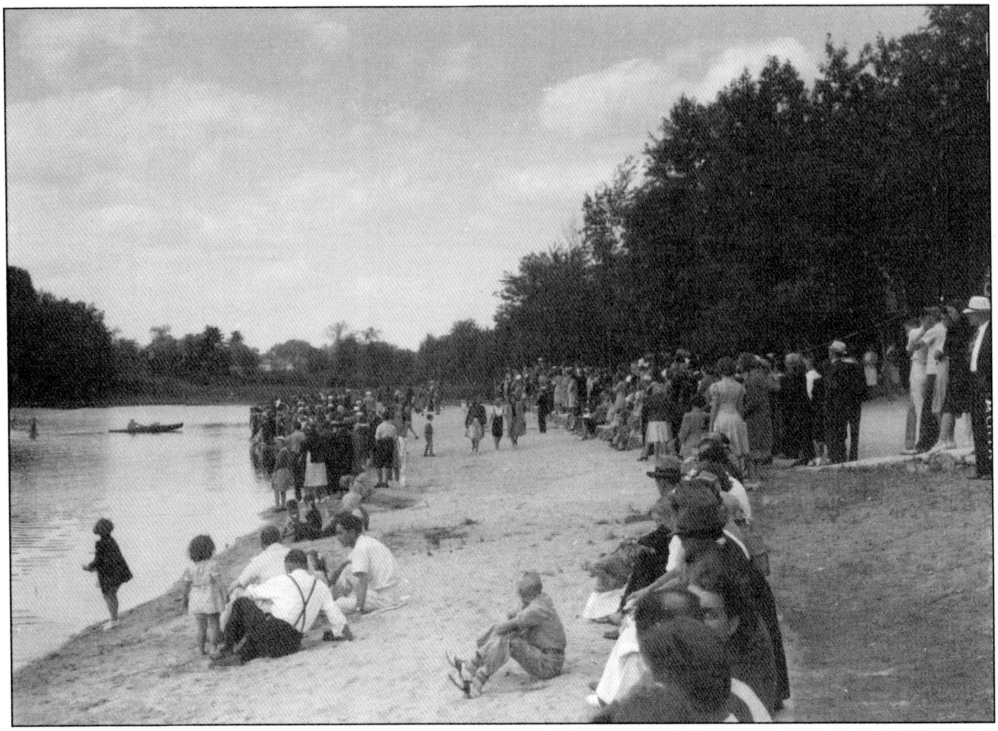

Over 2,000 people turned out for the August 1940 dedication of the new Hood Park. The park was the inspiration of George "Red" Lambert. The land was given by Mrs. Gilbert Hood and construction work was performed by the WPA. (Lear photograph)

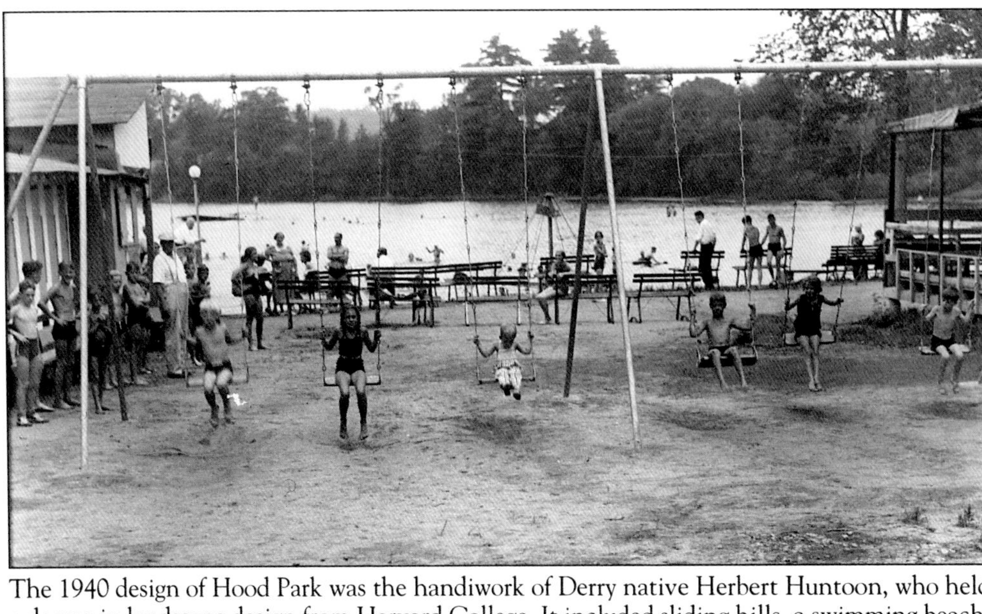

The 1940 design of Hood Park was the handiwork of Derry native Herbert Huntoon, who held a degree in landscape design from Harvard College. It included sliding hills, a swimming beach, and these large play areas.

Six

Social

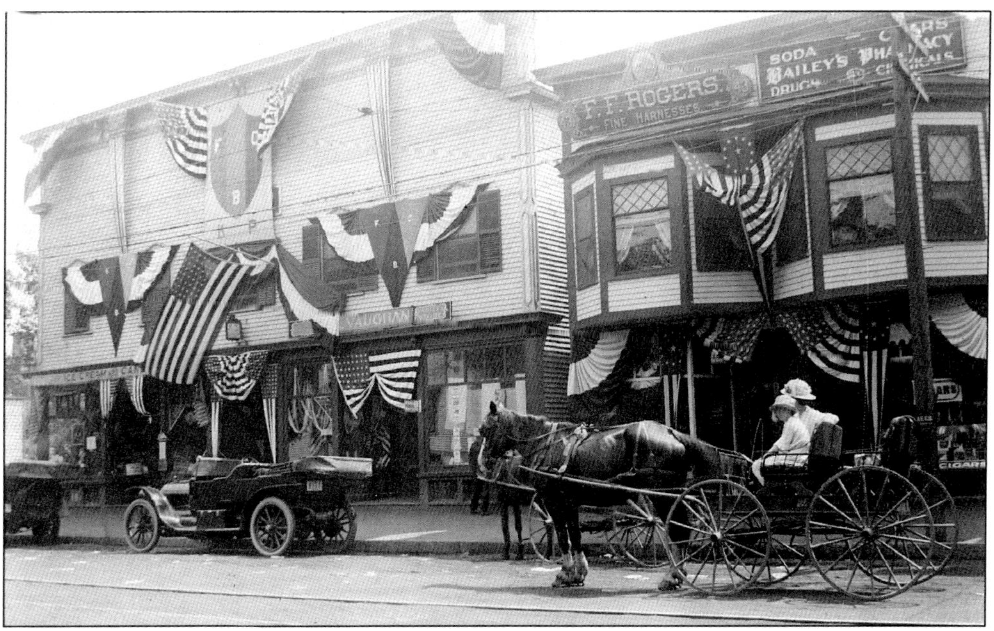

Old Home Week was a popular annual event from 1900 through World War II. It was designed as a time for scattered former residents to revisit their family and old friends in the town where they grew up. In this 1915 photograph, buildings are decorated with buntings and vehicles readied for a Broadway parade with five divisions and three bands. Many of the churches held Old Home services during the week, and a special dance was held at the Beaver Lake Pavilion. There was also horse racing and band concerts.

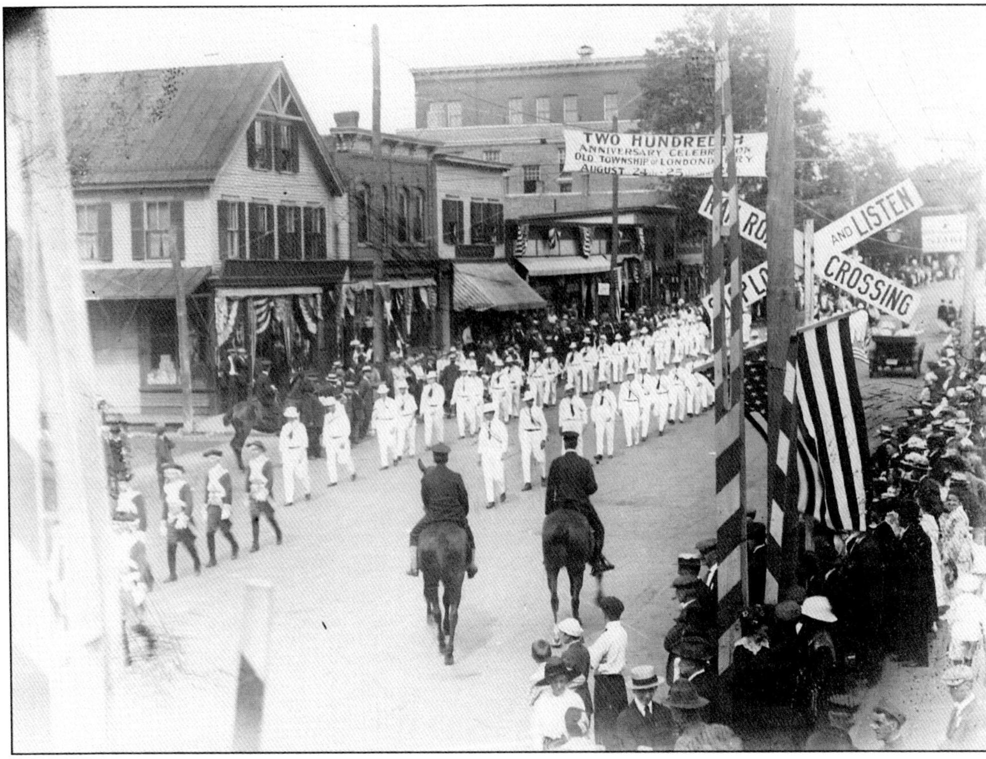

Broadway in 1919 was a very busy place as the town celebrated its 200th birthday. The parade (with eight divisions) was led by Lieutenant Alan B. Shepard, Sr. An airplane flying and parachute demonstration was cancelled because the plane was hit by lightning, and after being repaired, it got stuck in mud at Hood's meadow. (Grinnell collection)

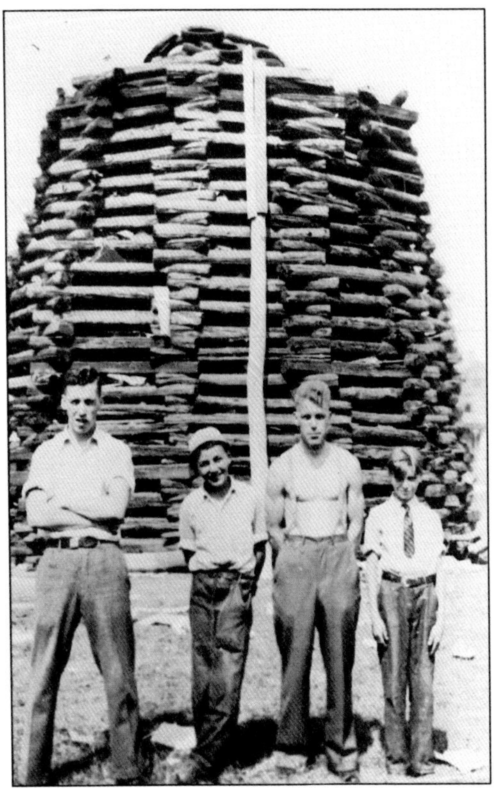

An Independence Day bonfire in 1938 at the so-called "Ward Five" district of the town (the site of the modern salt shed on Fordway). At the pavilion that night fireworks were fired from a barge in the center of Beaver Lake. Enjoying the festivities are, from left to right, Russell Holm, George Kachavos, Bernard Holm, and Leon Bunker.

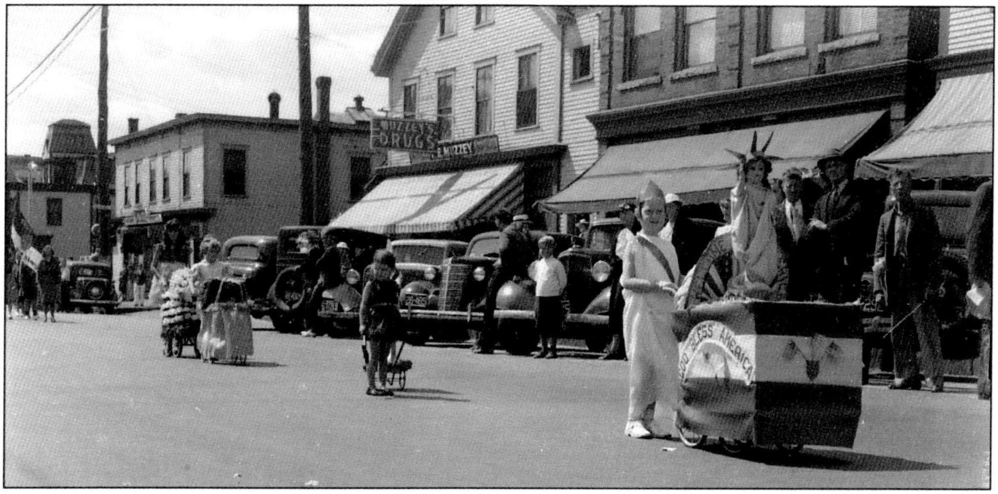

An August 1940 parade dedicating the new Hood Park. In the doll carriage division Eleanor Mae Dumont (right) won for prettiest. Most original was Little Barbara Potter (center left), who carried a tiny hatchet and a sign asking, "Has anyone seen Hitler?" (Lear photograph)

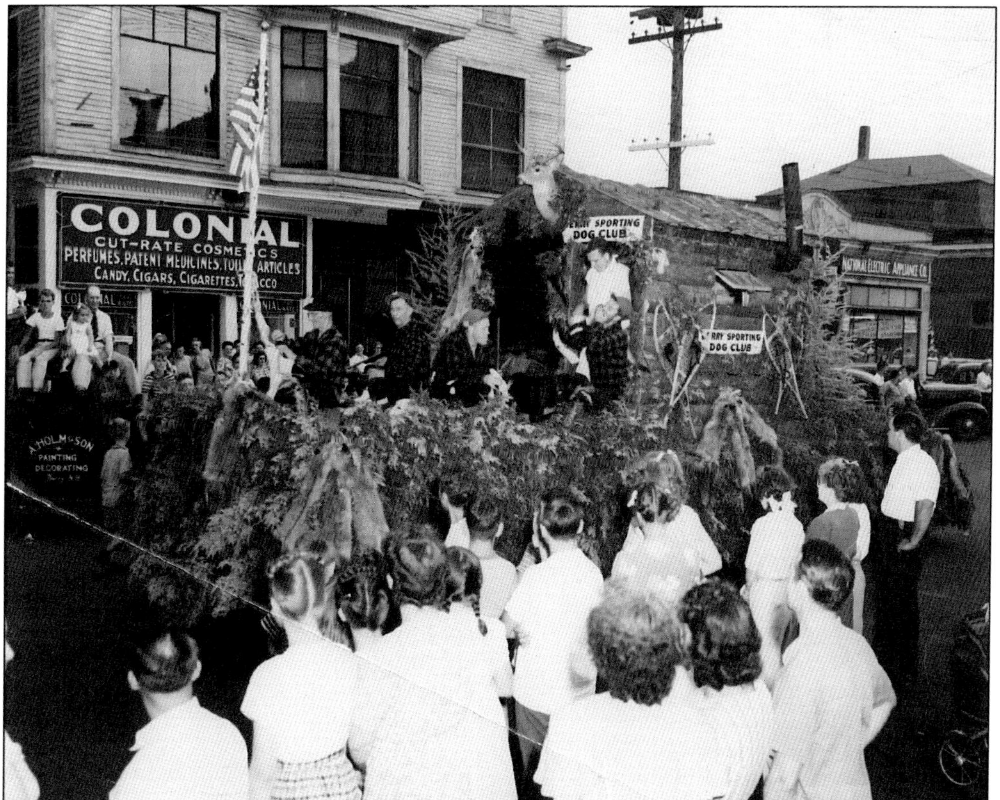

The Derry Sporting Dog Club float featured Derry sportsman Alfred Paquette (on the extreme left) skinning a rabbit. The V.J. Day parade was seen by 5,000 people and contained 50 units. Later that night a sky rocket accidently came down in the crowd slightly injuring three spectators and blowing up an empty baby carriage.

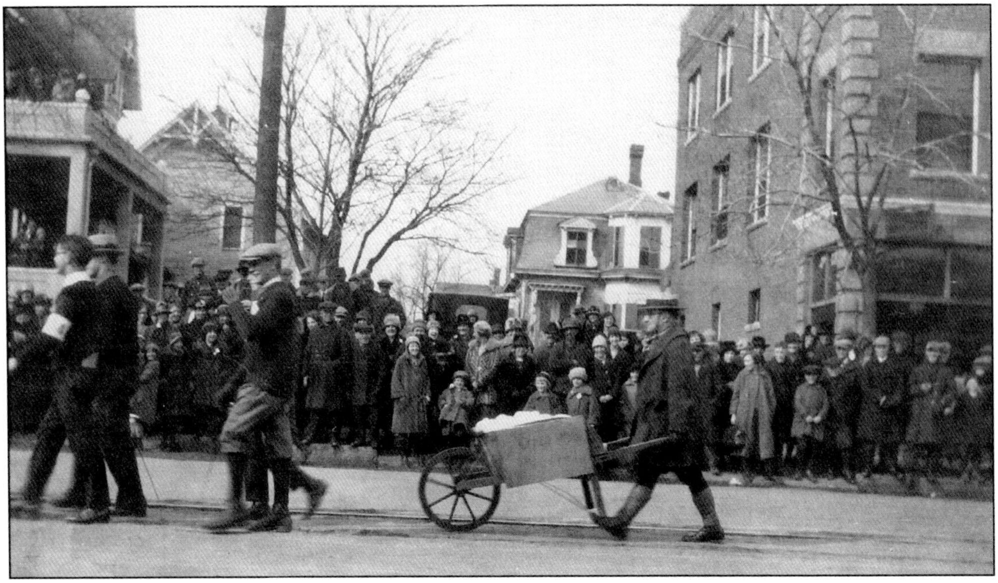

The Derry Athletic Association's winter carnivals started in 1924 as a townwide celebration. Joe Edwards is seen here marching in the 1925 parade: he had promised snow for the weekend but due to a warm spell he was forced to make good his pledge by delivering a wheelbarrow full of snow.

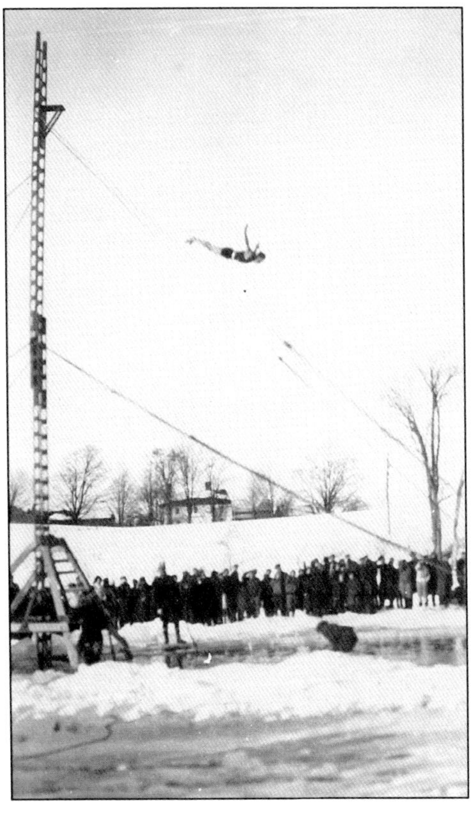

A stunt diver at the February 1926 winter carnival dove off a 50-foot ladder. Members of the Manchester Brownies swam in Beaver Lake like it was summer while nearly 1,000 spectators shivered in a cold wind that blew across the open area.

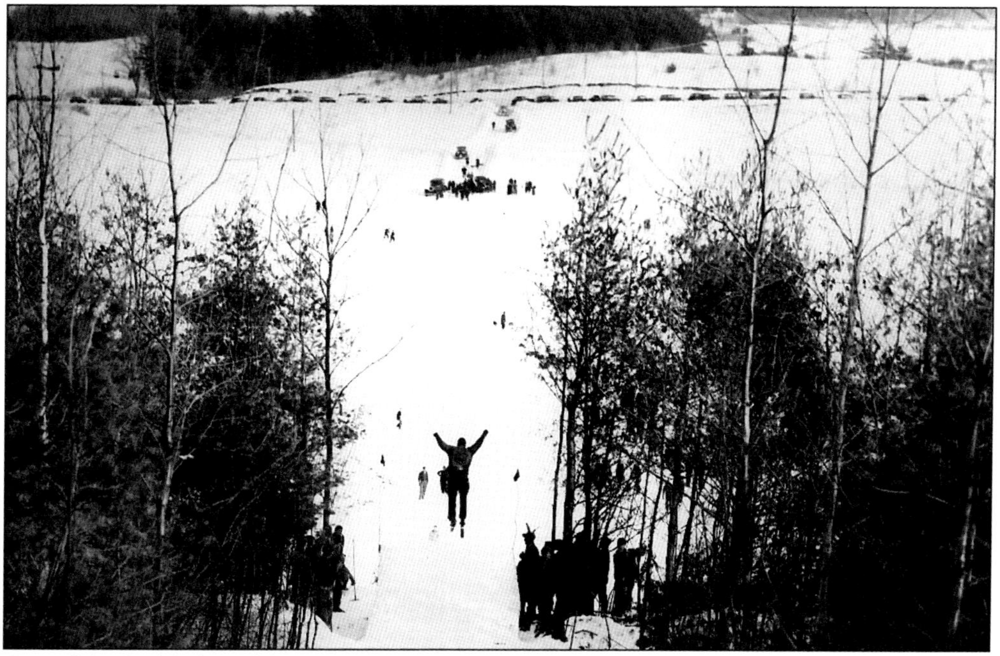

One of the highlights of the 1938 DAA winter carnival was ski jumping. Coming off the ramp on Ela's Hill was the flying judge, George Grinnell. In the distance is Route 102.

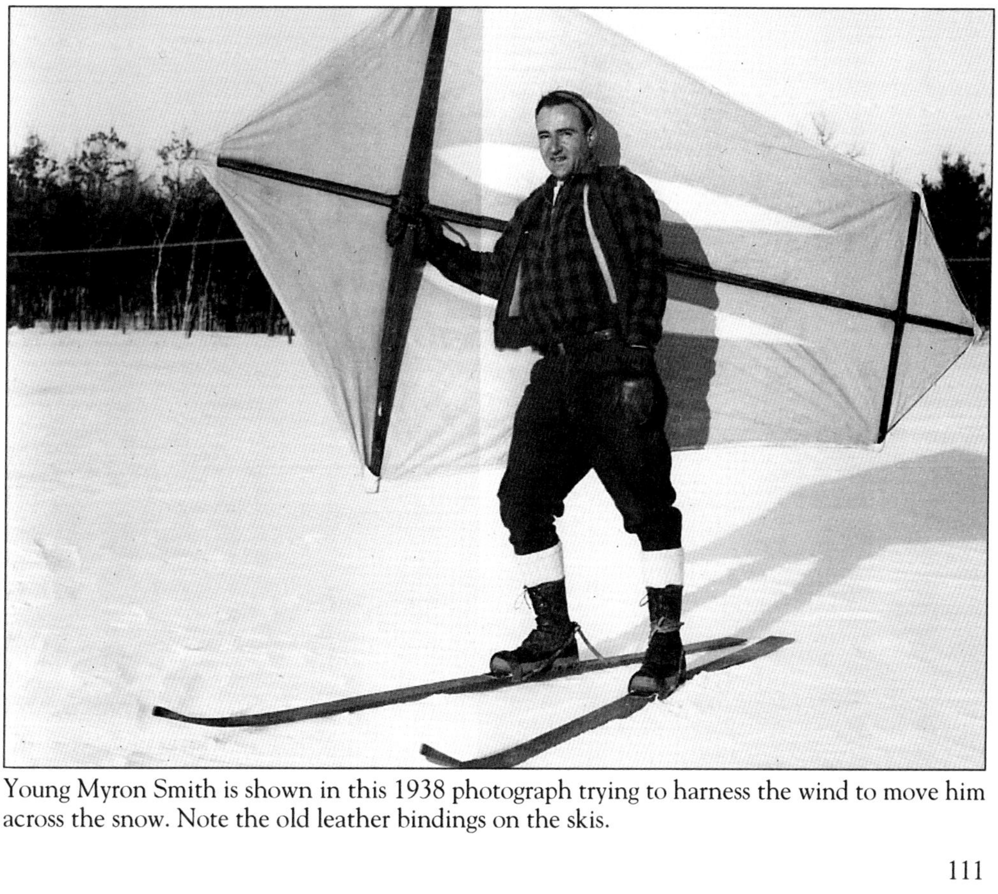

Young Myron Smith is shown in this 1938 photograph trying to harness the wind to move him across the snow. Note the old leather bindings on the skis.

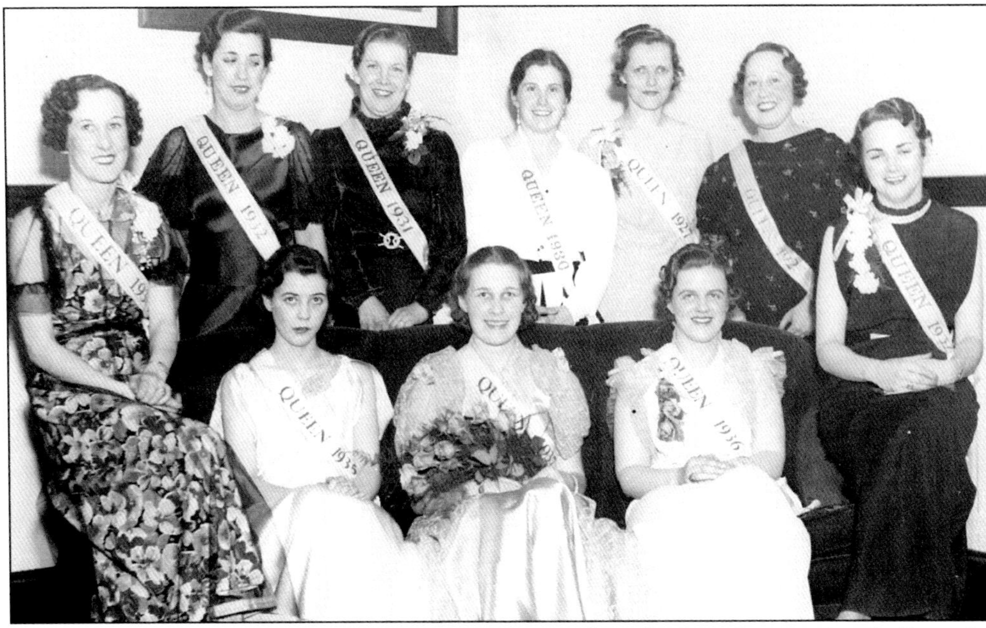

At the 1937 winter carnival nine former queens surround newly elected queen Amelia Romeiko Tobec (front row with roses). Queens were elected by votes earned by selling carnival buttons and collecting coupons from the *Derry News*. May Casten, the lovely young queen of the 1941 carnival, eventually became Derry's mayor.

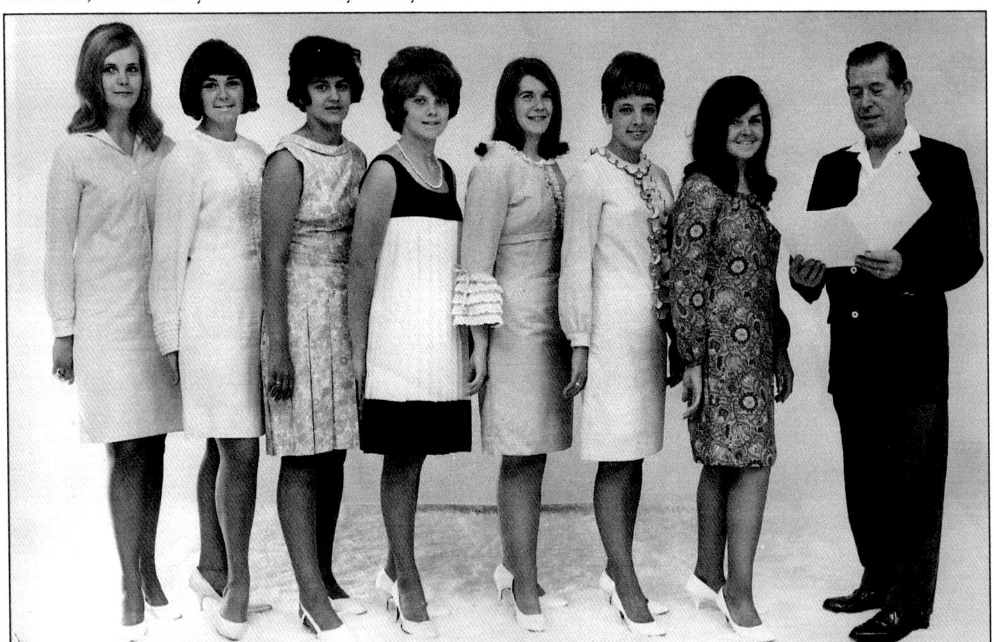

The contestants for Labor Day Queen in 1967 being presented by "Woody" Barrieau. The winner was Diane Harrison (extreme left). The Labor Day festivals ran from 1964 to 1971 attracting crowds estimated at over 20,000. Television star Rex Trailor gave a free show for many years. Also featured were sky divers (who would sometimes land in trees), helicopter rides, dancing, and track and field events.

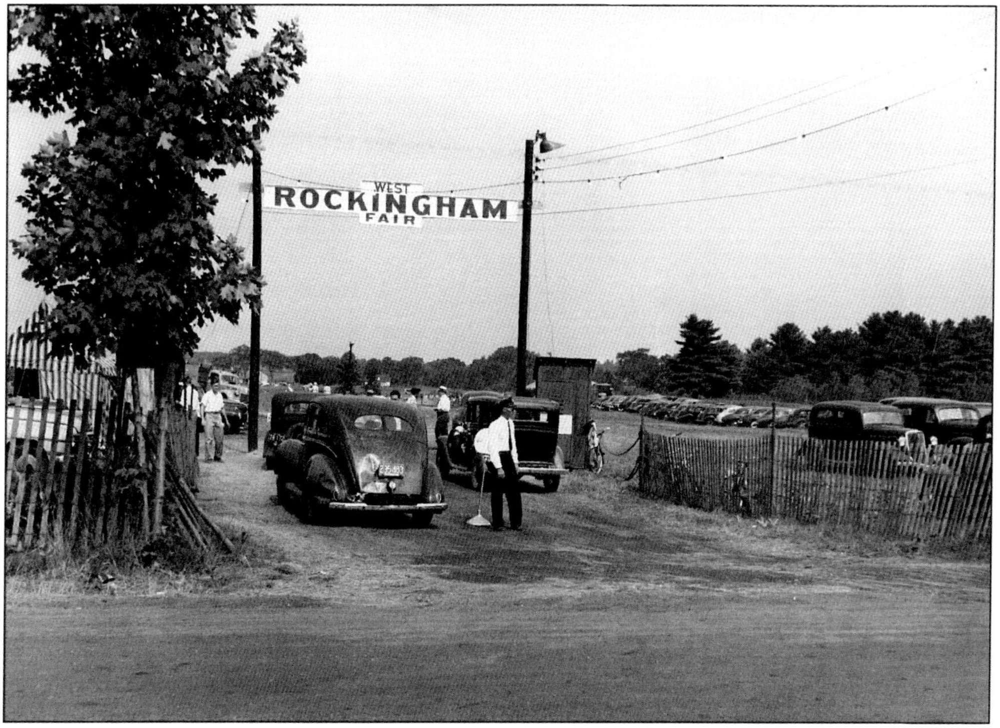

An estimated 8,000 spectators descended on a field located on Franklin Street for the West Rockingham Fair in October 1947. (F.J. Sullivan photograph)

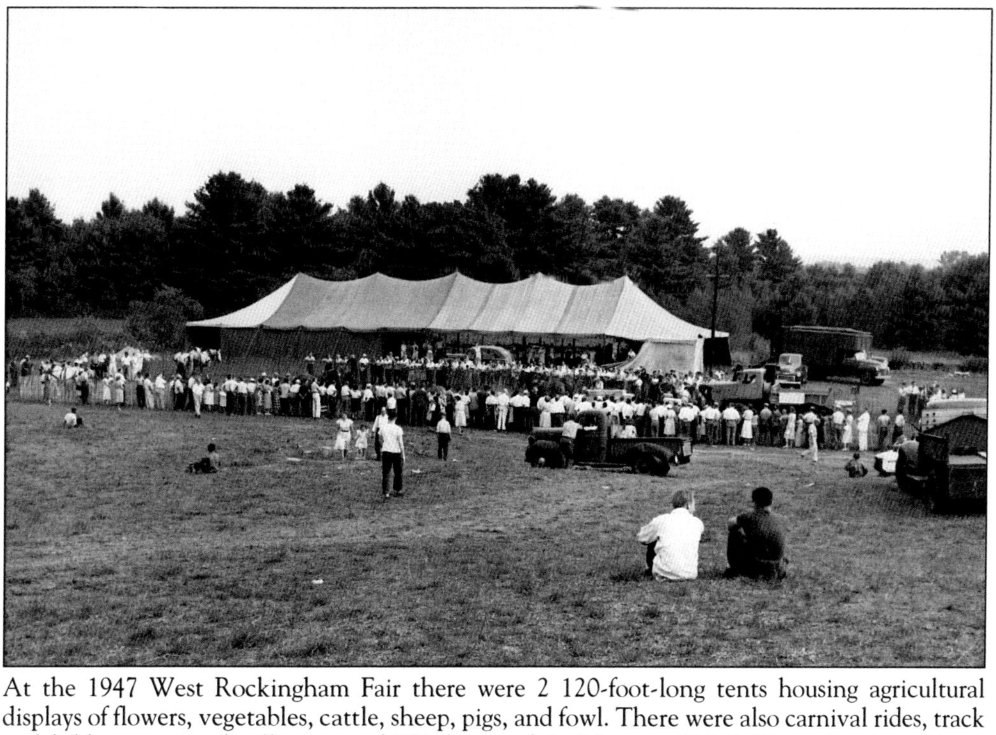

At the 1947 West Rockingham Fair there were 2 120-foot-long tents housing agricultural displays of flowers, vegetables, cattle, sheep, pigs, and fowl. There were also carnival rides, track and field events, vaudeville acts, and 250 show and draft horses. (F.J. Sullivan photograph)

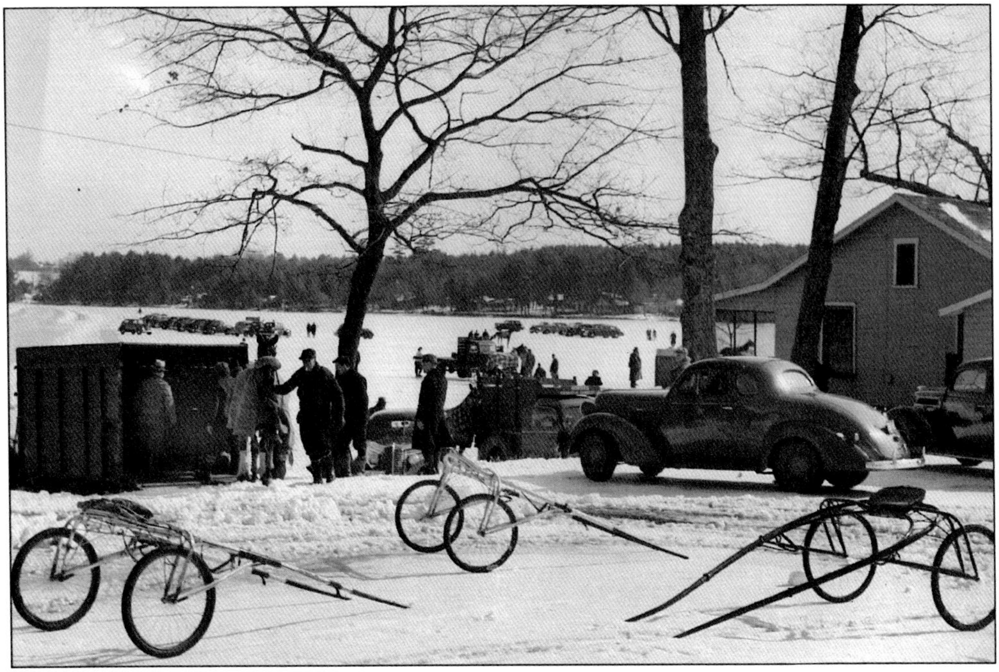

Sportsmen getting their sulkies ready for a 1939 race on Beaver Lake. To the right is the summer camp of County Commissioner Albert "Pokey" Fuller. The Derry Driving Club also raced that year in Amesbury, MA; Manchester, Nashua, and Newmarket, NH; and at Rockingham Park, Plymouth Fair, and the Deerfield Fair. (Lear photograph)

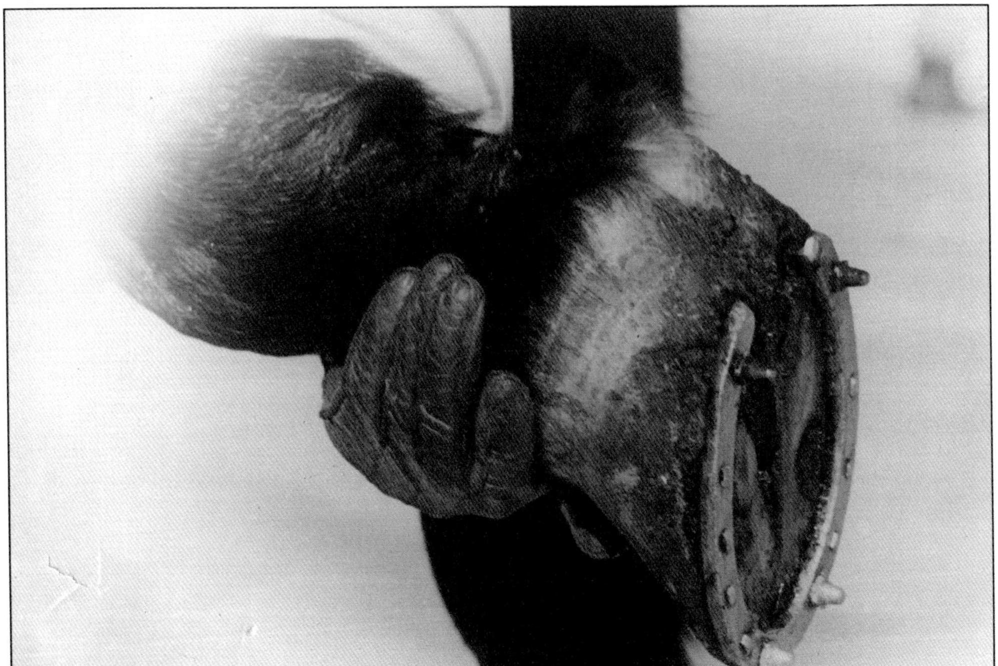

The secret of racing on ice: each of the horseshoes were fitted with special conical-shaped screws which prevented slipping. (Lear photograph)

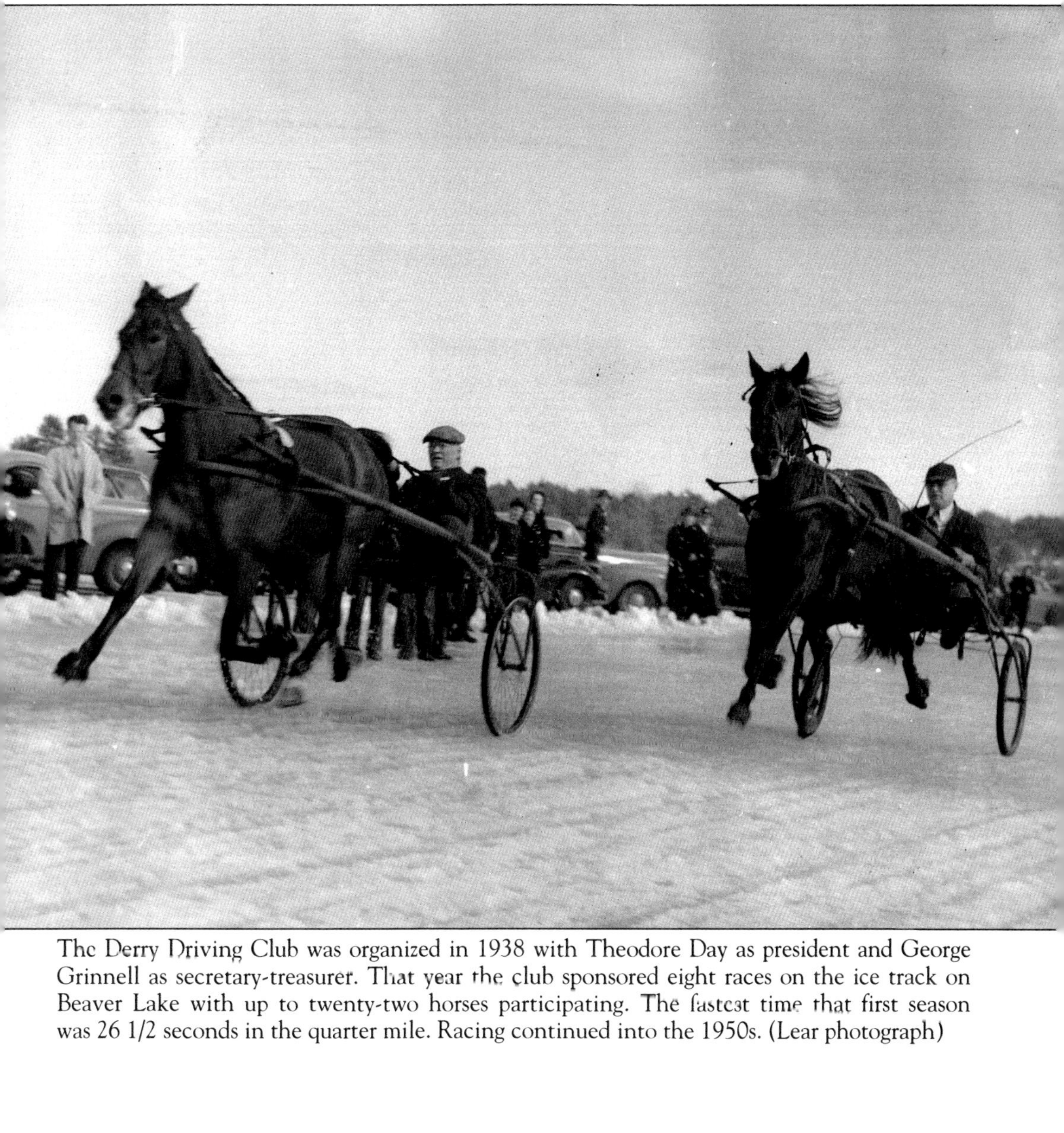

The Derry Driving Club was organized in 1938 with Theodore Day as president and George Grinnell as secretary-treasurer. That year the club sponsored eight races on the ice track on Beaver Lake with up to twenty-two horses participating. The fastest time that first season was 26 1/2 seconds in the quarter mile. Racing continued into the 1950s. (Lear photograph)

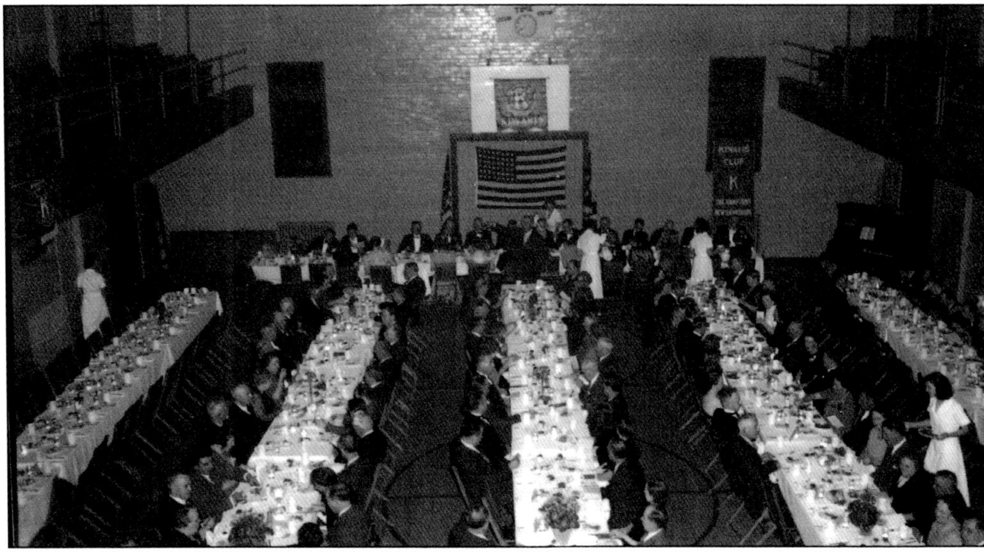

On December 7, 1939, the Derry Kiwanis Club received its charter at a banquet for two hundred people at the Veteran's Memorial Hall. The founding officers were Clive C. Sonnell (president), Alan B. Shepard, Sr. (vice-president), and Reverend Harold Bentley (secretary-treasurer). There were thirty-eight charter members. (Lear photograph)

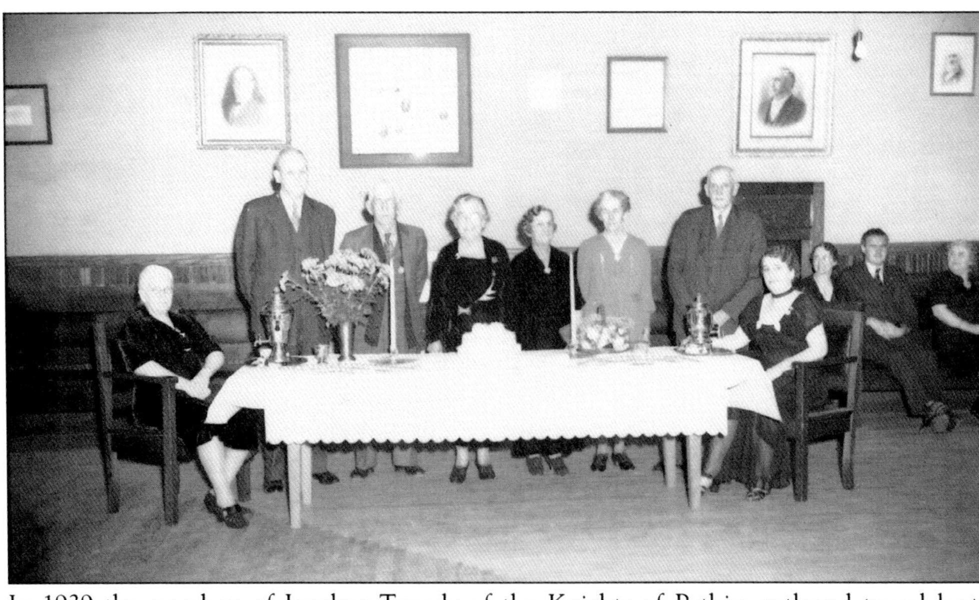

In 1939 the members of Ivanhoe Temple of the Knights of Pythias gathered to celebrate their 50th anniversary. Six of the original nineteen charter members attended and are shown standing at the table: Zanetta A. Rose, Edgar and Annie Osborne, Mr. and Mrs. Arthur Abbott, and Frank McGregor. (Lear photograph)

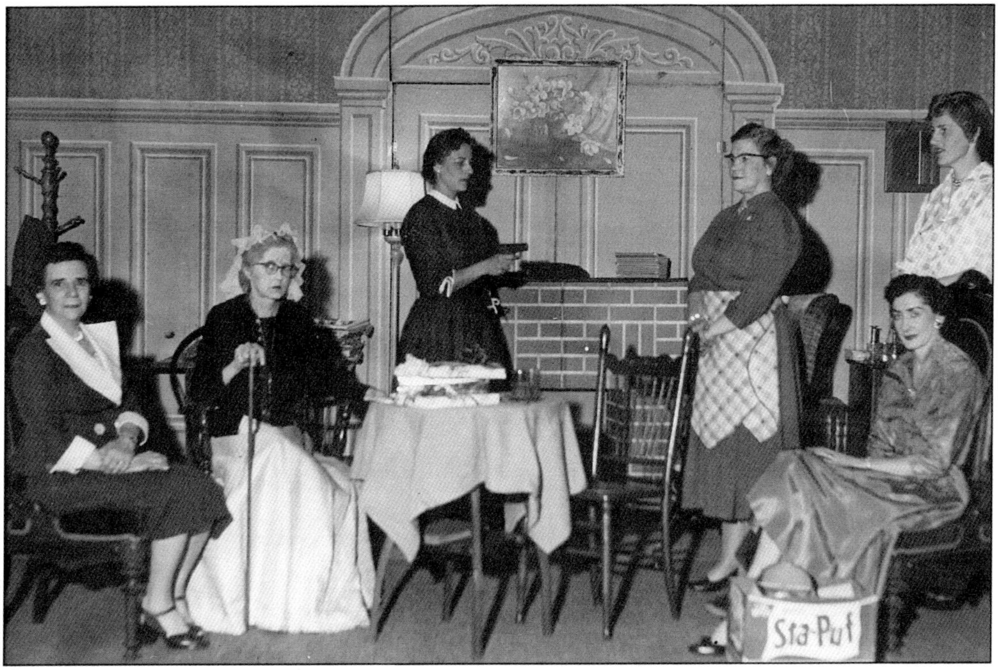

Members of the Women's Club in 1957 present the play My *Aunt Agatha* at the Association Hall. From left to right are Mrs. Harry S. Dyson, Mrs. Walter Harding, Mrs. Frank S. Breen, Mrs. William G. Smith, Mrs. Leon Day, and Mrs. Charles Audette.

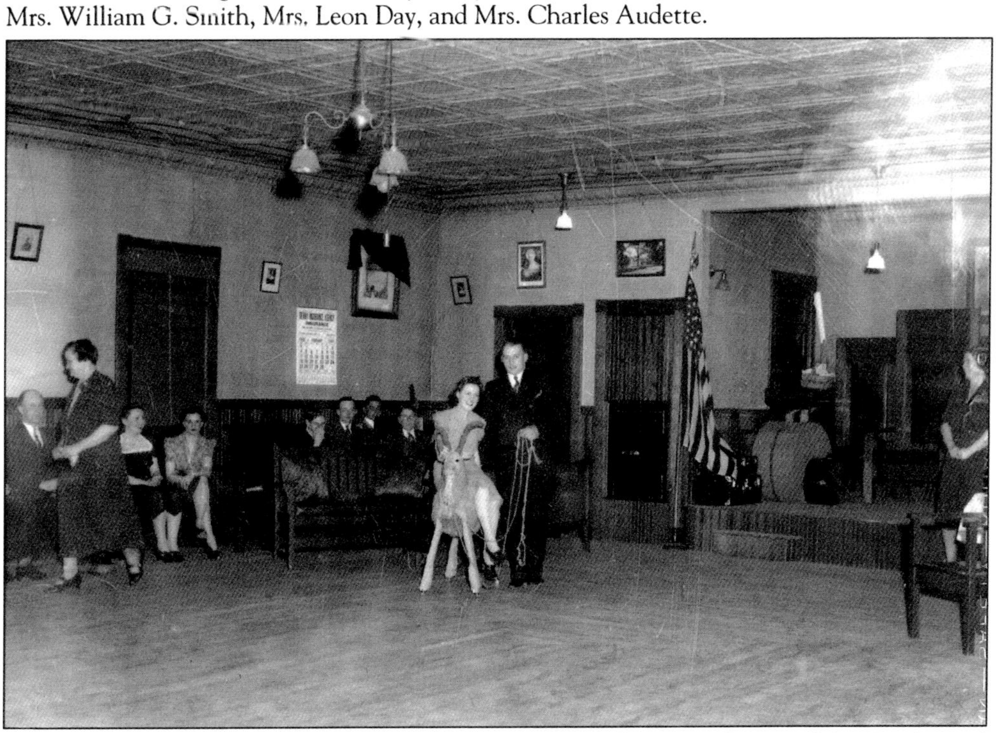

It is hard to determine exactly what is going on at this March 1939 gathering of the Knights and Sisters of Pythias. Why is the newly married Wesley Bean standing in the middle of the temple with his bride riding a wooden goat? A stunt? A ritual? A skit? (Lear photograph)

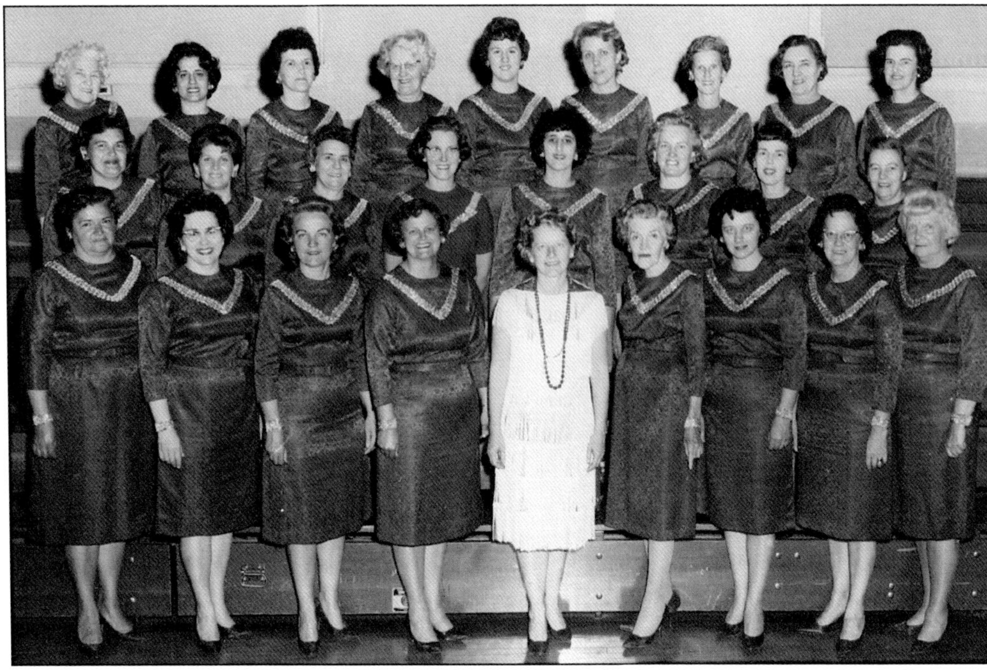

From 1954 to 1974 the Sweet Adelines of Derry were the local branch of a national singing organization. In 1958 and 1961, under the direction of Marilyn Lamson (front row in white), they won first place in the Northeast Division. In 1959 Derry hosted the Northeast Division Convention.

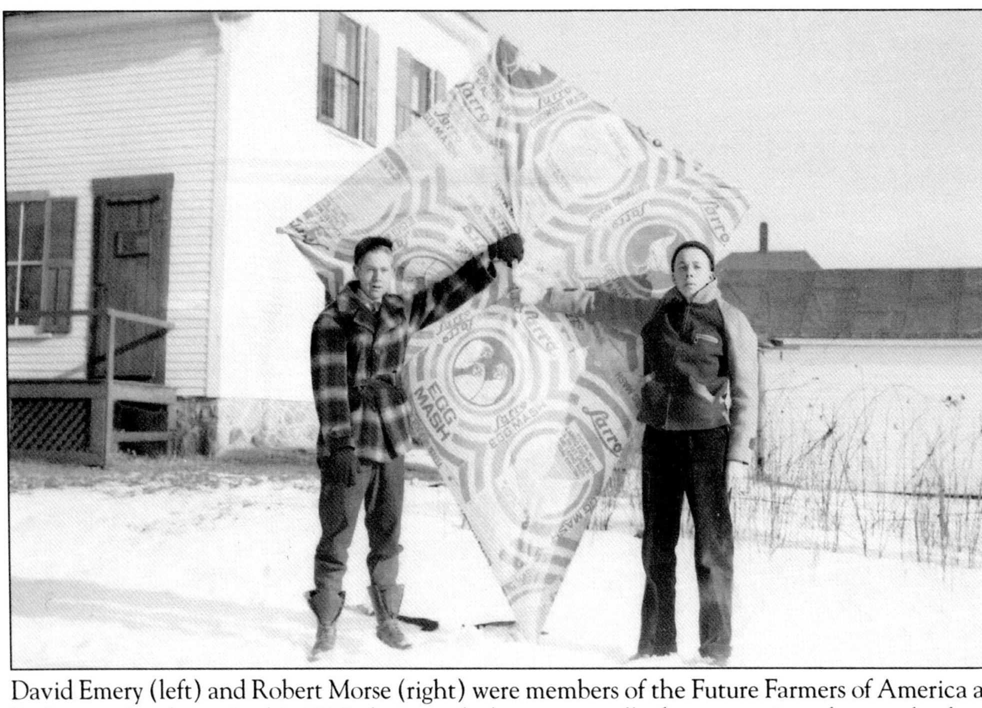

David Emery (left) and Robert Morse (right) were members of the Future Farmers of America at Pinkerton Academy. In this 1939 photograph they are proudly demonstrating what can be done with grain sacks. Their kite stood 10 feet high and was 7 feet wide. (Lear photograph)

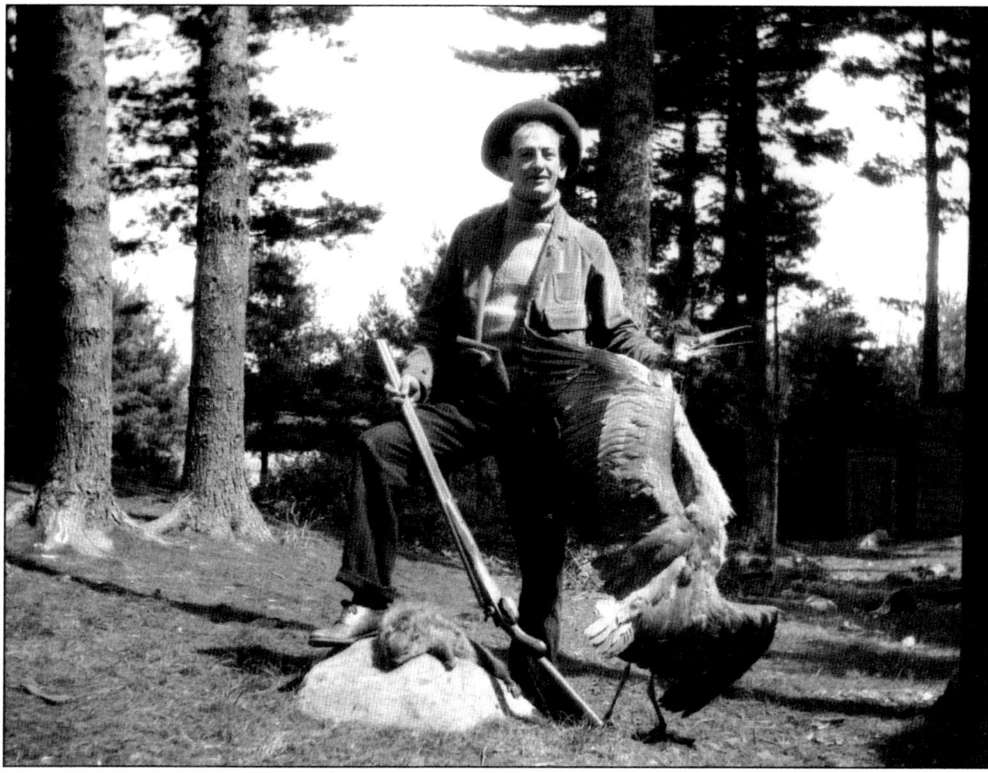

Not all of Derry's sportsmen wrapped themselves in glory. This Derry hunter, recorded only as "Steve," returned at the end of the day with two kills—a blue heron and a woodchuck—that he had dispatched with a double-barreled shotgun. (Lear photograph)

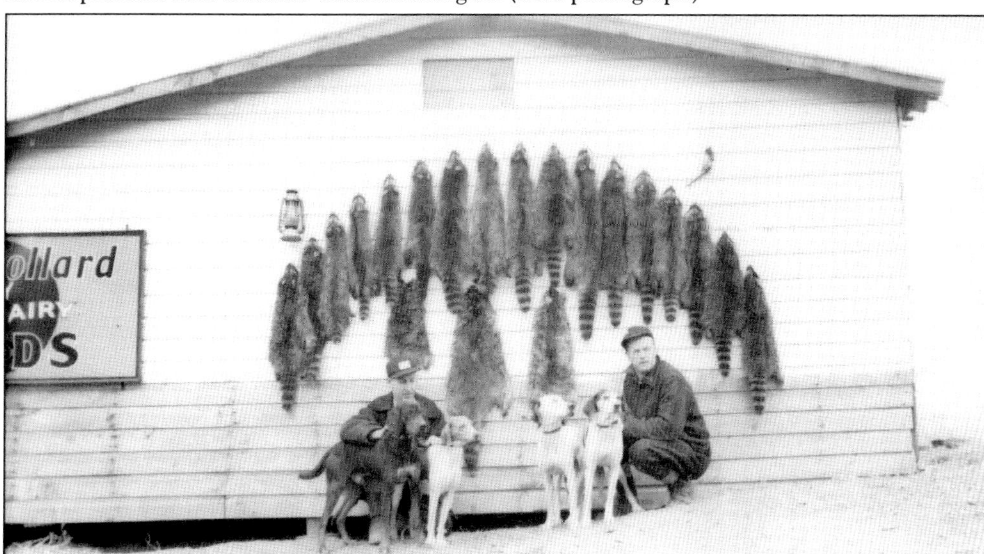

Surrounded by the lanterns, revolvers, and dogs they used during the 1939 raccoon hunting season are Ray Butterfield (left) and Leon Whitney (right). The pair managed to kill twenty raccoons long before the end of the season. The largest was a mighty 23-pounder. (Lear photograph)

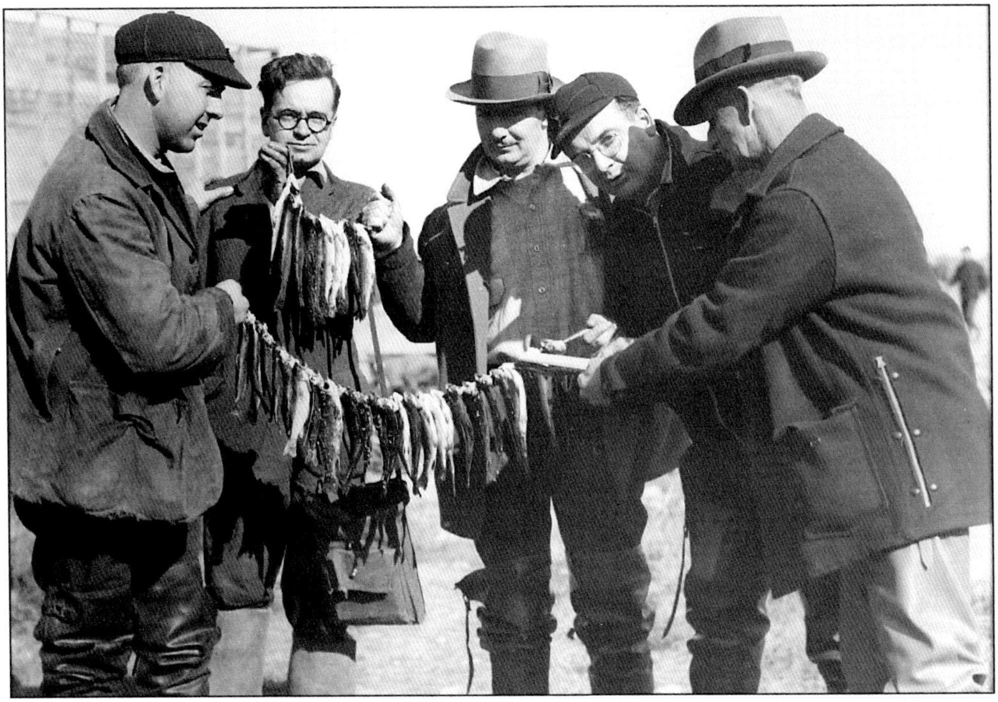

Sportsmen get their day's catch logged in by the judge at a 1938 fishing derby. It would appear that the working man with the cap caught twenty-five trout while the businessman in the felt hat landed less than a dozen fish.

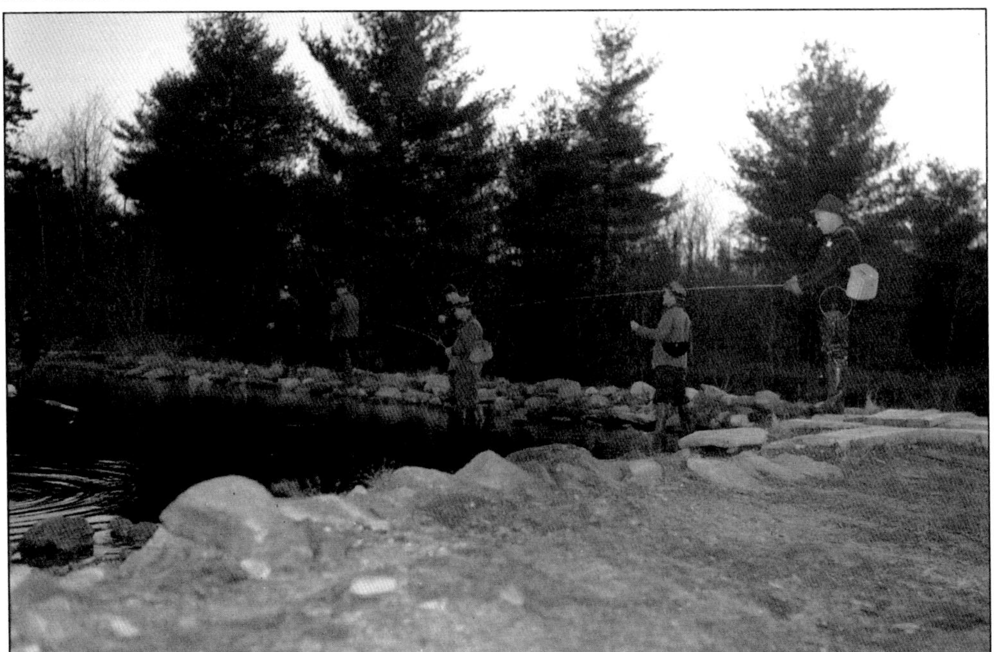

The 1939 opening day of the fishing season was, as usual, a well-attended event at nearby Scobie Pond. During the 1920s the state had killed all the "junk" fish and restocked the pond with trout. (Lear photograph)

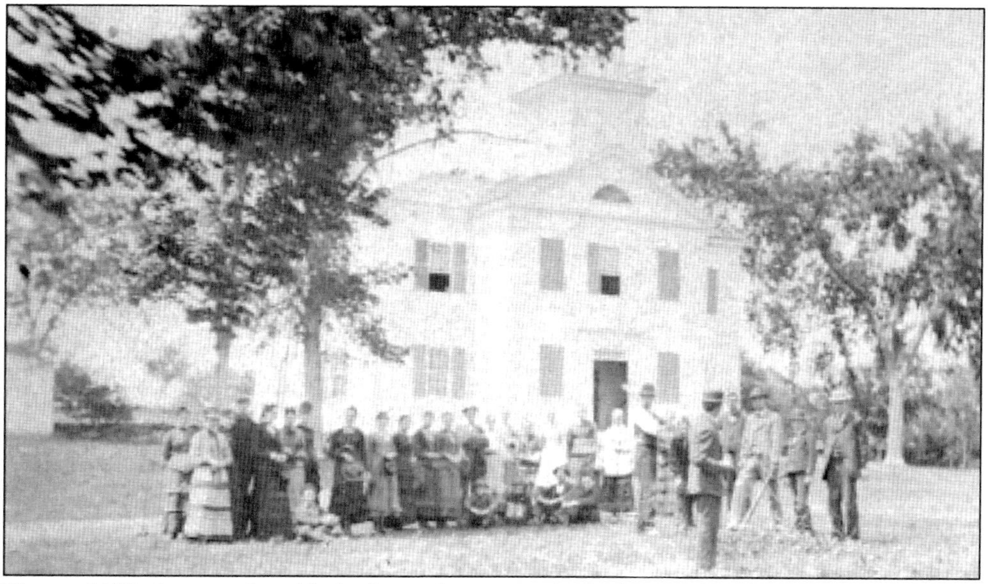

This c. 1870 photograph is likely the earliest one of a Pinkerton Academy sports team. The academy men are playing baseball in front of the original academy building. This building was moved to its present site in 1886 and the new brick Pinkerton building built in its place.

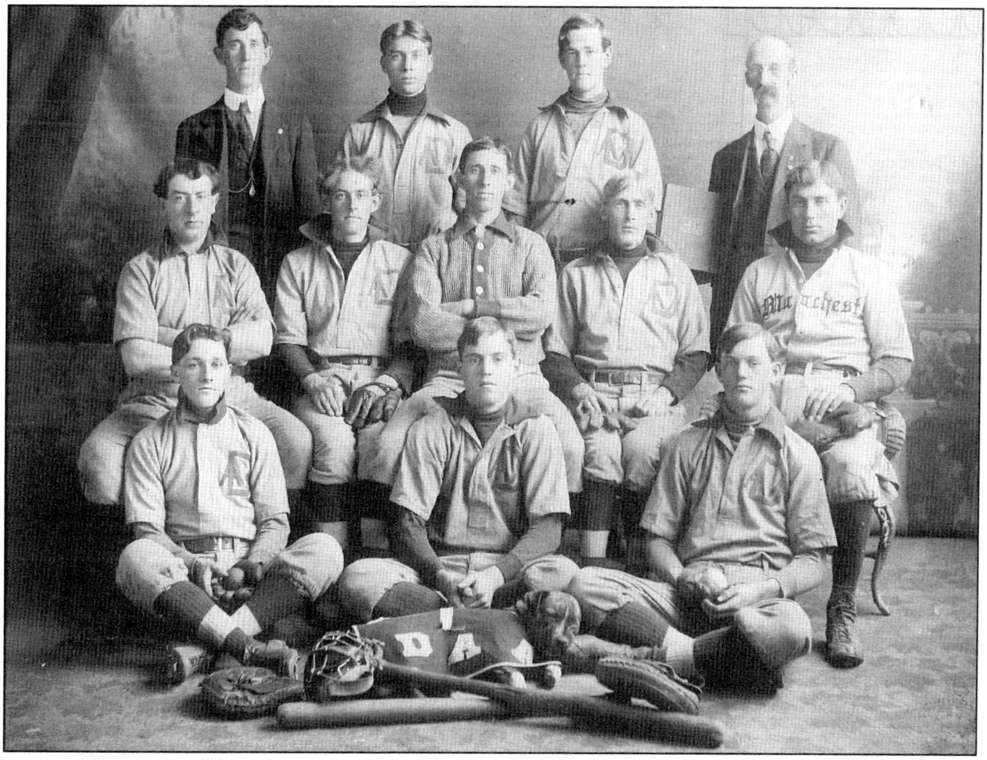

The 1907 Derry Athletic Association baseball team, under the coaching of George Burdette, was considered the area's best. Star pitcher George "Lefty" Tyler (bottom row, far right) eventually pitched in two World Series for the Chicago Cubs and later the Boston Braves. The DAA team played all over New England and in 1907 and 1908 had perfect seasons.

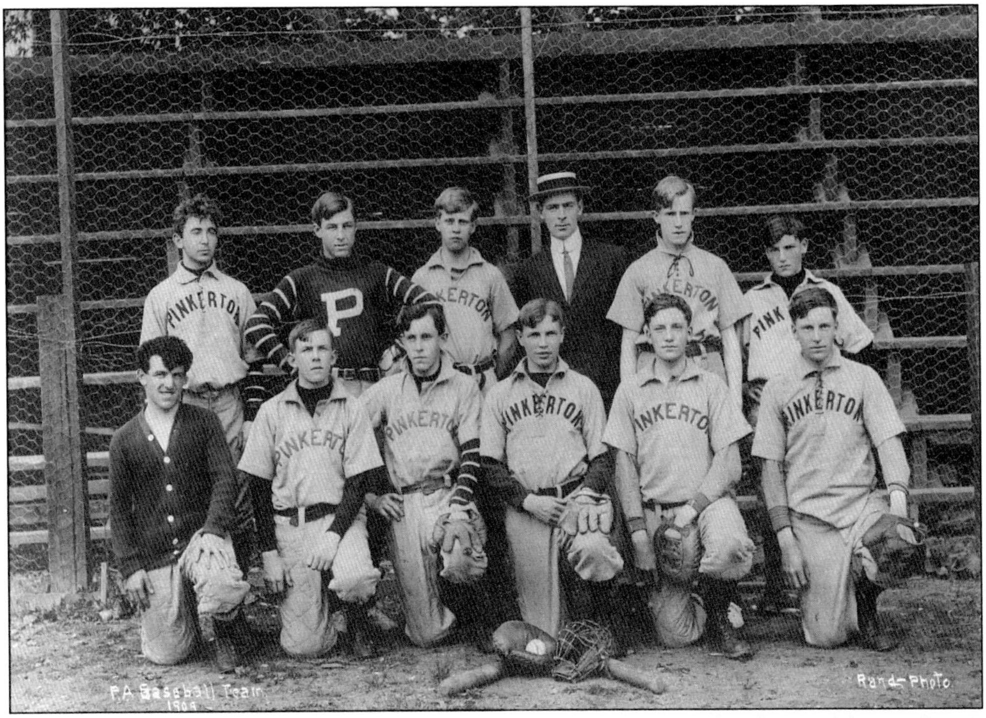

The 1909 Pinkerton baseball team under Coach Brice was not considered one of the academy's most memorable. That year it committed the nearly unpardonable sin of losing to chief rival Sanborn Seminary in their annual series. (Rand photograph)

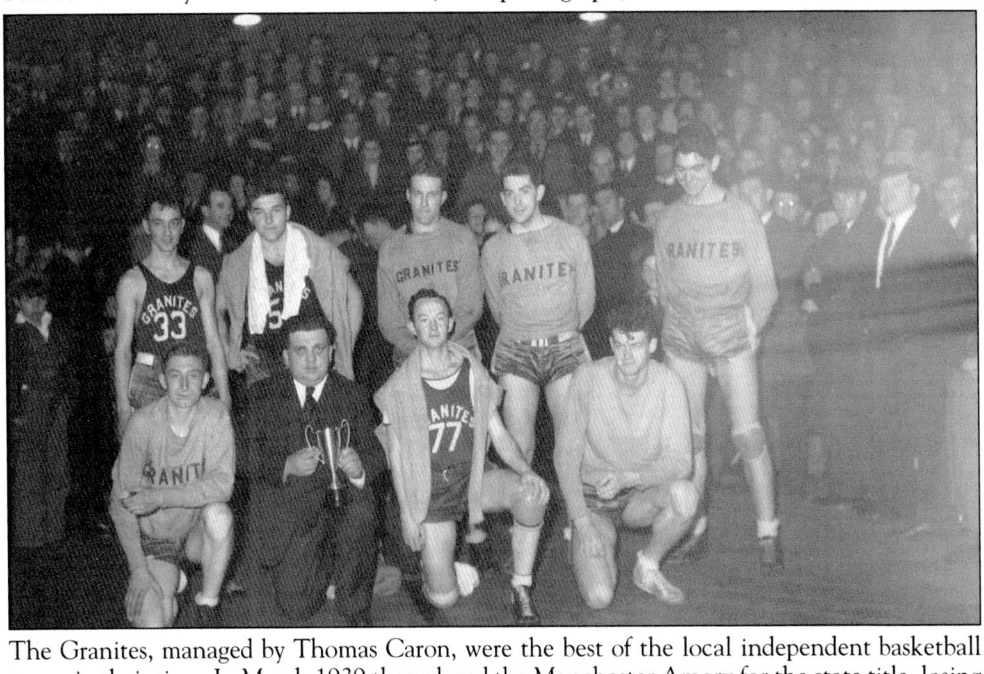

The Granites, managed by Thomas Caron, were the best of the local independent basketball teams in their time. In March 1939 they played the Manchester Amory for the state title, losing in the finals to the Claremont VFW team. The team consisted of Hepworth, Gonye, Michaud, Travers, Trobec, Levandowski, Jones, and Morrison. (Lear photograph)

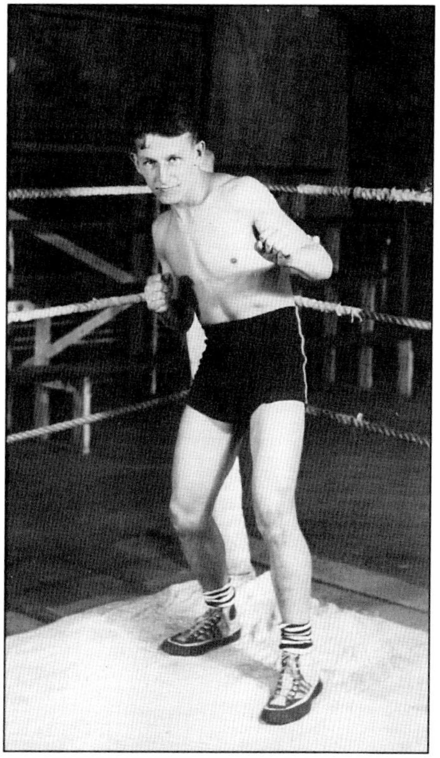

Club boxing was a very popular diversion during the Depression. Among the best of the local bantamweight contenders was James "Jocko" Sutton, who weighed in at 118 pounds for his April 1936 fight for the Derry Boys Club on Railroad Avenue.

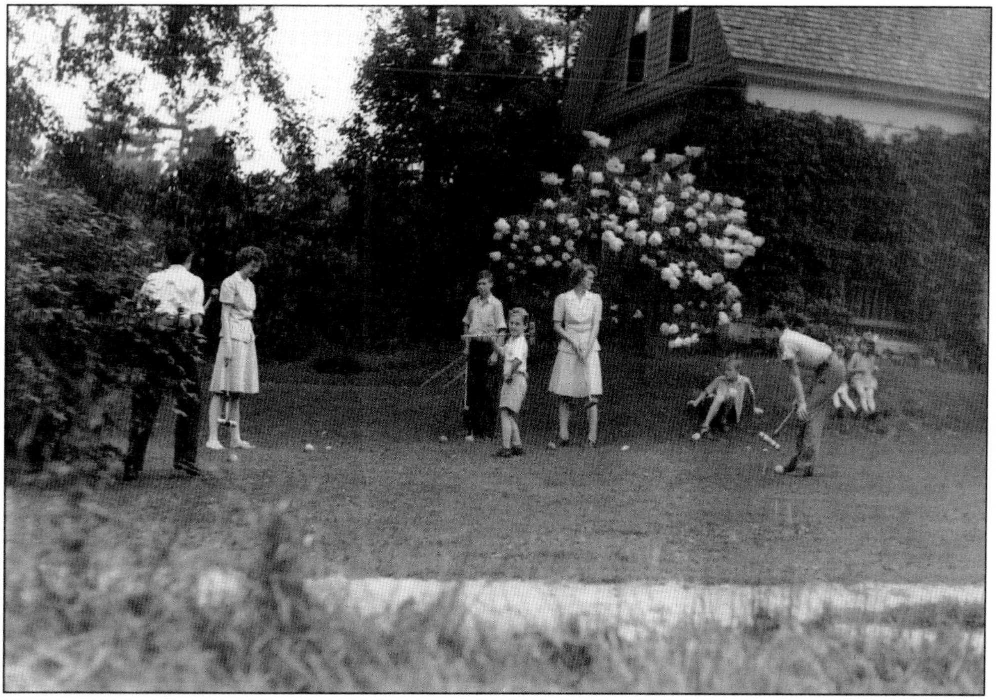

With the men away at war, pleasure driving was severely restricted and many families stayed close to home for entertainment. This photograph, taken in August 1943, shows a neighborhood croquet match. (Lear photograph)

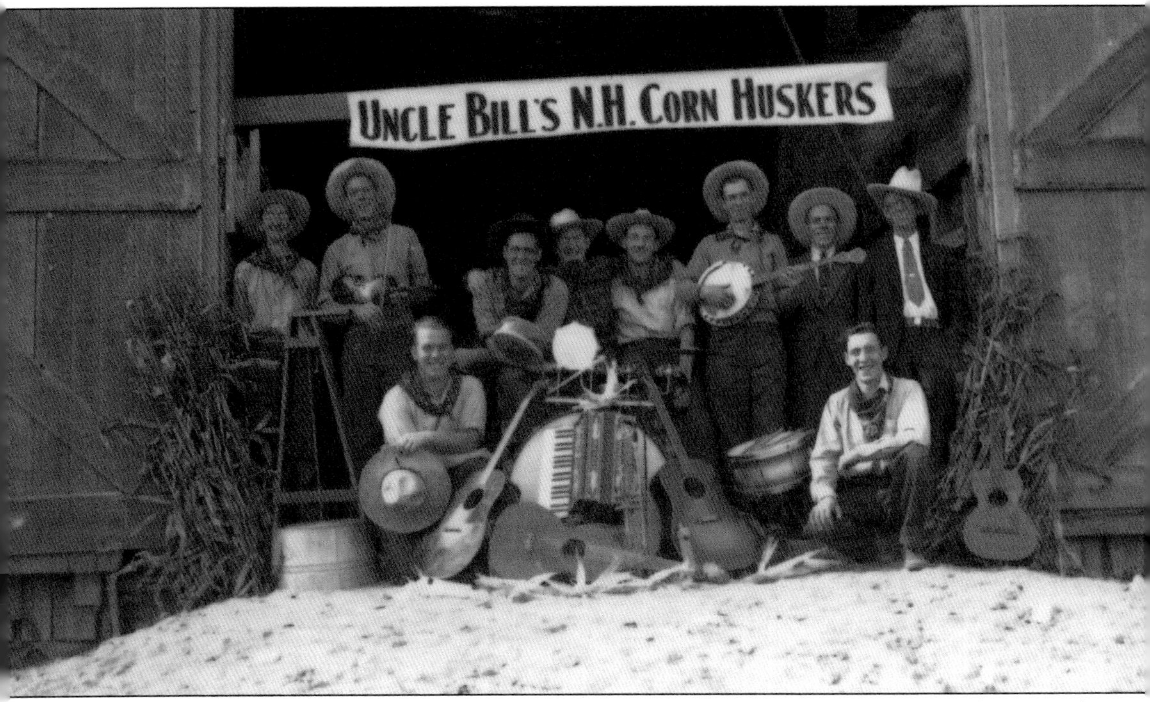

Uncle Bill's New Hampshire Corn Huskers played modern and old time music at area dances and were led by William Davies of Derry. They had two shows every week on radio stations in Lowell and Lawrence. Other members included Merle Mentor, Buddy Madden, George Allard, Leo Gallion, Frenchie of DesMaris Avenue, Joe Martin, and Russell Scribner. (Lear photograph)

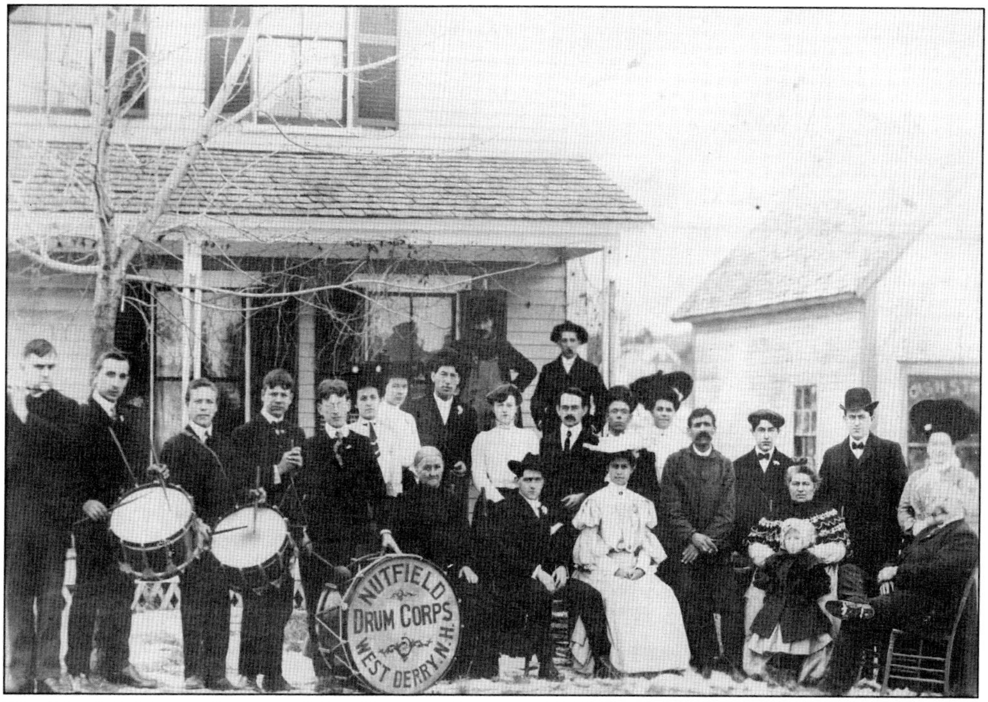

The Nutfield Drum Corps in West Derry is shown *c.* 1905. James E. Sutton, with bright red hair and glasses, is shown standing behind his big bass drum.

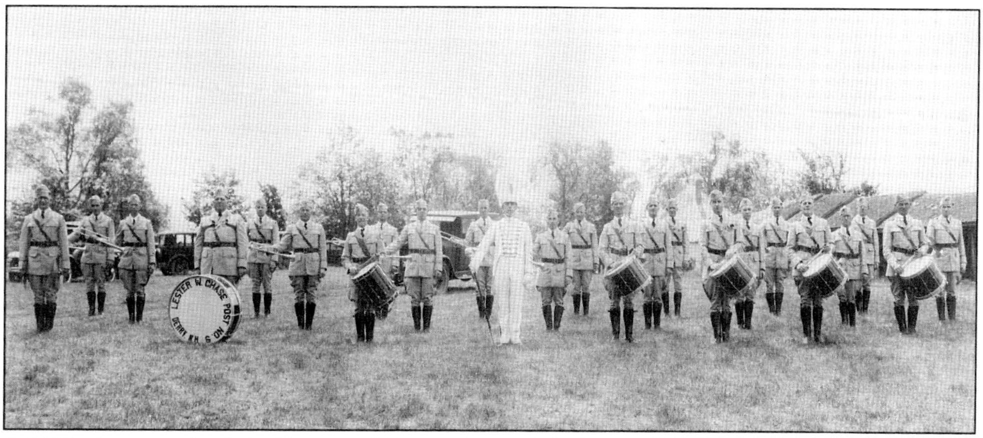

A 1932 photograph of the Drum and Bugle Corps of the Lester W. Chase part of the American Legion at a state competition. They are wearing their bright blue cavalry-style uniforms with Sam Browne belts.

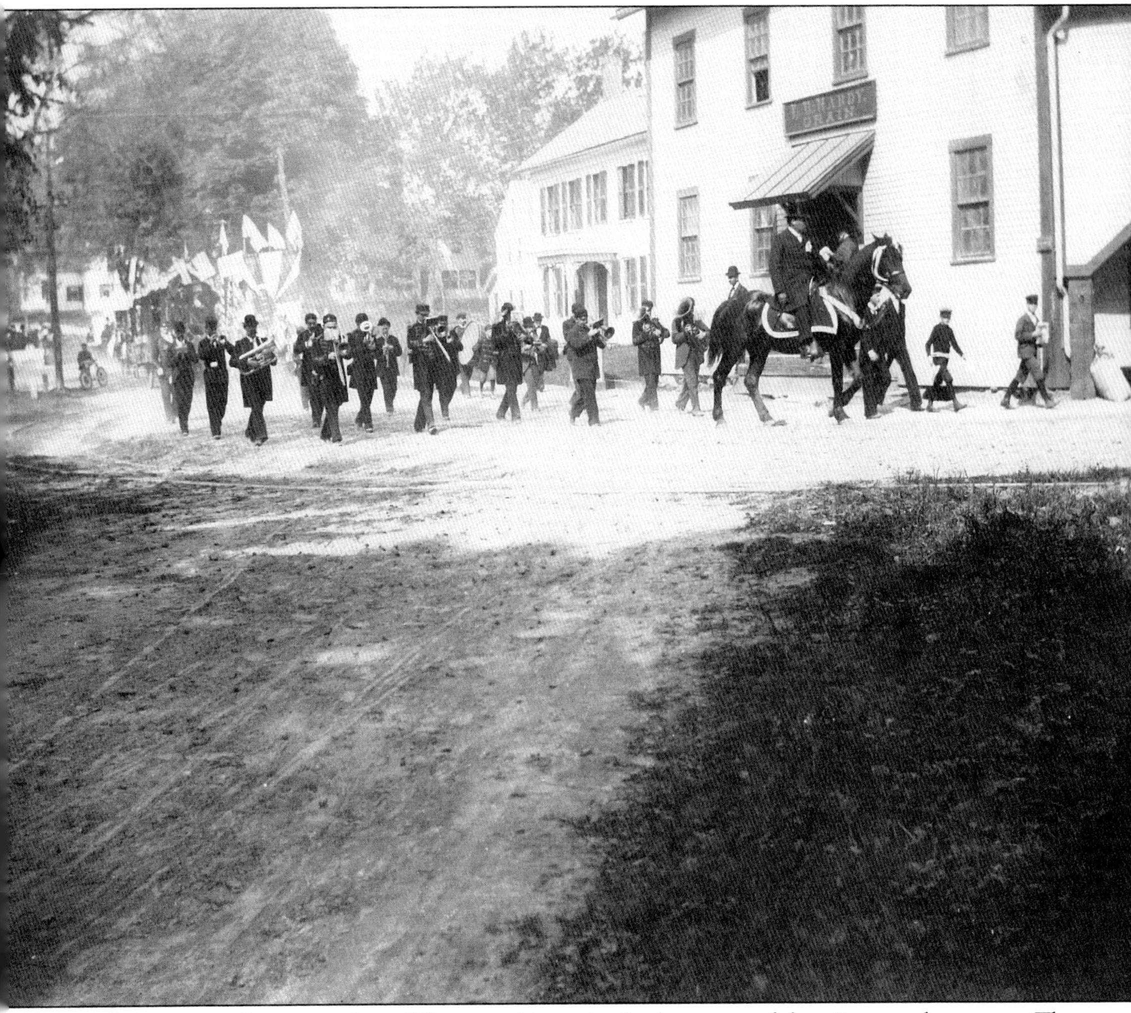

A circus parade passing down Thornton Street in the last years of the nineteenth century. The ringmaster (on horseback) leads an eighteen-piece brass band, and is followed by a long line of circus wagons. Several boys walk ahead passing out flyers.

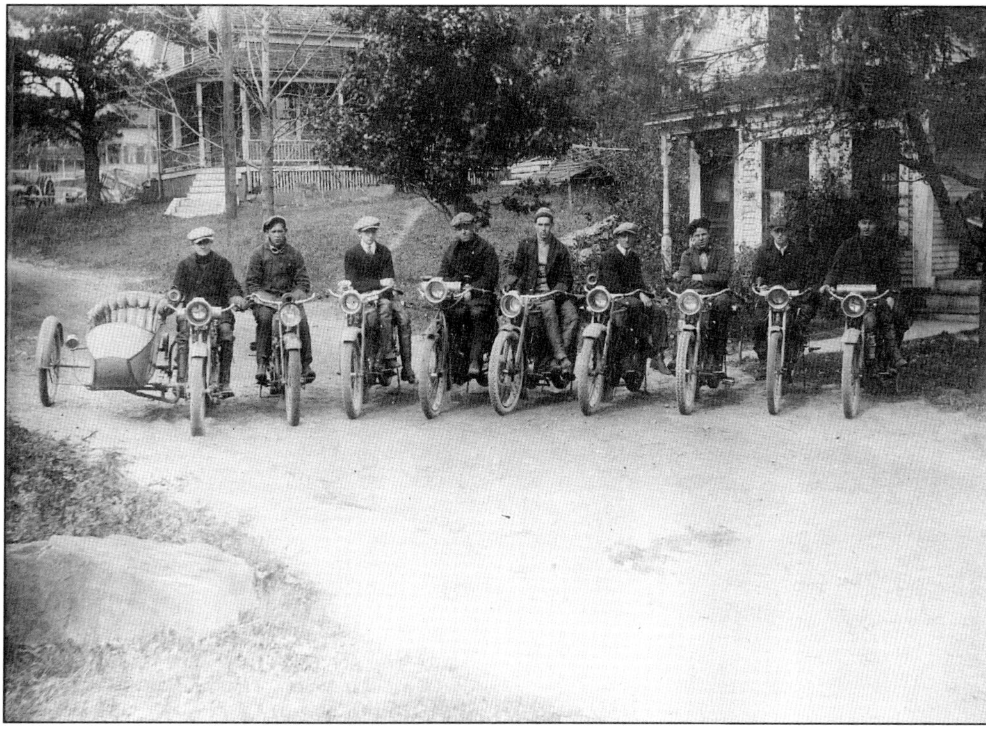

For these young men on Grove Street in 1915 Indian and Harley-Davidson motorcycles were the vehicles of choice.

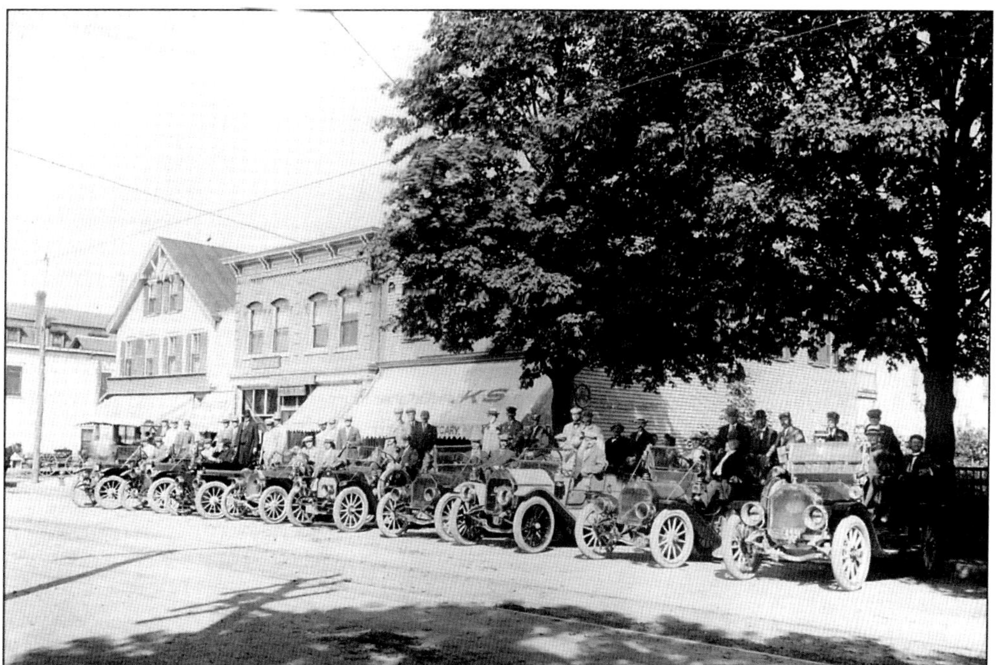

In August 1911, when automobiles were still a novelty, area drivers organized a caravan tour from Derry to Hampton Beach. This became an annual event up until World War I.

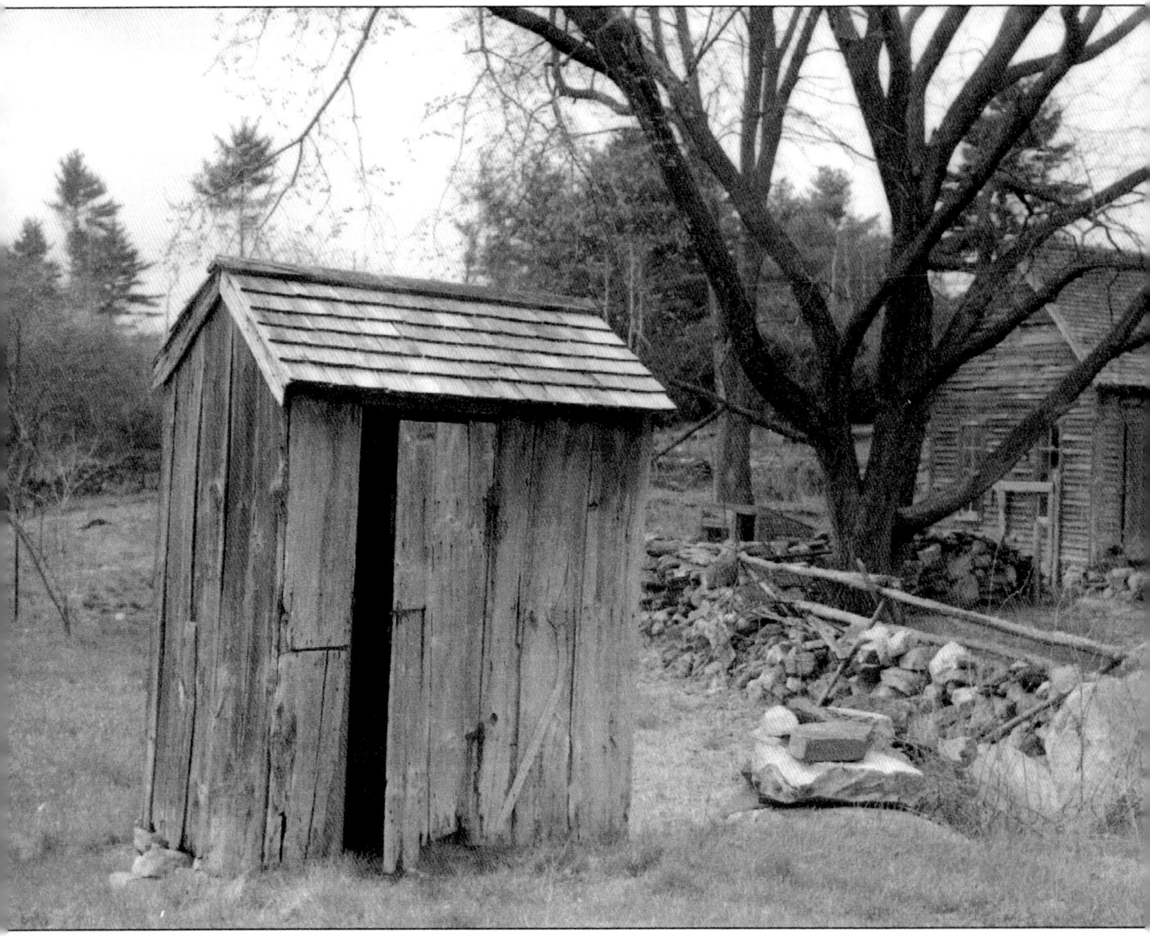

Many of the most interesting places in old Derry have disappeared during the last few years. Fire has taken its toll, along with the ravages of time, but the most damage has been done by the relentless march of so-called progress. We have lost so much and gained so little: gone are those classic Victorian buildings on Broadway, the A & P, the corner groceries, the cows and barns of the Hood Farm, the Broadway Theater, the vast shoe shops, the sound of the trains rushing through town, the local eccentrics—we miss them all.

There are, however, some things we are glad to see go. Children today are spared the suffering of polio. We don't miss unheated bedrooms, food rationing, the Great Depression, and all those wars. This April 1941 picture captures the outhouse of the two hundred-year-old Armstrong farm. Some progress is good. (Lear photograph)